INSIGHT GUIDE

EDINBURGH

APA PUBLICATIONS
Part of the Langenscheidt Publishing Group

INSIGHT GUIDE
EDINBURGH

Editorial
Managing Editor
Jane Ladle
Editorial Director
Brian Bell

Distribution

UK & Ireland
GeoCenter International Ltd
The Viables Centre, Harrow Way
Basingstoke, Hants RG22 4BJ
Fax: (44) 1256 817988

United States
Langenscheidt Publishers, Inc.
46–35 54th Road, Maspeth, NY 11378
Fax: (718) 784 0640

Canada
Thomas Allen & Son Ltd
390 Steelcase Road East
Markham, Ontario L3R 1G2
Fax: (1) 905 475 6747

Australia
Universal Press
1 Waterloo Road
Macquarie Park, NSW 2113
Fax: (61) 2 9888 9074

New Zealand
Hema Maps New Zealand Ltd (HNZ)
Unit D, 24 Ra ORA Drive
East Tamaki, Auckland
Fax: (64) 9 273 6479

Worldwide
Apa Publications GmbH & Co.
Verlag KG (Singapore branch)
38 Joo Koon Road, Singapore 628990
Tel: (65) 6865 1600. Fax: (65) 6861 6438

Printing

Insight Print Services (Pte) Ltd
38 Joo Koon Road, Singapore 628990
Tel: (65) 6865 1600. Fax: (65) 6861 6438

©2002 Apa Publications GmbH & Co.
Verlag KG (Singapore branch)
All Rights Reserved
First Edition 1993
Third Edition 2001
Updated 2002

CONTACTING THE EDITORS
We would appreciate it if readers
would alert us to errors or out-
dated information by writing to:
**Insight Guides, P.O. Box 7910,
London SE1 1WE, England.
Fax: (44) 20 7403 0290.
insight@apaguide.demon.co.uk**

www.insightguides.com

ABOUT THIS BOOK

This guidebook combines the interests and enthusiasms of two of the world's best known information providers: Insight Guides, whose titles have set the standard for visual travel guides since 1970, and Discovery Channel, the world's premier source of nonfiction television programming.

The editors of Insight Guides provide practical advice and general understanding about a destination's history, culture, institutions and people. Discovery Channel and its popular website, www.discovery.com, help millions of viewers explore their world from the comfort of their own home and also encourage them to explore it first hand. This fully updated edition of *Insight Guide: Edinburgh* is carefully structured to convey an understanding of the city and its culture as well as to guide readers through its sights and activities:

◆ The **Features** section, indicated by a yellow bar at the top of each page, covers the history and culture of the country in a series of informative essays.

◆ The main **Places** section, indicated by a blue bar, is a complete guide to all the sights and areas worth visiting. Places of special interest are coordinated by number with the maps.

◆ The **Travel Tips** listings section, with an orange bar, provides detailed information on travel, hotels, restaurants, shops, and more.

EXPLORE YOUR WORLD

The contributors

This new edition was developed by **Jane Ladle**, who is based just outside Edinburgh and has worked on a number of Insight's Scottish titles. *Insight Guide: Edinburgh* has been extensively revised by Ladle and a team of specialist writers, all of them resident in the city.

The history of Scotland's capital has been brought up to date by journalist and broadcaster **Keith Aitken**, editor of the magazine *Enterprise Scotland* and former chief leader writer for *The Scotsman*. Aitken also wrote the Scottish Parliament essay, and revised features on people, schools and poverty. New chapters on the New Town are by **Hamish Scott**, who has also written on architecture for London's *Daily Telegraph* and Readers Digest books on

Britain. **Giles Sutherland**, a writer and lecturer on the visual arts in Scotland, surveyed art in Edinburgh.

Mark Fisher, editor of the Edinburgh and Glasgow events magazine *The List*, revised the Edinburgh Festival chapter and supplied the Festival Fringe "diary". Staffers at *The List* also contributed: music writer **Mark Robertson** revised Pubs and Performers, and **Louisa Pearson**, **Kelly Apter**, **Helen Monaghan** and **Abigail Bremner** overhauled the Travel Tips.

This edition builds on the success of the first edition, which was conceived and edited by **Brian Bell**, now Insight's editorial director. Novelist, historian and journalist **Allan Massie** wrote the original history chapters; the late **W. Gordon Smith**, writer, playwright and songwriter, wrote the essay on the Festival, and reported on the Traverse Theatre and the city's medical innovators. The Places section was penned by two of Scotland's leading journalists. **George Rosie** wrote chapters on the city centre, The Tenement Landscape, and Leith and Newhaven, as well as illuminating the Edinburgh Character, The Disruption and the problems of municipal housing; **Julie Davidson** covered the suburbs, green spaces and the surrounding area.

The book's main photographer, Edinburgh-based **Douglas Corrance**, is one of Scotland's most sought-after photographers. Other credits go to **Julie Morrice**, for the original Travel Tips, on which the current listings are based, **Brian Morton** for Literary Edinburgh, **Alastair Clark** for Pubs and Performers, and **Conrad Wilson** for Scottish Cuisine. This edition was updated by **Hilary Fraser**, proofread by **Alison Copland** and indexed by **Isobel McLean**.

Map Legend

— —	State Boundary
– – –	Region Boundary
–•–	National Park/Reserve
– – –	Ferry Route
✈ ✈	Airport: International/Regional
🚌	Bus Station
❶	Tourist Information
✉	Post Office
† ⴕ	Church/Ruins
†	Monastery
☾	Mosque
✡	Synagogue
🏰	Castle/Ruins
∴	Archaeological Site
∩	Cave
𝟏	Statue/Monument
★	Place of Interest

The main places of interest in the Places section are coordinated by number with a full-colour map (e.g. ❶), and a symbol at the top of every right-hand page tells you where to find the map.

CONTENTS

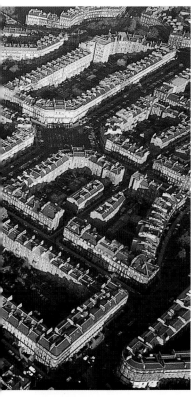

St Mary's Episcopal
Cathedral in the formal
pattern of the West End.

Insight on ...

Information panels

Places

Travel Tips

◆ **Full Travel Tips index
is on page 249**

THE CONFIDENT CAPITAL

Edinburgh has been called haughty and pathologically thrifty.

How is devolved government changing its image?

The idea of Edinburgh as a "real" capital like London, Paris or Washington may, prior to the re-establishment of the Scottish Parliament in 1999, have struck some visitors as a slightly ludicrous pretension – more especially as it is a city of less than half a million people. But throughout the three centuries it was denied control of Scotland's government Edinburgh remained enough of a capital to convince itself at least of its continuing importance. It was, after all, still the undisputed home of both the Church of the nation and the venerable Scottish legal system, which were never superseded by their English equivalents, and it was an important financial centre. And the influence Edinburgh wielded in Britain and Europe during the extraordinary flowering of intellect that took place in the city during the 18th and early 19th centuries must be regarded as being of equal value to a political role.

Now that Edinburgh is tasting political power again, albeit of a limited nature while Scotland remains within the United Kingdom, the pertinent question is: can the capital of Scotland carry off its elevation with aplomb in the 21st century?

For a number of years it was fashionable to deride Edinburgh for its perceived snobbery and meanness of spirit. The Marxist writer Tom Nairn characterised the city's soul as "bible-black, pickled in boredom by centuries of sermons, swaddled in the shabby gentility of the Kirk (Church)". But this image is surely incompatible with the verdict of quality-of-life surveys carried out in the 1990s, which put Edinburgh at the top of the league of British cities. Already the venue for the pre-eminent international festival of the arts, in recent years it has joined the 24-hour society, acquired two magnificent new theatres (the Playhouse and Festival Theatre), spawned the most important museum of the last hundred years (the Museum of Scotland) and commissioned an acclaimed architect to create a state-of-the-art parliament house.

Is Edinburgh truly re-energised or is it a beautiful relic of past achievements? Judge for yourself.   ❑

PRECEDING PAGES: the Military Tattoo on the Castle Esplanade; the choir of St Mary's Music School, whose patrons have included Sir Yehudi Menuhin; making lamps for period homes; swimming across the Forth.
LEFT: Festival clowns in the High Street.

Decisive Dates

BEGINNINGS–HOUSE OF STUART

AD 160 Ptolemy's *Geography* mentions the town of Dunedin (Edinburgh) in the Forth Valley.

1058–93 Reign of Malcolm III, who built a hunting lodge on the site of Edinburgh Castle.

1128 Holyrood Abbey is founded by David I for Augustinian monks.

1295–1314 Edinburgh Castle held by the English during the Wars of Independence.

1314 Scots forces under Robert the Bruce defeat the English at the Battle of Bannockburn.

RULING HOUSES OF SCOTLAND

ALPIN 843–1034: Indulf MacAlpin (reigned 954–62) captured Edinburgh from the English.

DUNKELD 1034–58: Duncan I; Macbeth (subject of Shakespeare's play); Lulach (The Fool)

CANMORE 1058–1290: Malcolm III; Donald Ban; Duncan II; Edmund; Edgar; Alexander I; David I; Malcolm IV; William; Alexander II; Alexander III; Margaret (Maid of Norway)

BALLIOL 1292–96: John Balliol

BRUCE 1306–71: Robert I (The Bruce); David II

STUART (STEWART) 1371–1603: Robert II; Robert III; James I; James II; James III; James IV; James V; Mary, Queen of Scots; James VI

1329 Robert the Bruce grants a Royal Charter to Edinburgh and awards it Leith harbour.

1440 William, Earl of Douglas, and his brother David are summarily executed at Edinburgh Castle after the "Black Dinner" hosted by James II.

1513 James IV invades England and is defeated and killed at the Battle of Flodden, prompting the building of the Flodden Wall around Edinburgh.

1544 Henry VIII sacks Edinburgh Castle in the Rough Wooing of the infant Mary, Queen of Scots, an attempt to force a marriage to his son Edward.

1559 John Knox founds the Protestant Church of Scotland and is appointed Minister of St Giles'.

1561 Mary returns from exile in France to claim her inheritance.

1566 Mary, Queen of Scots gives birth to James, later king of Scotland and England, at Edinburgh Castle.

1571–73 After Mary's abdication and flight to England, Edinburgh Castle is held for her by the Keeper and is besieged for over a year.

1583 Edinburgh University, the first non-religious university in Britain, is opened with 80 students.

THE DUAL MONARCHY

1603 Union of the Crowns. James VI becomes James I of England and leaves Edinburgh to set up court in London.

1633 Charles I visits Edinburgh with the Archbishop of Canterbury, confirming it as the Scottish capital and granting St Giles' the status of an Episcopalian cathedral.

1638 The National Covenant, a petition objecting to the imposition of Episcopalianism over Scottish Presbyterianism, is signed in Greyfriars churchyard.

1645 Edinburgh is ravaged by the plague.

1650 The royalist Marquis of Montrose is executed for treason at Mercat Cross. Cromwell seizes power in England; Scotland proclaims Charles II as king. Cromwellian troops occupy Holyroodhouse and a fire destroys much of the palace.

1672 Reconstruction of the Palace of Holyroodhouse is begun by Charles II.

1679 Covenanters are imprisoned for five months in Greyfriars churchyard.

1681 The Edinburgh-based Royal College of Physicians is founded.

1695 Bank of Scotland is founded in Edinburgh.

AFTER THE UNION

1707 Union of the Scottish and English parliaments. Scotland ceases to be governed from Edinburgh.

1722 Last burning of a witch on Castlehill.

1736 Porteous Riots result in the lynching of the Captain of the City Guard by the Edinburgh mob.
1745 Jacobite rebellion: Prince Charles Edward Stuart arrives in Edinburgh with his Highland army and takes up residence at Holyrood. He wins the Battle of Prestonpans then marches into England.
1752 Pamphlet published proposing the building of the New Town, inspired by Lord Provost George Drummond.
1759 Drainage of the Nor' (North) Loch begins.
1767 James Craig wins competition for a plan to build the New Town of Edinburgh.
1772 The first North Bridge is completed.
1786 Robert Burns publishes the first edition of the Kilmarnock Poems and visits Edinburgh to rapturous welcome.
1788 William Brodie, Edinburgh magistrate and burglar, is hanged from a gallows he designed himself.
1791 Robert Adam is commissioned to design Charlotte Square.
1802 Founding of the *Edinburgh Review*, which became highly influential throughout Britain.
1818 Sir Walter Scott discovers the Honours of Scotland in a locked chest in Edinburgh Castle.
1822 State Visit to Edinburgh of George IV, the first reigning monarch to set foot on Scottish soil since 1641, masterminded by Sir Walter Scott.
1824 Fire destroys most of the buildings on the south side of the High Street.
1829 The Royal High School, Edinburgh's oldest school, moves to a new neo-classical building on Calton Hill.

THE VICTORIAN AGE

1840–46 The Scott Monument is erected.
1842 Edinburgh joins the railway age with a line to Glasgow. The North British Railway publish plans for routes on a network connecting with London.
1843 Disruption of the Church of Scotland. The established Church is split and 470 ministers secede to form the Free Church of Scotland.
1851 Population of the Old Town peaks at over 40,000, around half the city's total population.
1881 Census shows that domestic servants make up 20 percent of Edinburgh's population.
1890 The Forth Rail Bridge opens, providing a direct rail link with the northeast coast of Scotland.

PRECEDING PAGES: late 18th-century view of the Old Town, by Philip Mercier.
LEFT: Mary, Queen of Scots, who reigned 1542–67.
RIGHT: Mary's son and successor James VI (James I of England).

MODERN TIMES

1914–18 150,000 Scots die in World War I, remembered by the Scottish National War Memorial (1927) at Edinburgh Castle.
1920 The Edinburgh Boundaries Extension Act redefines the city to include villages on its south and west sides and Leith on the Firth of Forth.
1939 The Scottish Office is transferred from Whitehall to Edinburgh.
1947 Edinburgh International Festival and Edinburgh Military Tattoo are inaugurated.
1961 Publication of Muriel Spark's *The Prime of Miss Jean Brodie*, set in Edinburgh.
1964 The Forth Road Bridge opens.

1970 New Town Conservation Committee is formed.
1979 Referendum rejects devolution in Scotland.
1985 Old Town Conservation Committee is formed.
1995 Edinburgh city centre, including the Old and New Towns and Dean Village, is declared a World Heritage Site by UNESCO.
1996 The Stone of Destiny (Stone of Scone), Scotland's ancient coronation seat, is transferred to Edinburgh Castle from Westminster Abbey.
1997 Referendum results in vote in favour of a Scottish parliament with tax-varying powers.
1998 The Museum of Scotland opens in Edinburgh on St Andrew's Day.
12 May 1999 The new Scottish Parliament convenes in the Assembly Hall on The Mound. ❏

BEGINNINGS

Edinburgh became established after it was favoured by successive kings,

but its southern location meant it fell prey to frequent English invasions

Two early chroniclers of Scottish history, John Stow and Andrew of Wyntoun, asserted that Edinburgh had been established in 989 BC when a mystical (if reputedly much-married) King Ebrauke built a "Mayden Castel" on its famous rock. The first genuine historical reference to the city comes more than 1,000 years later, in Ptolemy's *Geography* (AD 160); he wrote that the Votadini (Goddodin) inhabited a town called Dunedin in the Forth Valley.

This reference disproves the later claim that the city takes its name from Edwin, King of Northumbria, who conquered the Lothians in AD 638. The resemblance of Edwin's burgh to Edinburgh is mere coincidence, Edinburgh being in reality the anglicised version of the Celtic "Dunedin".

The Scots King Indulf MacAlpin captured Edinburgh from the English in the 10th century, but for several hundred years the kings of the Scots continued to hold their courts further north. It would be premature to talk of a "capital" of their kingdom, as monarchs tended to travel from place to place, but in the 11th and 12th centuries they were certainly more likely to be found across the Firth of Forth in Dunfermline (or later Stirling) than in Edinburgh. (Kings were crowned at Scone Abbey near Perth, traditionally seated upon the Stone of Destiny until it was lost to the English in 1296.) Edinburgh was unsuitable as a permanent base for the court because it was too insecure, being so close to the English border.

Royal castle and abbey

After Edinburgh became a part of the Scots' realm, it is not mentioned in any records until the reign of Malcolm III (who was known as "Canmore"), which lasted from 1058 to 1093. He built a castle in Edinburgh, on the site of the present castle, to serve principally as a hunting lodge. A chapel within the castle walls – by far the earliest building which still stands – is dedicated to his English wife Margaret. "Saint" Margaret was a devout queen who is said to have secluded herself in the chapel after hearing of the deaths of her husband and eldest son in battle at Alnwick. However, architectural

evidence indicates that the surviving chapel was not built during her lifetime, but (probably) by David I as a memorial to his mother, who was canonised in 1250.

David I, king from 1124 until 1153, who "illumynyd in his dayis/ His landys with kirkis and abbayis", built the Abbey of the Holy Rood (Holy Cross) below Arthur's Seat, the city's volcanic hill supposedly named after the legendary King Arthur; and the Royal Mile is the name still given to the street that runs from the Castle to the palace later built beside David's abbey.

The Abbey's charter makes it clear that Edinburgh was already a town sufficiently important to pay tax, as its financial burden included

LEFT: Robert the Bruce sends a defiance to Edward III of England.

RIGHT: St Margaret, Queen of Malcolm III, from a 15th-century illumination.

40 shillings a year for the Abbey. The Augustian monks who ran it were also granted permission to build another town between the abbey and Edinburgh, which grew up at the bottom of the Canongate. (It would remain a separate burgh until 1856, long after it had become physically one with Edinburgh.)

Commerce and war

So, from early times, medieval Edinburgh was held between the two poles of Castle and Abbey, the stronghold and the civilising church. St Giles' Church was founded at about the same time (or perhaps earlier) though the present building dates from the 15th century. There were also other monasteries and convents in medieval times. Meanwhile, Edinburgh became a successful trading centre, making use of nearby Leith to import and export goods by sea.

The Castle, dominating Lothian and commanding the Forth estuary, inevitably came under attack during the English invasions of Scotland. During the Wars of Independence it was held by them from 1295 until it was recaptured in 1314 by Thomas Randolph, Earl of Moray, who scaled the rock in a daring night assault. Randolph was the nephew of Robert the Bruce, whose successful struggle to attain

BURGESSES OF EDINBURGH

By the time Edinburgh was granted a Royal Charter by Robert the Bruce it had already evolved into a thriving burgh whose traders had begun to develop a form of self-government. The charter and its forerunners enshrined the special rights of the "burgesses" (generally established residents who had purchased a property tenure). They enjoyed certain privileges, the most important of which was a trading monopoly which excluded non-burgesses, namely outsiders; another was the right to elect magistrates. In return the burgesses had to undertake duties such as the night watch, and abide by rules including a stipulation that goods for sale had to be openly displayed, either in a window or at the town market. But the poet William Dunbar complained, around the turn of the 15th century, that "craftis vyll" defiled the streets and merchants crowded together too closely alongside the "luckenbooths" (locked booths) of the High Street.

Medieval Edinburgh was very cosmopolitan; it imported (and exported) customs as well as goods from continental Europe, and attracted foreign immigrants and visiting merchants, ambassadors and craftsmen. Meanwhile merchant guilds and craft guilds were established. Burgesses had to pay substantial taxes to the Crown, yet business was frequently interrupted by English invasions.

Scotland's throne is remembered in the tale of his inspiration while in exile from observing the persistence of a spider weaving a web in a cave.

When in power, Bruce was so impressed by the ease with which the English could advance on Edinburgh and then dominate the country from the Castle that he demolished it, except for St Margaret's little chapel. Perhaps by way of compensation, he granted Edinburgh its earliest surviving Royal Charter in 1329, the last year of his life. Significantly, the port of Leith was given to Edinburgh under the charter, sparking strife between the two which continues to this day.

Windsor Castle, near London, and the fortification of Edinburgh imitated Windsor in several respects. Meanwhile, in the late 14th century, after the English had withdrawn, Robert II of Scotland gave the Edinburgh burgesses permission to build houses within the Castle walls and to pass freely in and out without paying a toll.

The Castle was never to be a regular royal residence. It was an armoury and a stronghold; the Parliament met there and courts of justice were held in its great hall, but it was not adapted for even a modest degree of domestic comfort: the room where Mary, Queen of Scots gave birth to her son James in 1566 is tiny.

England's mark

By the end of the 14th century the Castle had been re-built, though it is a curiosity of history that much of its fortification was the work of English armies. They always found the Castle more useful as a means of controlling the Lothians than the Scots found it an effective defence.

Enlargement of the enclosed area was made by the English king Edward III. He had previously embarked on great building works at

LEFT: David II shakes hands with Edward III of England after the Scot's defeat in 1346.
ABOVE: David's father, Robert the Bruce, was victorious in battle.

When in Edinburgh, kings generally preferred to reside at the Abbey of the Holy Rood.

Nevertheless, the Castle was the setting of one of the nastiest political murders in Scottish history. In 1440 the young William, sixth Earl of Douglas, and his brother David were lured there under promise of safe conduct, seized and summarily beheaded without a trial on the orders of the Castle's Keeper, Sir William Crichton, who was a member of a rival family. This deed was known as the "Black Dinner" because the signal of the brothers' fate was reputedly given by the bringing in of a black bull's head to the dinner table while they were being entertained by the juvenile James II. ❏

QUARRELS WITH THE CROWN

During the 16th and 17th centuries Edinburgh was, by turns, the seat of sovereign power and at the centre of religious and political strife in Scotland

By the beginning of the 16th century, Edinburgh was established as the capital of Scotland, albeit unofficially, and the Old Town had assumed its present shape. Following James IV's doomed invasion of England and defeat (and death) at the Battle of Flodden in 1513, construction of a new defensive wall around Edinburgh (the "Flodden Wall") was embarked upon. Although the wall took some 47 years to complete – and proved inadequate to keep the English out – it was to define the boundaries of the burgh for 250 years. (Only a few stretches of the Flodden Wall remain; the best preserved tower is at the Vennel in the West Port above the Grassmarket.)

Edinburgh and the Canongate were still separate burghs, but even then the Royal Mile (which is properly four streets – Castlehill, Lawnmarket, High Street and Canongate) was regarded as a unity. It was, however, in a state of continuous change and redevelopment. St Giles' in the High Street was the High Kirk of the City, the parish church (later the church of four parishes) which only became a cathedral (defined as the seat of a bishop) at the order of Charles I in 1633. In this year too, Edinburgh was finally confirmed as the capital of Scotland.

Aristocrats' homes

St Giles' was substantially rebuilt in later years but some other buildings from this period survive in a state approximating to their original appearance. Among the oldest buildings in the High Street are John Knox's house, Moubray House and Tweeddale House; they have, of course, been altered over the years, yet all retain their air of antiquity *(see page 115)*. So, too, does Moray House in the Canongate, built about 1630 for Mary, Dowager Countess of Home. It was in its Garden Pavilion that the Treaty of Union was signed in 1707.

Many of the Scots nobility had their houses in the Canongate; others favoured the Cowgate,

which runs parallel to the Royal Mile but at a lower level. Cardinal Beaton had his palace there, long since demolished, on the corner with Blackfriar's Wynd, while the Regent Morton's House can still be found, greatly altered, in Blackfriars Street, which runs between the High Street and the Cowgate.

Both Cardinal and Regent (the fourth to stand in for the young James VI) met violent deaths in the turbulent – indeed revolutionary – 16th century. It was also the last century in which Edinburgh had a resident monarch, though royal palaces outside the city, namely Linlithgow and Falkland, were also favoured. James IV was an enthusiastic builder in the Renaissance style and he left his mark on Holyrood; during his reign the monks of the Abbey were pushed to the periphery of the building by the royal household, and by the time the king married Mary Tudor, in 1503, it had developed into a substantial palace. His son James V presided over further expansion of the palace, which was

---

LEFT: John Knox admonishing Mary, Queen of Scots.
RIGHT: Lord Darnley courting the Queen.

subsequently sacked during Henry VIII's "Rough Wooing" of the infant Mary, Queen of Scots on behalf of his son Edward.

Blood at Holyrood

It is Mary, Queen of Scots' own eventful sojourn at Holyrood that is chiefly remembered, for much of the drama of her brief reign was concentrated in Edinburgh. It was at Holyrood that she argued with the Protestant leader John Knox for her right to practise her own Roman Catholic religion, and it was at Holyrood that she was compelled to witness, while pregnant, the brutal murder of her Italian secretary and

her army at Carberry Hill outside Musselburgh, Mary was returned captive to Edinburgh, where she encountered an angry mob shrieking "Burn the hoor (whore)". Nothing in Edinburgh's history is quite so moving as its association with the unfortunate queen, who was later to be imprisoned for 20 years and finally executed on the orders of Elizabeth I of England.

Two thrones

Holyrood saw yet more drama during the reign of Mary's son, James VI: he was besieged there by his mad and dangerous cousin, Francis Stewart, Earl of Bothwell, who was a nephew

confidant, David Rizzio. It was in the Castle that her son was born, and in the Provost's house of Kirk o'Field on the outskirts of the city (where Edinburgh University's Old College now stands) that her second husband, Darnley, was murdered. Within a week, a placard was nailed to the door of the Tolbooth in the High Street, naming the Earl of Bothwell as his murderer, though an Edinburgh court subsequently acquitted him of the charge, intimidated by his armed retainers.

Innocent or not, when Bothwell, a Protestant, almost immediately divorced his wife and married Mary – perhaps forcibly – the Queen's subjects were outraged. So, after the evaporation of

of Mary's husband. But it was also there that he was awakened on the night of 27 March 1603 by the Englishman Sir Robert Carey, who had galloped north from Elizabeth of England's deathbed to hail James as "King of Great Britain, Ireland and France".

The throne of England was a prize which James had long coveted and which he knew could be his because Elizabeth, the Virgin Queen, had no heir – and his great-grandmother was the daughter of Henry VII of England. Nine days later James left Edinburgh to take possession of his new inheritance, and neither Scotland nor Edinburgh was ever the same thereafter. The King was enamoured of the pomp and ceremony of the English court and he returned to Scotland only once after becoming James I of England. Scots have speculated ever since about how differently history might have turned out had James made Edinburgh rather than London his base.

Yet, though the kingdoms were united under one man, they remained two independent sovereign states, and Parliament continued to function in Edinburgh. More important still, the city was the regular meeting-place of the General Assembly of the Church of Scot-

A GOOD IMPRESSION

In 1636 an English traveller, Sir William Brereton, wondered at "the glory and beauty of this city … and the longest street [the Royal Mile] that ever I have seen".

provoked a riot in Edinburgh, set off when a woman called Jenny Geddes threw a stool at the preacher in St Giles' Cathedral for daring to "say the Mass in my lug (ear)". Subsequently the mob tried to lynch the city's Bishop.

Resistance to the king's innovations grew fiercer, and in 1638 the National Covenant, binding its signatories to defend the Scots form of worship "against all sorts of persons whatsoever", was drawn up; the people flocked to Greyfriars Churchyard to sign it. This led to

land. It was the attempt by James's son Charles I to impose a uniformity of religion on his two kingdoms which aroused fury in Scotland and precipitated the civil wars that provided Edinburgh with some of its most dramatic moments.

Religious rebellion

In 1633 Charles visited his Scottish capital, bringing with him his new Archbishop of Canterbury, William Laud. They ordered that a new prayer book be used in Scottish churches. This

the Bishops' Wars which secured the independence of the Scots Kirk and the re-establishment of St Giles' as the mother church of Scottish Presbyterianism (and banishment of bishops).

In 1641 Charles, alarmed by the opposition now aroused in England also, returned to Edinburgh to attempt to reconcile his native land. It was while playing golf on Leith Links that he received news of the Irish Rebellion; this precipitated the civil war in England and Scotland which ended in his defeat and execution.

LEFT: Robert Herdman's depiction of the execution of Mary, Queen of Scots.
ABOVE: Charles I, who reigned 1625–49, by Van Dyck.

Montrose's story

Edinburgh was spared fighting, but in 1650, the year after the king's death, the city was the setting for one of the most memorable and dramatic scenes in Scottish history. The central figure was the great Marquess of Montrose. He had been one of the first signatories of the Covenant, and prominent in the Bishops' Wars. But, believing that these wars had secured the liberties of Scotland, and suspicious of the ambitions of the Marquess of Argyll and some of the other Covenanting leaders, he had taken the King's side in the subsequent civil war.

In 1644–45 he had conducted a remarkable campaign which had terrified his Covenanting enemies and made him for a few weeks master of Scotland, until his little army was defeated in

attending a wedding there, looked out, caught Montrose's eye, and turned away. An English soldier cried that "it was no wonder they started aside at his look, for they durst not look him in the face these seven years".

Montrose was taken to the Tolbooth, now a museum, and three days later was hanged at the Mercat Cross nearby. His body was dismembered and the trunk buried beside the public gallows on the Boroughmuir, on a spot later occupied by the printing-works of the publishers Thomas Nelson & Sons. His head was placed on a spike protruding from the west front of the Tolbooth.

Philiphaugh. Five years later he returned to try to win support for Charles II, but he was captured and brought to Edinburgh for execution.

His entry to the city was made by the Watwergait, at the foot of the Canongate. "The street," in the words of his best biographer, John Buchan, "was lined by a great crowd – the dregs of the Edinburgh slums, the retainers of the Covenanting lords, ministers from far and near – all the elements most hostile to the prisoner. But to the amazement of the organisers of the spectacle there was no sign of popular wrath. Rather there was silence, a tense air of sympathy and pity and startled admiration." As they passed Moray House, Argyll, who was

Eleven years later, after the monarchy was restored under Charles II, Montrose's head was replaced by Argyll's. Montrose's remains were then collected to lie in state in the Abbey Kirk of Holyrood, before being interred in St Giles'. There are now monuments to both great marquesses there (see page 167).

Royal building works

Charles II's reign was notable for the reconstruction of Holyrood House, undertaken in

ABOVE: a Covenanter preaching, by Sir George Harvey.
RIGHT: Covenanters being taken to execution during "the killing times".

1672 to the design of Sir William Bruce and carried out by Robert Mylne, the King's master mason. The palace, as it now stands, is their work. It was occupied for two years by Charles's brother, James, Duke of York (the future James VII of Scotland and II of England), who was sent to govern Scotland during the last Covenanting rebellion of 1679–80. Some 1,200 unfortunate Covenanting prisoners were held for five months, in miserable conditions, in the Churchyard of Greyfriars, awaiting transportation to the West Indies.

James, who was a Roman Catholic, also converted the Abbey Church at Holyrood into a Catholic chapel for the Knights of the Thistle. Its displaced congregation was handsomely rehoused in the new Canongate Church, designed by James Smith in 1688, but that same year the Edinburgh mob wrecked the Holyrood chapel to purge it of its extravagant Catholic ornamentation.

The road to Union

The monarchy came back in line with the Protestant majority when James VII was deposed in favour of his son-in-law William of Orange, but his successor Queen Anne was childless, prompting fears that supporters of the Stuarts – the Jacobites – would attempt to break away from England and put a Catholic claimant on the throne instead of the approved choice of successor. It was partly this fear – and partly for economic reasons – that the Scottish Parliament was eventually persuaded to vote itself, reluctantly, out of existence.

At the same time, anti-English feeling was strong and the popular mood was vehemently opposed to the Union. At the close of the 17th century, after a decade of economic hardship, many Edinburgh financiers and merchants were ruined by the collapse of the Darien Scheme – a Central American trading venture – whose failure was widely blamed on the hostility of the English Court and Bank of England. Yet some influential figures concluded that Scotland could only prosper in future if it united with England.

The century-old, increasingly stressful Dual Monarchy was terminated in 1707, when the Treaty of Union with England was accepted (with the help of bribes). This was "the end of

the auld sang (old song)", Scotland's last Lord Chancellor gravely commented.

Parliament House, which had been built between 1632 and 1639 to serve the double purpose of a Parliament and High Court of Justiciary, was now abandoned to the lawyers alone. The handsome building, as seen today *(see page 115)*, is the result of extensive remodelling in the early 19th century, which aroused the ire of Lord Cockburn; who wrote that "no one who remembers the old exterior can see the new one without sorrow and indignation". However, some of the interiors – in particular Parliament Hall, and the Laigh Hall beneath – retain their original features. ❑

THE ANTI-UNION MOB

When the Scottish Parliament approved the Treaty of Union with England in the autumn of 1706, the Edinburgh mob went on the rampage trying to track down the "traitors" who, they felt, had sold Scotland out to the "Auld Enemy" (the English). They trapped at least one prominent pro-Union civic leader in his home, reported the English government's agent Daniel Defoe (the author of *Robinson Crusoe*), who was himself pelted with stones when he ventured to look out of the window of his lodgings at Moubray House in the High Street. "A Scots rabble," Defoe wrote to the Secretary of State for the Northern Department, "is the worst of its kind".

THE ENLIGHTENMENT

After the loss of its political status, Edinburgh grew in physical and intellectual stature, becoming a hugely influential centre of Scottish culture

The Union marked the end of one Edinburgh, and the birth pangs which would lead to the development of a new, richer and more splendid city. At first, people were most aware of what they had lost: it was hard to make their grievances heard effectively when the reins of power were held 400 miles (640 km) away in London. But the benefits of the Union were soon to be experienced in an expanding economy and a new prosperity.

There are, however, three interludes in Edinburgh's development which seem properly to belong to the old city, and which will therefore be dealt with first. Each of them illustrates the strength of nationalist feeling that persisted in some quarters, despite a general easing of political tension after the early years of the 18th century.

Aftershocks of the Union

The Porteous Riot of 1736 was a spontaneous and yet disciplined outburst of popular feeling which challenged London's right to dictate policy to the erstwhile Scottish capital. Captain Porteous of the City Guard had been convicted of murder after firing shots into the rabble-rousing crowd at the scene of an execution in the Grassmarket. When London intervened to stay his own execution, the mob took the law into its own hands, broke into his prison cell and marched him to the gallows. This shook the Government in London, which demolished the Netherbow Port on the Royal Mile to make it easier for its troops to enter the city in the event of future rebellions. The best account of the episode is in the opening chapters of Sir Walter Scott's finest novel, *The Heart of Midlothian.*

The second interlude took place nine years later, when Holyrood House became for a few weeks again a royal palace. Its occupant was Prince Charles Edward, the grandson of James VII and champion of the exiled line of native

kings. He faced little resistance when he seized the city (but not the Castle) with his Highland army, which was quartered in the King's Park outside the palace, after which he announced his Regency, proclaiming his father as King. The prince's army then marched out to defeat the Hanoverian army under Sir John Cope at

Prestonpans, before the "royal court" left Edinburgh to make an ill-fated advance into England.

Finally, during the Napoleonic Wars, the "Auld Alliance" between Scotland and France was revived. When many French prisoners were held in the Castle, Holyrood was the refuge of the claimant to the French throne, the future Louis XVIII, and his brother the Comte d'Artois; the latter returned there for 18 months in 1830, when as Charles X, he had been driven from his throne by the July Revolution.

The Golden Age

Predominantly, however, the 18th century was Edinburgh's Golden Age, and the Age of Reason

---

LEFT: Raeburn's famous portrayal of the Rev. Robert Walker skating on Duddingston Loch (1784).
RIGHT: Allan Ramsay's portrait of David Hume.

rather than Romance. Having ceased to be a political capital, it became a cultural and intellectual centre of unprecedented influence. It was said that a man could stand by the Mercat Cross and "in a few minutes take 50 men of genius by the hand". This was testimony both to the cultural riches of the city and its small size.

Until the middle of the century it was still confined within its late medieval limits – to the Royal Mile, the Cowgate, the Grassmarket, and the closes and wynds running off these streets. In the words of Daniel Defoe, the author of *Robinson Crusoe* and a Government spy who left a full account of the city just before the

medieval city. It spread first to the south with the building in 1763–64 of George Square (where Walter Scott would live as a child) and then of Buccleuch Place from 1772. Only the west side of the square now survives of the original design, the other three sides having been barbarously redeveloped by Edinburgh University in the 1960s. Among the notable buildings of this period is the Old College of the university, designed by Robert Adam in 1789. But only the street frontage on South Bridge is his work, the single court within having been designed by William Playfair and completed in 1834.

Union, it stood "on the narrow ridge of a long ascending mountain". He added: "I believe … that in no city in the world do so many people live in so little room as at Edinburgh."

It was a filthy city – "as if the people were not willing to live sweet and clean as other nations", said Defoe – but, by its close-knit nature, it was also a city still ignorant of the segregation of classes: tradesmen, lords, merchants, clerks and labourers might all inhabit the same tenement *(see Gentry in the Stink, page 37)*.

Great expansion

In the middle of the 18th century Edinburgh at last broke the bounds of the overcrowded

More audacious, however, was the decision taken by the Town Council, at the instigation of Lord Provost Drummond, to build a completely new town on the north side of the loch (now Princes Street Gardens) which at that time defined Edinburgh's northern limits.

A competition for the design of the New Town was won by a 22-year-old architect, James Craig. His plan was for single-sided terraces facing over gardens to the south and north: Princes Street and Queen Street respectively.

ABOVE: the Porteous Riot of 1736.
RIGHT: portrait of James Craig, architect of the New Town, by David Allan.

Between them ran a street of unprecedented breadth, George Street, completed at either end by expansive squares, St Andrew Square and Charlotte Square. Other streets ran north and south on a grid pattern and between the main thoroughfares were two narrow service streets. The original design provided for a great circus in the middle of George Street, but this was never built.

Early in the 19th century, further expansion to the north would take place below Queen Street Gardens, and this larger development – which is mainly residential – is now also referred to as part of the "New Town" *(see The Greater New Town, pages 147–153)*.

New confidence

The building of the New Town was an expression of the intellectual and economic confidence characteristic of 18th-century Edinburgh. It was a consequence of the Scottish Enlightenment, several of whose luminaries, such as the philosopher and historian David Hume, came to live in the New Town.

The history of Walter Scott's dwelling-places in Edinburgh may be taken as an illustration of how the city changed during his lifetime. He was born in the dark and squalid College Wynd in the Old Town, lived as a child in George Square, moved after marriage to Castle Street in the New Town, and then, after his financial crash in 1826, to lodgings in Walker Street, then recently built to the west of Charlotte Square. It had been open country when he was a young man. Among his younger contemporaries who resided at this time in the New Town were fellow writers Thomas Carlyle (who lived in

Comely Bank) and Thomas De Quincey (Great King Street).

Old Town networking

For most of the 18th century, though, social life was concentrated in the taverns of the Old Town. Claret was the favoured drink there, for Scotland had kept its links with France sufficiently for gentlemen to continue to favour Bordeaux wine rather than the coarse port which was the usual drink of the English gentry. It was a small society where anonymity was impossible. Everyone in 18th-century Scotland enjoyed an extensive cousinage; pride

of family was powerful, and any degree of secrecy was impossible.

In this atmosphere it was no wonder that ideas were stimulatingly exchanged. Everyone knew that knowledge was being rapidly expanded, and both in the taverns and through the agency of learned societies people came to realise that they were living in an age of improvement.

In the second half of the century, the university – though at that time the youngest in Scotland, having been founded only in 1582 – began to acquire a reputation as the most progressive school of learning in Britain (despite the fact that Hume had earlier been denied a

sovereign state, and they sought a new understanding which would give them some validity in their new condition.

One consequence was that intellectuals came to be regarded as natural leaders of society. Contemporaries frequently commented on the high status they enjoyed, and it was generally recognised that Edinburgh's reputation rested on its contribution to philosophy, history, art and science. Nevertheless it was still an aristocratic city. The greatest nobles might have followed Court and Parliament to London, but many landed families maintained a house or flat in Edinburgh.

Chair on account of his reputed atheism). But it was less formal bodies such as The Honourable Society for Improvement in the Knowledge of Agriculture and The Select Society – founded by Hume, Allan Ramsay and Adam Smith, among others, to discuss general moral and political questions and the improvement of Scottish society – which were the principal focuses of the city's intellectual life.

Such developments were common, both in Europe and America; similar clubs were found in, for example, Dijon, Bordeaux, Boston and Philadelphia. The Scottish clubs, however, felt a special urgency: they were aware of how Scotland had lost its historic identity as a

Power and professions

There was little in the way of formal administration of Scotland by the Government: when a Scottish Secretary was appointed in 1762, for instance, he found that there were no papers relating to Scottish business. In fact the members of the Faculty of Advocates managed what there was of public business, and for more than a century and a half the Lord Advocate was, in effect, the Government's man in Scotland.

Meanwhile, other Edinburgh lawyers, the Writers to the Signet, achieved a dominant position as men of business acting for the Scottish nobility. By the end of the century Edinburgh was on the way to becoming a city dominated by the professions, especially law and medicine.

The Royal College of Physicians had been founded in 1681, and the Edinburgh Medical School was founded at about the same time. Under Alexander Monro (1697–1767), who taught anatomy there for 40 years, the latter acquired a reputation which attracted students from other parts of Britain and even from the Continent; in the 20th century the attraction became world-wide. Not even the scandalous involvement of the Professor of Anatomy, Robert Knox, with the body-snatchers and murderers Burke and Hare in the 1820s *(see page*

Horner, and a Church of England clergyman Sydney Smith, who was then resident in the city. The fact that the first three were advocates provides further evidence of the importance of the legal profession in Scottish cultural history; Jeffrey eventually became Lord Advocate and Brougham Lord Chancellor of England in the Whig Ministry of 1832.

The *Review* was published by Archibald Constable, to whom Lord Cockburn (another advocate and later a judge) said: "the literature of Scotland has been more indebted than any other of his vocation". It quickly established itself as the leading periodical of its day. Within

167) seriously checked the growing reputation of Edinburgh medicine.

Intellectual forum

Edinburgh's reputation as an intellectual and cultural centre was reinforced when *The Edinburgh Review*, a periodical that promoted Scottish literature and philosophy, was established in 1802. Its founders were three advocates: Francis Jeffrey, Henry Brougham and Francis

LEFT: engraving, by Paul Sandby, of the Castle and city from the northwest before the New Town was built.
ABOVE: high society promenades on Princes Street and admires the view of the old city, *circa* 1810.

ENLIGHTENED SCIENCE

The Enlightenment in Edinburgh was not restricted to philosophy, the arts and medicine. Some important scientific figures also lived and worked in the city. They included Joseph Black (foremost of several eminent chemists), the father of quantitative chemistry who helped Watt develop the steam engine and discovered carbon dioxide, and James Hutton, whose *Theory of the Earth* (1785) is considered the foundation of modern geology. William Smellie of Edinburgh, the editor and principal author of the first edition of the *Encyclopaedia Britannica*, was a fountain of knowledge of both science and the arts.

five years its circulation was 7,000; by 1818 it had monthly sales of over 18,000. It decreed the canons of taste – not only in Scotland but throughout Britain – for the expanding middle class, but its politics were Whig. It soon had a Tory rival in *Blackwood's Magazine*.

The Age of Scott

The first three decades of the 19th century are regarded as the second phase of the Enlightenment, often referred to as the Age of Sir Walter Scott. First as a poet, then as the author of the Waverley novels, he presented a new and Romantic picture of Scotland to the world. His

self died in 1832, the same year that Thomas Carlyle, the outstanding figure in the next generation of writers, settled in London. That date may conveniently be taken as marking the decline of the Scottish Enlightenment. It was significant that Carlyle could not find sufficient intellectual sustenance in Edinburgh.

Cockburn was to declare that "the 18th century was the last purely Scotch age. Everything that came after was English." There was some truth in this judgement, though it was grossly exaggerated. But it was not entirely a bad thing: Scotland had achieved a new confidence as part of the United Kingdom.

influence was profound, extending far beyond literature: he organised the visit of George IV to Scotland in 1822, the first by a reigning monarch since Charles I had come north in 1641. For that visit, Scott put half of Edinburgh into tartan, the fashion for which soon extended to Paris. The influence of Scott's medieval novels, and of the code of chivalry they revived, was so great that Mark Twain held him responsible for the American Civil War.

End of Enlightenment

The literary reviews remained influential throughout the 19th century, but their great days were over by the end of the 1830s. Scott him-

The idea of Britishness was strengthened by the experience of the wars against Napoleon. Significantly, the eastward continuation of Princes Street was called Waterloo Place, and a fine equestrian statue of the Duke of Wellington was erected outside Robert Adam's Register House. Some, however, may discern a darker, but more accurate, symbol of the relationship between Scotland and the rest of the UK in the National Monument to commemorate Waterloo built on the Calton Hill; it was left unfinished due to a lack of funds. ❑

ABOVE: Princes Street and its gardens, graced by a monument to Scott 14 years after his death.

Gentry in the Stink

From late medieval times into the 19th century the Old Town was like a past version of Manhattan, in which the aristocracy, gentry, merchants and common folk of Edinburgh lived cheek by jowl in highly stacked tenements or "lands". Often they shared the same lands, the "quality" in the middle reaches, and hoi-polloi at the bottom and the top. Despite the presence of the upper classes standards of hygiene were appalling and one particular (in)sanitary arrangement was notorious: the emptying of slops from high windows into the street. A famous street-cry was "gardyloo", a local version of the French "gardez l'eau" (look out for the water), yelled to warn passers-by of the impending shower. "Haud yer hand!" any lingering pedestrians would shout back. Many travellers commented on the stench of the streets.

The tenements were also prone to disastrous fire, although the fact that the staircases were built of stone helped to reduce the risk. After one catastrophic fire in 1824, which gutted much of the south side of the High Street and wrecked the steeple of the Tron Church, the city fathers formed Britain's first-ever municipal fire brigade. In November 1861 the tenements between 99 and 107 High Street collapsed, killing 35 of the inhabitants. One man buried under the rubble told his rescuers to "Heave awa' chaps, I'm no' deid (dead) yet", words which are inscribed over the entry to Paisley Close.

The close quarters in which men and women of widely different stations lived had a marked impact on how society functioned, for all and sundry rubbed shoulders in the dark stairways, and knew one another in a way that was impossible in England. Beggars and pullers of sedan-chairs lived in the closes where earls and dowagers had their apartments; lawyers' clerks mingled drunkenly with porters and joined in outbreaks of mob rule. Any Lord of Session (high court judge) whose verdict was unpopular could expect to be harangued, or even pelted with mud, as he made his way home.

Likewise, politicians, the aristocracy, church leaders and various power brokers came under close scrutiny. With the Scottish Parliament meeting in a building located in the middle of the High Street (just behind St Giles') it was impossible to avoid the eye of the public. Political questions were not only debated by the educated classes; the masses kept abreast of the issues of the day, too, and were frequently involved in street demonstrations. In fact the Edinburgh mob was a formidable political force.

For part of the 18th century it was led by one "General" Joe Smith, a bow-legged cobbler who believed passionately in the inferiority of women (his wife had to walk several paces behind him) and who could drum up a crowd of thousands within a few minutes. With the mob at his back Joe Smith could lay down the law to the magistrates of Edinburgh, and ran a kind of rough justice against thieving landlords and dishonest merchants.

Not that life in the Old Town was entirely dominated by mob rule. Far from it. Until the end of the 18th century the Old Town was the epicentre of fashionable society, a tight little metropolis of elegant drawing rooms, fashionable concert halls, dancing academies and a bewildering variety of *howffs* (taverns), coffee houses and social clubs.

A peculiar Edinburgh institution, the "caddies", were men and boys who acted as street messengers, guides and general factotums (and carried golf clubs). Although the poorest of the poor, the caddies were fiercely honest. One 18th-century English writer credited the caddies with the fact that "there are fewer robberies and less housebreaking in Edinburgh than anywhere else". ❏

RIGHT: residents spilled into the street in overcrowded Libberton's Wynd.

GROWTH AND DIVISIONS

Victorian Edinburgh was characterised by creeping expansion,
prosperity and learning for some, and a hard life in the slums for others

The Victorian Age, which may be considered in this context as lasting until the outbreak of World War I, was a period of paradox in Edinburgh's history. On the one hand, the city's expansion continued; on the other, it declined from occupying the position of an intellectual metropolis to the condition of a provincial capital.

It grew vastly – though far more slowly than did Glasgow or many English provincial cities. The area north of the Meadows was covered with lofty stone terraces, and, in Grange and Morningside, with substantial villas; the city now extended almost to the base of the Pentland Hills. To the west it stretched out to include the once rural village of Corstorphine. Working-class tenements covered Gorgie and Dalry, and the fringes of Leith Walk and Broughton (*see page 150*).

Unlike Glasgow, however, the city had very little heavy industry. There was ship-building in Leith, still a separate burgh, but Edinburgh was predominantly a commercial and professional city, not an industrial one. Brewing and printing were the main industries. The *Encyclopaedia Britannica* was first published here, as was *Chambers Encyclopaedia* and maps, including *The Times Atlas*.

Age of the train

Edinburgh handled the printing for most London publishers, sheets being carried on the steam packets that now ran between Leith and London. The railway arrived in the 1840s, drawing Scotland and England even closer together. Rival companies established their own stations, Princes Street at the west end and Waverley at the east end of the city's main thoroughfare, and in the first decade of the 20th century the two great railway hotels at either end of the road, the Caledonian and the North British, were built to serve the customers of the respective companies.

The city's growth hastened the decline of the Old Town, which soon became a territory of insalubrious slums. In 1851 half the population, about 40,000 people, still lived there, crammed into tenement blocks which lacked any kind of

sanitation. The old social homogeneity had gone. In his essay *Edinburgh: Picturesque Notes*, Robert Louis Stevenson remarked that "to look over the South bridge and see the Cowgate below full of crying hawkers is to view one rank of society from another in the twinkling of an eye".

Probably this loss of homogeneity was inevitable. It affected most great cities in the 19th century, which saw a sharp delineation taking place between the districts inhabited by a growing, ever more prosperous, bourgeoisie and the expanding working class.

There were, of course, distinctions within this class, too: between the respectable and

LEFT: *The Rev. Thomas Guthrie on a Mission of Mercy*, by James Edgar.
RIGHT: Princes Street was Edinburgh's busiest thoroughfare in the late 19th century, as it is now.

The Disruption

In the porch of elegant, neo-classical St Andrew's and St George's church, at the east end of George Street in Edinburgh, is a modest sign which explains that, on 18 May 1843, this building was the scene of one of the most dramatic events in 19th-century Scottish history – the "Disruption" of the Church of Scotland. On that day almost 500 ministers startled Britain by turning their backs on salaries, homes, careers and social standing and walking into the wilderness to set up the Free Church of Scotland.

The Disruption was the culmination of decades of bruising, politically charged argument which split Scotland's established church down the middle and led law-abiding men to mount a fierce (and successful) challenge to the power of the British government and aristocracy. In fact, it has been argued that the Disruption of 1843 was the only rebellion in 19th-century Britain that succeeded. It projected on to the international stage Presbyterian divines like Thomas Chalmers (whose statue stands at the crossroads of George Street and Castle Street) and Thomas Guthrie (whose image graces the west end of Princes Street Gardens). The church they created underpinned the key differences between Scottish and English societies.

It all began with the Patronage Act of 1712, a notorious piece of Jacobite-inspired law-making which gave the Scottish gentry the right to appoint (or "intrude") clergymen of their own choosing on Church of Scotland congregations – a right the English gentry had enjoyed for hundreds of years. The Scots were outraged. Since John Knox's Reformation of 1560 the election of ministers by their congregations had lain at the heart of the Scottish Presbyterian Church, and the Patronage Act was a flagrant violation of treaties with England. But the English-dominated parliament could see nothing wrong with bringing Scotland into line with England.

In the late 18th century the General Assembly of the Church became dominated by the "moderate" party, most of whom were appointees of the gentry. But eventually the "moderates" gave way to the "evangelical" party led by Dr Thomas Chalmers, a brilliant theologian, mathematician and orator. After 10 years of unsuccessful political and legal battles with the British establishment, Chalmers and some 470 "evangelical" ministers walked out of the General Assembly of the Church of Scotland, in 1843, to set up the Free Church of Scotland. This took the Establishment by surprise, but it was no romantic gesture. Chalmers and his colleagues were brilliant organisers and tireless money-raisers, and within a very few years the Free Church had built hundreds of new churches, manses (homes for the clergy) and schools, plus three substantial theological colleges.

Not that Chalmers and company had it all their own way. In many parts of Scotland, and particularly in the Highlands, the lairds refused to give (or sell) the Free Church any land on which to build churches. Like their 17th-century ancestors, many adherents were forced to hold their services in the open air, often in foul weather and usually harried by the laird's men. Eventually, in 1847, parliament set up an inquiry into why so many of Queen Victoria's most pious subjects were being denied the right to worship, and the aristocracy were embarrassed into dropping their resistance.

In 1874 the Patronage Act was scrapped, and in 1929 most of the Free Church congregations returned to the established Church of Scotland. But not everybody accepted the new order: a minority, particularly in the Highlands, clung to their independence and remain the democratic (if somewhat stern) Free Church of Scotland. ❏

LEFT: a detail from Lorimer's classic painting *Ordination of the Elders*.

regular wage-earners, who mostly inhabited the rows of new tenements, and the indigent poor, many only working at casual trades, who thronged the slums of the Old Town. As a city with a high proportion of the middle class, Edinburgh also housed huge numbers of domestic servants; according to the 1881 census they amounted to more than 20 percent of the total population.

Men of principle

In this religious age Edinburgh was also a city of churches, and the more so after the great event of the middle part of the century, the Dis-

themselves the Free Church of Scotland. The great number of churches in Edinburgh, many now converted to other uses, was the consequence of this secession, for the Free Kirk at once embarked on a policy of church building, which resulted in duplication of the existing parish churches.

The great political figure of mid-19th-century Edinburgh was Duncan McLaren, several times Lord Provost and one of the city's Members of Parliament. He was a Gladstonian Liberal, and the brother-in-law of the great English Liberal advocate of free trade and pacifism, John Bright. At that time the Liberals were pre-

ruption of the Kirk (Church) in 1843. This split in the Church of Scotland was brought about by a dispute over patronage (the right to appoint the minister of a parish). The seceders were led by Dr Thomas Chalmers, Professor of Theology at Edinburgh University and the most famous churchman of the day.

Chalmers led some 470 ministers, 40 percent of the whole number in Scotland, out of the Church's General Assembly meeting in George Street and down Hanover Street to Canonmills, where in a hall they proclaimed

ABOVE: John Wilson Ewbank's depiction of George IV's descent into Edinburgh from Calton Hill.

THE FIRST TOURISTS

Curiously, while some of the distinctions that made Scotland Scotland were being whittled away by electoral and municipal reform – and even as the Old Town spiralled into ignominious decline – Edinburgh was acquiring a reputation as a tourist destination. When rail travel became possible the romantically inclined began flocking to the city, emerging from Waverley Station to be greeted by the recently built gothic Scott Monument. Some may have been encouraged by the reports of the young Queen Victoria, who visited Edinburgh with Prince Albert just before the railway was opened in 1842, and was full of praise for its grand and handsome architecture.

dominant in Edinburgh, as indeed they were throughout Scotland.

McLaren favoured the extension of the franchise to most householders, free trade and legislation to control the sale of alcohol (the great cause of vice, it was widely thought, of the Scottish working class). He was a Free Kirk man and suspicious of trade unionism. In 1873 he was described by the Trades Council of Edinburgh as "a traitor to the working-class interest" because of his part in the Criminal Law Amendment Act which had outlawed picketing; a great demonstration against him and his policies was held in the Queen's Park outside the Palace of Holyroodhouse. This was evidence of the divisions within the city.

School classes

The social stratification of the city was also evident in its schools. Scotland has always boasted a democratic tradition of education, and in the 19th century it was undoubtedly easier for a poor boy to get an education in Scotland than in England. Nevertheless, social distinction between different schools became more marked in Victorian Edinburgh.

The Royal High School, where Scott and Cockburn had been educated, moved in 1829

THE HIDDEN MORALITY

There was a moral division in Victorian Edinburgh that was so sharp it may be called a duality. Towards the end of the century, at a time when marriage was regarded as the only acceptable basis for sexual relationships, around 7 percent of babies born in the ostensibly virtuous God-fearing city were illegitimate.

Moreover, the city was abundant in brothels. In 1842 Dr William Tait claimed that there were 200 of them in Edinburgh. Hypocrisy was rife: it was said that the brothels in Rose Street enjoyed their best trade during the week of the annual General Assembly of the Church. In 1862 an Act of Parliament empowered the police to close brothels and drive prostitutes from the streets. Even so, in 1901, Edinburgh police reported 424 known prostitutes and 45 brothels operating in the capital.

No one was more conscious of the two faces of Edinburgh morality than the writer Robert Louis Stevenson. Though his masterpiece of duality, *The Strange Case of Dr Jekyll and Mr Hyde*, is set in London, no one has doubted that its inspiration came from Edinburgh *(see page 65)*. As a young man, Stevenson himself had frequented the brothels and disreputable taverns of Leith Walk and had even fallen in love with a prostitute called Kate Drummond.

from the Old Town to a noble neo-classical building *(see page 152)* on Calton Hill. (In the 1960s the school would move again to the middle-class suburb of Barnton, and a decade later the old building would be prepared for the first, unsuccessful attempt in the 20th century to set up a Scottish Assembly.) But dissatisfaction with the High School had led, in 1824, to the creation of the Edinburgh Academy, which became the pre-eminent school for the sons of the professional classes. The schools owned by the Edinburgh Merchant Company also became more socially exclusive, and three public schools

great Edinburgh clubs, Heart of Midlothian and Hibernian, were both formed before the end of the century.

The name of the latter, from the Roman for Ireland, calls attention to the Irish Catholic immigration which took place in the 19th century, mostly after the famine in Ireland of 1846. Although sectarian passions did not run as high in Edinburgh as Glasgow, where even more Catholics went, "Hearts" was the Protestant club and "Hibs" the Catholic club. (In time the distinction between them would dwindle to a geographical one, Hearts representing the west side of the city and Hibs the east.)

on the English model, Loretto, Merchiston and Fettes, were in being by 1870.

It was in these schools that rugby was first played, the sport that would become the team game favoured by the middle classes. The working-class game, Association Football, came into being a little later, as a result of greater leisure and the realisation on the part of employers that sport provided a valuable recreation and diversion for their workers: the two

LEFT: the busy Port of Leith with a distant view of Edinburgh, by Paul Jean Clays.
ABOVE: the Old Town through the steam from trains emerging from Waverley Station, *circa* 1870.

Higher learning

Edinburgh University flourished throughout the 19th century, particularly in the areas of law, philosophy, history, medicine and natural science. Its greatest alumnus was James Clerk Maxwell, the outstanding theoretical scientist of the century; but, though born and wholly educated in Edinburgh, he was never given a chair at the University.

The greatest figure in medicine was Sir James Young Simpson, Professor of Midwifery, and promoter of anaesthetics. He discovered the efficacy of chloroform in the laboratory in his house in Queen Street, which now bears a plaque recording the event. ❏

FROM WAR TO HOME RULE

After a century of ambitious schemes and conservatism, civic mistakes and
spectacular successes, the new millennium offers a fresh start for the capital city

The Edinburgh that welcomed the 21st century with a dazzling binge of music, fireworks, rhetoric and whisky was, in important respects, very different from the dank Victorian city of a hundred years earlier. Though it had never ceased to think of itself defiantly as the nation's capital, it had finally regained the parliament whose abolition almost three centuries earlier had undermined the claim.

It had sprawled significantly from its focus around the Castle Rock and had officially absorbed communities like Corstorphine, Colinton and Leith, as well as building, with variable results, new settlements in what had been its surrounding countryside. The city centre, too, had gained many new buildings, ranging as elsewhere from the splendid to the abject. Most of its unsanitary slums had been demolished or, more often, gentrified. The pall of tarry smoke that had earned Edinburgh the nickname of "Auld Reekie" (Old Smoky) had gone, and many of its finest buildings had been scrubbed clean of their sooty patinas.

Old character preserved

Yet, in other respects, Edinburgh changed much less across a dynamic century than most British cities. It escaped the Nazi bombs that so transformed London, Coventry and Liverpool. Thanks to the twin blessings of awkward geography and unconsensual civic politics, it also escaped the worst of the mid-century grand planning designs that submerged so many city centres in characterless concrete precincts and urban motorways.

Many Edinburgh people, of all classes, continued to live in buildings erected in the Victorian era or earlier, which have now been lovingly restored. Even the villages that the city's urban sprawl had devoured tended to retain their character, though sometimes as rustic islands in oceans of bland bungalows. And

Edinburgh's natural boundaries of hills and the Firth of Forth stopped it sprawling too far.

It remained a city whose extremes of wealth and social standing had a polarity that seemed more vivid than elsewhere: a large middle class living, cheek by jowl, with a large working class. Where once they had shared the same

tenements, now they lived in different, though often adjacent, districts. Each retained the intuitive ability to identify one another by speech, appearance, education and manner, though the old demarcations of trade and profession were eroding. Above all, perhaps, Edinburgh remained a city with a rare talent for containing social, political and historical turbulence beneath a demure imperturbability.

The Great War nevertheless took its toll on Edinburgh as on the rest of the country, and the scale of the losses in both the 20th century's World Wars is recorded in the lists of the dead in the Scottish National War Memorial in Edinburgh Castle. The Memorial was the master-

LEFT: Scottish patriots campaigning for home rule.
RIGHT: an early 1900s postcard showing the view from the Rutland Hotel at the west end of Princes Street.

piece of Sir Robert Lorimer, one of the greatest Scottish architects of his generation.

The 20 years between the wars marked the first of the two periods (the second being the 1950s and 1960s) when Edinburgh's physical expansion was at its most marked. Old slums were cleared, while the growth in public transport saw housing developments unfold along what had previously been farm roads. Much of the new housing was built by the local authority, often to a high standard that would prove

THE NEW SLUMS

In the 1960s Edinburgh City Council built well-intentioned but woeful peripheral housing schemes which would have attracted wider condemnation had not Glasgow built worse.

impossible to sustain in the second surge of development after World War II. Gradually, the city stretched outwards: west along the Glasgow Road, south to the foot of the Pentland Hills, east towards Musselburgh.

Two faces of Edinburgh

Much of the Old Town remained *terra incognita* to the respectable middle class. David Daiches, literary critic and historian, who was a schoolboy at George Watson's College in the 1920s, remembered the Grassmarket and Cowgate as a "filthy slum with children with rickets and bare feet running around in obvious poverty, and ill-nourished women with threadbare shawls coming out of the jug and bottle entrance of a pub, trying to drown their sorrows in gin". Only in the last quarter of the century did the brooding closes of the Old Town begin to take on an air of chic.

It was middle-class Edinburgh that gave the city the face it presented to the world. This was the city of elegant villas and terraces, dignified hotels and great department stores (Jenner's and Forsyth's pre-eminent on Princes Street, Patrick Thomson's on North Bridge), of electric tramcars and a suburban railway, and, most famously, of tea-rooms. The sight of fur-coated ladies in forbidding hats taking afternoon tea in McVitie's was one of the most characteristic and imperishable Edinburgh images.

Status boosts

Meanwhile, the city's claim to capital status gained fresh force with the relocation of the Scottish Office to Edinburgh. Scotland had been accorded its own government department in 1885, but it was based in London and its senior minister only acquired Cabinet rank in 1926. In 1936 Walter Elliot, one of the more distinguished Secretaries of State for Scotland, initiated its transfer to Edinburgh, and from its imposing new premises on the slopes of the Calton Hill it steadily took on a distinctive approach to policy, particularly under Tom Johnston during World War II.

This was, wrote historian Michael Fry, "more than administrative reform. It had immense symbolic value, making Edinburgh once again a seat of government, truly a capital rather than just the headquarters of the Church and the judiciary." It also allowed Scotland to hold on to many of its most able administrators, and reinforced the distinctiveness which it had maintained in its educational, legal, judicial and cultural environments after the Act of Union.

The city's international prestige gained its most significant lift after World War II with the creation of the Edinburgh International Festival in 1947. Three men were responsible: Harvey Wood, Scottish director of the British Council, Rudolf Bing, general manager of Glyndebourne Opera, and Sir John Falconer, Lord Provost of Edinburgh. Sir John's involvement represented one of the most visionary acts on the part of the

City Council since the creation of the New Town almost 200 years before, though thereafter its commitment to the Festival, at least in financial terms, was less enthusiastic.

In particular, the lack of an opera house (despite sporadic schemes) became a standing reproach, prompting some critics to maintain that the Festival happened despite, not because of, the Edinburgh City Council. Only in the closing years of the century, with the impressive refurbishment of the Festival Theatre and the renovation of the Playhouse Theatre, Lyceum Theatre and Usher Hall, did the city appear at last ready to shoulder the responsibilities that went with the privilege of hosting the world's biggest arts festival.

Nevertheless the establishment of the Festival, and the extraordinary growth of the Fringe around it, set Edinburgh firmly on the world's tourist itinerary. Visitors came for the performances and were captivated by the backdrop. From the 1980s onwards, Edinburgh staked out another chunk of the calendar by extending a global invitation to what became the world's biggest Hogmanay party. By the end of the century, the city was well on its way to achieving the ultimate goal of all tourism authorities: a year-round season.

Bad planning

In other respects, though, the first two decades after World War II were unhappy. The city failed to come to terms with the hazards of congestion and pollution that the motor car presents to all historic towns, and the closure in the early 1960s of the suburban railway was a prime example of myopic folly.

Worse still, while Edinburgh's historic heart was spared systematic redevelopment, the city exhibited a depressing capacity in the century's middle years for being careless of its architectural heritage: Princes Street was debased by some unsightly frontages; the University, to its enduring shame, was permitted to destroy George Square and its environs; the St James Centre, a leading contender for the title of Scotland's ugliest construction, squatted balefully at the top of Leith Walk; even the New Town came under threat, though it would emerge rel-

atively unscathed. The Old Town was subject to redevelopment, benign in that it saved the fabric of the Canongate, less so in that it resulted in the expulsion of its traditional inhabitants.

Urban renewal

Fortunately, there was a reaction. The New Town Conservation Committee was formed in 1970, after an international conference, and the shadow of despoliation of the New Town gave way to conservation and renovation, which soon extended to the Old Town. There was, as always, a price to pay. Recognition of the New Town's Georgian elegance turned its town

houses into highly fashionable business premises for fund managers, lawyers, accountants and the like. As homes, they passed beyond the purse of all but the wealthiest, and the New Town lost much of its life-force outside office hours. The restored Old Town, equally, could occasionally resemble a heritage centre rather than a community during the tourist season.

Yet, the century closed amid hopes of redress for the city centre on both sides of the dividing Princes Street Gardens. Office fashion, driven by communications technology and management fad, shifted to a preference for purpose-built open-plan premises. The professions

LEFT: city road-sweeper in the mid-20th century.
RIGHT: a typical 1960s tower block, built for better housing but now considered an ugly eyesore.

consequently moved out of the New Town, and rows of vacant Georgian properties began to return to domestic occupation. Meanwhile, the coming of the Scottish Parliament, initially domiciled on The Mound but due to occupy futuristic new premises at Holyrood in 2003, has brought a fresh sense of purpose to the Old Town, reflected in the spread of chic little shops, restaurants and bars.

The main losers in these changes are the big chain-store retailers ranged along Princes Street, whose demands for concrete and plate-glass frontages perpetrated some of the worst architectural aberrations of a generation earlier.

Now they find the lunchtime shoppers lost to new business districts outside the city centre, and weekend shoppers preferring to travel outward to new developments dotted around the city bypass, rather than inward to a central zone in which the present policy is to make private cars unwelcome (the number of one-way streets and parking restrictions proving a source of constant frustration to those who continue to drive regularly into the city centre).

At the same time, the city authorities have tried to stem the haemorrhage of income with plans for new city-centre retail developments. However, a bizarre and unpopular scheme to

put a shopping mall under Princes Street failed to get planning permission, and in any case many people prefer a lived-in centre from which they can commute *out* to service the demands of mammon.

Regaining the initiative

On the flip side of the coin, the city has in several instances adopted a pioneering approach to social policy. One example is the needle-exchange scheme introduced to stem the onslaught of Aids *(see box, left)*; another is the licensing of saunas, which has shifted much of the city's prostitution trade off the streets and into regulated, health-checked premises.

THE AIDS CAPITAL

In the mid-1990s, the movie *Trainspotting* alerted a wider world to an unwholesome truth about Edinburgh. For 20 years the city had harboured a festering hard drugs culture; worse, the prevalence of needle-sharing was exposing addicts to a deadly new disease. By the late 1980s, Edinburgh was the Aids capital of Europe, with infection levels on a par with those of New York State. However, though drug abuse remains extensive, the threat of an HIV epidemic has been averted by bold initiatives which included setting up official needle exchanges where addicts could swap used needles for clean ones. It was a controversial but successful new approach.

Edinburgh has often been accused of hiding its seedier side. In recent years, it has not only been forced to acknowledge and confront its social problems, but has learned to take pride in its success in doing so. Edinburgh has rarely lacked self-confidence, but it has entered the 21st century with more spring to its step, and more justification for it, than in many decades. Having watched bemused in the 1980s while its old rival Glasgow reinvented itself as a modern hub of culture and commerce, Edinburgh regained the initiative in the 1990s.

Local government reorganisation restored the dignity of a unitary city council after 20

The new politics

In the early to mid-1990s the Conservative government of John Major, anxious to stave off home rule, flattered the city with international summits and even the return, to the Crown Room in Edinburgh Castle, of the Stone of Destiny *(see page 111)*. But in 1997 Major was swept from office by Labour's Tony Blair, who kept his promise of an early referendum on a devolved Scottish Parliament.

The result, in September 1997, was a resounding "yes", and on 1 July 1999 the Queen formally opened the first Scottish Parliament to convene since 1707, and the first ever to be

years when power had been shared within the frame of a wider regional authority. The city's various local economic development bodies showed a readiness to work in harmony that was rarely matched elsewhere in Scotland, and prestigious new developments ensued, including a new financial district, an international conference centre and a new out-of-centre business and retail sprawl at the Gyle (on the approach to the airport).

LEFT: traditional ceilidh dance in the Assembly Rooms, 1970s style.
ABOVE: Hogmanay fireworks: New Year celebrations were bigger than ever to greet the new millennium.

democratically elected. It took control over policy areas previously administered on Westminster's behalf by the Scottish Office, swiftly becoming both the focus of Scottish public life and the crucible for what many hoped would be a more consensual style of politics.

No less swiftly, it also demonstrated that such aspirations would be forever in contention with the disputatious, some would say cantankerous, elements of the Scottish character. Numerous controversies erupted, not least over the Parliament's own premises. It found a temporary home in the Church of Scotland's Assembly Hall on The Mound, while a futuristic complex was prepared a mile away at Holyrood. But shortly before the architect's sudden death in 2000 it emerged that the building would not be completed on schedule, nor for much less than three times its original budget (costs have continued to spiral since then).

This matter may have stirred voters less than it did their elected representatives, for whom it provided the makings of what Scots call a fine "stushie", or row. It was not the best start for the new Scottish politics, but in time it may seem a small affair. The bigger point was that Edinburgh's claim to be a capital city was at last fully realised.

VAGUE VISION

The new Parliament building was designed by the late Catalan architect, Enric Miralles, to a nautical theme that was perhaps more exciting in concept than it was specific to Edinburgh.

of Scotland and a splendid new Museum of Scotland, and has a rich artistic life.

Though it has many problems, though it retains a lingering envy for the renaissance of Glasgow, and though its extremes of privilege and deprivation remain largely unreconciled, Edinburgh exerts an enduring appeal which the excitement and confidence of its restored status can only enhance. It retains a unique ability to beguile the eye and the imagination that makes it an unde-

Things to be proud of

No less important has been Edinburgh's command of the other kind of capital. During the 20th century it built and consolidated a reputation as one of Europe's most important financial centres (see The Money Men of Charlotte Square, page 143). It also remains the headquarters of the Scottish legal system, and its reputation for academic distinction has been reinforced by a rise in its tally of universities from one to three, as first Heriot-Watt and then Napier College gained university status. It is pre-eminently the city of the professions, with its medical prowess in particular retaining a global prestige. It houses the National Galleries

niable gem of European civilization: not for nothing have both the Old Town and the New Town, as well as other nooks and crannies, been designated by UNESCO as a World Heritage Site.

Recent years have gilded that inheritance with a wholly contemporary exuberance that has not always been evident in the city's rather dour reputation. Edinburgh is always prepared to be disappointed, but for the moment it faces the future with its confidence and its spirits riding high. ❏

ABOVE: Donald Dewar, the first First Minister of the Scottish Parliament. Dubbed "Father of the Nation", he died suddenly of a brain haemorrhage in 2000.

A New Sang

Wednesday, 12 May 1999: "The Scottish Parliament, adjourned on 25 March 1707, is hereby reconvened." The speaker was the veteran nationalist, Winifred Ewing, and with those words the world's newest legislature, and a new Scotland, came into being. History is often made of simple sentences.

Mrs Ewing, as the oldest of the 129 Members of the Scottish Parliament (MSPs) just elected, had been pressed into service to get things going until a Presiding Officer (or Speaker) and First (or Prime) Minister had been elected. They were, shortly afterwards, in the persons of Lord (David) Steel, the former Liberal Leader, and Donald Dewar, hitherto Scotland's Labour Secretary of State.

In truth, the new legislature bore no resemblance to the old Scottish Parliament, whose passing in 1707 was described at the time as "the end of the auld sang (old song)". It was, for one thing, democratically (and proportionally) elected, in contrast to the rule of the aristocrats ("a parcel o'rogues", as Robert Burns called them) who populated the previous one. It also left Scotland explicitly inside the United Kingdom which the 1707 Union of the Parliaments had wrought.

Mrs Ewing's colleagues, the main opposition party in the new Parliament, wish things were otherwise, and Scotland fully independent within the European Union. But it is not. Responsibility for most of the key home policy areas have been transferred – "devolved", in the jargon – from the UK Parliament in Westminster. They include health, education, economic development, farming and fishing, local government, the environment, law and order, and the courts. But foreign affairs, defence, economic and monetary policy, most taxation, business regulation and constitutional issues are retained, or "reserved", to Westminster. The tensions between the devolved and reserved powers seem destined to define the battlegrounds in the new Scottish politics.

Some think talk of a new politics is wishful. They point out, first, that London retains its fiscal grip over Scotland's purse-strings and, second, that the devolved powers are in essence the same things that the Scottish Office, a department of the Westminster Government, used to run anyway from its base in Edinburgh. Its officials now form the Par-

liament's civil service. After 1707 Scotland retained its own laws, judiciary, educational system and Churches: distinctive provision north of the border is hardly a novelty.

Yet, in other respects, the Parliament is very new in style and newer still in aspiration. Its procedures were agreed by two broad-based bodies, the Scottish Constitutional Convention and the Consultative Steering Group, and both determined that it would reject the archaic pantomime rituals of Westminster, and instead be informal, constructive, family-friendly, accessible and consultative. More importantly, there can be no repetition of the position in the 1980s and early 1990s, when Scot-

land was governed by policies it had comprehensively rejected at the polls.

Initially, the Parliament is occupying the Church of Scotland's gothic Assembly Hall at the top of The Mound until a stylish new building is ready, probably in 2003. When the Parliament is in session, it generally meets on Wednesday and Thursday each week, though committees are at work on other days. The public is welcome to watch, and can acquire tickets at the Visitor Centre on George IV Bridge, worth a visit in its own right. For those who prefer virtual visiting, both the Parliament (www.scottish.parliament.uk) and the Executive (www.scotland.gov.uk) maintain useful websites: new technology for a new sang. ❑

RIGHT: piping in a new era.

THE FESTIVAL FRINGE: ARTS FOR EVERYONE

The spirit of the Fringe is in the adventure of the spectator who takes a leap in the dark, tries out the unexpected and stays tuned to its artistic pulse

Imagine a day on the Fringe. You keep the morning free for sight-seeing, then at lunchtime the spirit moves you to buy a ticket for Shakespeare's *Richard III*. It is performed in a dusky hall with a cast of five who have set the tragedy in a kindergarten. On Richard's ascension to the throne, a bouncy castle appears on stage. You realise it is a work of genius.

Afterwards you notice that, within an hour, you can see an award-winning new student comedy about football fans in the same venue. You do and it's delightful. Within half an hour of the end you rush to catch a much-praised show about a woman obsessed by her pet Japanese pocket monster. It's not great but it shows promise.

STAMINA TO PARTY

Two shows on, and having grabbed a bite to eat in between, you emerge exhilarated, realising that it's not yet 9.30pm. A city of laughter, drama, music and dancing still beckons.

Fantasy? Not at all. It's a real day from the diary of a dedicated fringe-goer, selected at random.

▷ **WALKING TALL**
Physical dexterity and circus pizzazz are qualities admired just as much as the cerebral.

▽ **PARK LIFE**
One week into the Fringe, Holyrood Park is the venue for a day of family entertainment. A highly popular event, Fringe Sunday lets you sample the best of the fest for free.

△ **BLOWING HOT**
Don't underestimate the performers you can see for free on the streets; many are award-winning artists happy to find a receptive audience for their work.

◁ ALL MADE UP

Colourful street performers from around the world congregate on the High Street and The Mound, all seeking to attract the largest crowd. Only the most exuberant succeed.

△ AND SOMEWHERE TO GO

International Fringe drama, from the esoteric to the mainstream, can be found in the least likely places, be they church halls, Masonic lodges or purpose-built theatres.

THE MECCA OF STAND-UP COMEDY

Although theatre makes up the largest section of the Fringe programme, it is comedy that makes the loudest noise. It has always been there – Alan Bennett, Peter Cook, Dudley Moore (pictured above) and Jonathan Miller sealed their reputations here as satirists in 1960 – but since the mid-1980s, when Ben Elton, Rik Mayall and Adrian Edmondson first appeared, stand-up has grown ever more prominent.

With all eyes on the annual Perrier Award for the funniest act, the Fringe is a three-week industry bonanza easily the equal of Montreal's Just For Laughs in terms of importance, though never formally constituted as a comedy festival in its own right.

For the punter, it means a non-stop flow of newcomers and top names, and the chance to see unknowns on the brink of stardom. Julian Clary, Frank Skinner, Fred MacAulay, Jo Brand ... few comics have made it without the helping hand of Edinburgh.

▷ CHILD'S PLAY

Young people are increasingly well catered for on the Fringe. The Fringe Society office produces a separate children's programme, as does the Book Festival.

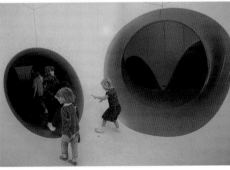

◁ STREET LIFE

There's so much on offer during August, it can be hard to keep to your budget, but it doesn't cost anything to enjoy the festive buzz on the streets.

▷ STAR-SPOTTING

Eddie Izzard is now an Emmy Award-winning celebrity comedian, but not so long ago he was playing the smallest Edinburgh venues.

THE EDINBURGH CHARACTER

An image of the typical Edinburgh man or woman may spring to mind, but to what extent does the reality match the reputation?

Those who set out in search of the essence of Edinburgh usually pitch their first (and sometimes last) camp on the irresistible territory of *Dr Jekyll and Mr Hyde*. It seems somehow inevitable that the great parable of the divided self was written by an Edinburgh man. Robert Louis Stevenson may have set the story in London, but the character was inspired by one of Edinburgh's more notorious 18th-century citizens, William Brodie, Deacon of Wrights and Masons. Like Dr Jekyll, Brodie was a pillar of society during the day; like Mr Hyde, he was a ruthless villain at night. He ended his days at the end of the hangman's rope, suspended from an "improved" gallows which he himself had designed and built.

Pride and paradoxes

Many have seen Stevenson's famous tale as a handy metaphor for Edinburgh itself. Where else does a semi-ramshackle, late medieval town glower down on such Georgian elegance? What other British city combines such civic pride with intractable social problems? Which European city (except London) juggles so many billions of pounds, dollars, euros and yen, but never has quite enough money to keep the streets clean?

Could any other city in Europe stage the world's biggest festival of music and drama for 47 years while refusing to build a decent opera house or even a new theatre? (The gap was finally filled in 1994 with the the magnificent, multipurpose Playhouse, and embellished shortly thereafter when the much-mourned Empire Theatre reopened as the stylish Festival Theatre.) Edinburgh may be one of Europe's urban jewels, but on its periphery are some of the bleakest housing estates in the whole of Britain. Yet southern liberals, expecting a bas-

tion of Calvinism, are startled instead to find pubs open all day and half the night, licensed saunas that have effectively decriminalised prostitution, and clergy who have been leading campaigners for communitarian politics.

Residents can find the contrasts as hard to reconcile as do the visitors. Edinburgh's rich and poor, its legislators and labourers, its judges and junkies, sometimes seem to inhabit different universes rather than the same city, and their encounters tend to be circumspect on all sides. Yet Edinburgh's diversity is undoubtedly part of its charm, and much of what is gracious about it is available to all, regardless of income. Some of its finest golf courses are publicly owned. Edinburgh's superb botanical gardens, most of its museums and galleries and its great libraries are, by tradition, both free to visit and determinedly visited by all.

In wearing its social divisions so openly, Edinburgh can be an oddly egalitarian place. Privilege is often evident, yet superiority is

PRECEDING PAGES: supporting the national football team is a passion in Edinburgh, as in all Scotland.
LEFT: eccentricity in an antique shop in St Stephen Street, Stockbridge.
RIGHT: contrasting ethnic traditions.

rarely claimed and never conceded. In contrast to Glasgow's mercantile elite, Edinburgh's wealthy classes tend to regard ostentation as being in poor taste, an echo perhaps of Knox's zeal in driving idolatry from the churches during the Reformation.

Or perhaps the modesty is founded in mere apprehension. For much of its history, after all, the aesthetes' playground was also the city of the "blue blanket", legendary rallying standard for the urban mob. In some respects, the most "typical" of all Edinburgh's corners is the Grassmarket, where smart boutiques and bistros share street space with hostels for the homeless.

The bourgeois myth

Yet, somehow, Edinburgh has acquired a reputation which has little to do with the facts. On the world stage, it is the prim little city of Muriel Spark's novella *The Prime of Miss Jean Brodie*: a sniffish, cold-hearted place, full of petit bourgeois pretension and intolerance, lacking Glasgow's (tirelessly self-promoted) proletarian warmth and urban raffishness. To Glaswegians especially, Edinburgh is a "west endy, east windy" kind of place, "all fur coats and nae knickers (no underwear)" as the old jibe goes, a town of chilly streets stalked by flinty lawyers, hard-eyed accountants and

THE ENGLISH IN EDINBURGH

Since the Union of the Parliaments in 1707, and more particularly since the 1745 Jacobite Rebellion *(see page 31)*, Englishness has been synonymous in Scotland with the perceived values and vices of the ruling classes. Even today's Scottish adults (though, happily, not today's Scottish children) were taught in school that they could never hope to prosper in life unless they shed "common" Scots words and vowel sounds in favour of "speaking proper English". That prejudice, not entirely unjustly, has been particularly associated by the rest of Scotland with Edinburgh, its schools and its social milieu. The city's attractions – especially its cosmopolitan universities – retain an

exceptional appeal to people from England. Reports in early 2000 that Prince William was considering studying at Edinburgh University immediately increased its cachet with the metropolitan smart set (to whom St Andrews has traditionally exerted a greater appeal).

But English people of more modest means also continue to find Edinburgh a civilised and congenial city in which to settle. The last census, surprisingly, described only a tiny percentage of Edinburgh households as being in "multi-ethnic areas", yet were one to expand the definition to include the English it would certainly be well over half. It is, by and large, a pretty amenable arrangement.

terrifying dowagers. They regard it as a mean-spirited place, even though it is home to most of Scotland's charities. "A toon (town) wi' ideas above its station" was the verdict of one West of Scotland businessman (possibly just after Edinburgh had beaten Glasgow in a fiercely-fought contest to site a branch of the ultimate posh British emporium, Harvey Nichols).

None of which Edinburgh folk will admit to recognising. In fact, it is hard to know quite where the notion of Edinburgh's monied respectability originated. Edinburgh is widely regarded as the natural home for Scotland's urban middle classes, yet the evidence for this

of owner-occupation in its housing stock, yet it has fewer than average detached, semi-detached or terraced houses. Most of the homes (nearly 58 percent) are tenement flats of the sort Glasgow spent so much of the 1960s energetically demolishing.

Maybe the impression of cultivated urbanity grew out of the 19th-century boom in middle-ranking clerical jobs in banking, insurance and government, in contrast to the heavy industry then dominating the rest of Scotland's central belt. These remain important employers, though job numbers are falling. More likely, though, it has to do with Edinburgh's ability to attract

bourgeois domination is at best patchy. Certainly, the city hosts some of Scotland's priciest private schools, yet many of their pupils come from very far afield. Certainly, it is stiff with dignified professionals (11.3 percent of households, according to the 1991 Census, against 6.4 percent for Scotland as a whole), yet few of them command the fancy commercial salaries of the regenerated Glasgow. Certainly, it has a higher proportion than the Scottish average (66 percent, against under 60 percent)

LEFT: music lesson in the hallowed hall of Stewart's Mellville College.

ABOVE: a board meeting in Charlotte Square.

more than its share of middle-class educated incomers from England, drawn to jobs in academia, publishing, finance and administration.

Self-importance

Even prior to the restoration of a Scottish Parliament in 1999, Edinburgh retained most of the dignity and some of the attributes of a capital city. It was always the focal point of Scots Law (though the laws themselves were made in London) and of the Scottish judiciary. It was home to the Scottish Office, the suave officials who would transform themselves in 1999, so smoothly and speedily, into the civil service of the Scottish Executive. Once a year, when royalty comes to the Palace of Holyroodhouse, Edinburgh even takes on the trappings of a Court city. Anyone in Scotland wishing to consult official records has to come to Edinburgh (though increasingly the information is available on-line).

The "Edinbourgeois" are always keen to emphasise their role as guardians of Scotland's historic capital, but outside observers have detected parallels between the city's unfulfilled potential and the perceived reserve of its citizens. "There is

only 18th-century Madrid rivalled Edinburgh for sheer squalor. As late as 1944 the Chinese writer and traveller Chiang Yee found the inhabitants of Edinburgh sociable and garrulous to the point of being alarming. (They kept trying to force whisky down his throat.)

For centuries the Edinburgh mob was notorious for spontaneous assembly at the slightest grievance, and, while its capacity to lay down the law to authority has been exaggerated by legend, it did once hunt down

no one really alive in Edinburgh yet/ They are all living at the tiniest fraction of the life they could easily have", wrote the great polemical poet, Hugh MacDiarmid. He saw a city of people in great houses, "who prefer to live in their cellar and keep all the rest sealed up". Mocking the city's Victorian pretensions as the "Athens of the North", Marxist writer Tom Nairn labelled it the "Reykjavik of the South".

Past reputation

Yet, the idea of pious and genteel Edinburgh is a fairly modern one. Daniel Defoe said that "the nastiness of this place" could not be denied. Captain Edward Topham thought that

the Captain of the City Guard (the equivalent of the Chief Constable) and lynch him from a barber's pole in the Grassmarket after he had ordered his troops to fire on demonstrators. Even then, there was perhaps a flash of Edinburgh respectability, in that the mob left the chandler the money for the rope!

A rougher side

While this kind of turbulence no longer plagues Edinburgh, the city still has two of the busiest police stations in Britain (Drylaw and Craigmillar) and late-night discos and pubs can be a focus for lawlessness, though the worst excesses of drunkenness are generally reckoned to have been resolved, to the surprise of some, by the more liberal drinking laws that followed the Clayson Commission in the 1970s. Prior to that, the city's hostelries all closed at 10pm, thus encouraging drinkers to get as much liquor on board as they could load in the available time.

This rougher side to the city was well captured by the poet and playwright Donald Campbell, who wrote: "In the Morningside chippie/ I was confrontit by nae feugher than ten/ o the reuchest and the teuchest/ o yer haurdest-haurd men/ and (O Gode!) How I wished I was in Glasgow." Somewhat puzzlingly, Morningside

in art, social welfare, education or religion." And Italian Fascism, Miss Brodie's predilection, was just one such "new idea". The same period found agitators like MacDiarmid exploring the outer reaches of communism and nationalism, often simultaneously.

There is a further paradox. Edinburgh has, of course, produced more than its share of great philosophers, writers, doctors, lawyers and divines. But for a city which is supposedly straight-laced it has also given the world some colourful talent. The Glasgow comedian Billy Connolly has argued that the Scottish/Irish interface in Glasgow, like the English/Jewish

is generally regarded as one of Edinburgh's most respectable districts.

Radicalism and humour

Even the ambitious Jean Brodie has been misrepresented. Muriel Spark makes it plain that Miss Brodie and her type were ladies of some complexity. "There were legions of her kind during the 1930s," she wrote, "women from the age of 30 and upward, who crowded their war-bereaved spinsterhood with voyages of 'discovery' into new ideas and energetic practices

LEFT: dressing up for a social occasion.
ABOVE: life on the streets for the less privileged.

mix in London, has produced a seam of natural comedy that Edinburgh's Scottish/English amalgam cannot match. Yet, a succession of funny men – running from the peerless film comedian Alistair Sim, through the diminutive Ronnie Corbett, to the Absolutely team of the 1990s – begs to differ.

Those who know Edinburgh only by its stuffy reputation might also be surprised to learn that it has produced a world lightweight boxing champion (Ken Buchanan), one of Britain's most enduring international film stars (former Fountainbridge milkman Sean Connery), pioneering folk musicians (Bert Jansch, Dick Gaughan, the Incredible String Band) and some of the biggest pop names of the 1970s (Bay City Rollers), 1980s (Simple Minds) and 1990s (Garbage).

Tolerating diversity

Like most European cities, Edinburgh's texture has been much enriched by immigration, at its height in the period prior to World War II when Leith was one of Britain's busiest ports. The biggest ethnic minority is the Irish (who flooded into Edinburgh in the 19th century in the wake of the Great Famine), but there are also lively communities of Poles, Ukrainians, Chinese, Norwegians, Sikhs, Jews, Pakistanis and Ital-

To the tourist, it is the city of the Military Tattoo and the Castle. To many Scots, it is the home of their Parliament, yet somehow alien to Scotland. To its inhabitants, it is a hundred nooks and crannies in a complicated jigsaw.

If the New Club, the city's oldest and most select community (now housed in the ugliest modern building in Princes Street) is one cameo of Edinburgh, then so are the junkies dealing smack in Warriston Cemetery, the gays drinking in one bar, the folkies playing bodhrans in another, the poets arguing politics in a third. You'll see typical Edinburgh faces and hear typical Edinburgh conversation in a Heriot Row

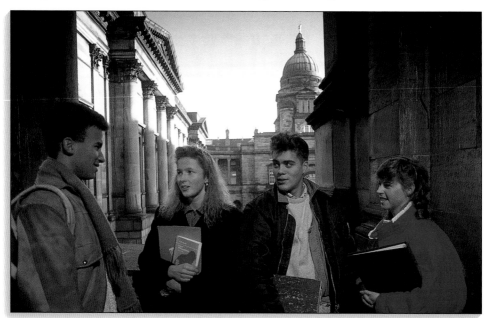

ians – and, of course, English. Many of these individuals have made a powerful impact on Edinburgh, and the city has a record of assimilating incomers more placidly than many a recipient town. Recent distinguished scions of immigrant communities include former Conservative Foreign Secretary Malcolm Rifkind (Jewish), art impresario Richard Demarco (Italian) and civic leaders like Mark Lazarowicz (Polish) and Eric Milligan (Irish).

The truth is that the character of Edinburgh, like that of other European cities, is a bewildering tapestry of subcultures, interests and traditions. Many have sought the single motif that encapsulates the place, but none has found it.

drawing room and a Wester Hailes bus shelter, and they won't resemble one another at all.

Edinburgh's capacity to tolerate such contrasts has sometimes shocked and sometimes beguiled visitors. But respectable Edinburgh and its rougher, tougher counterpart long ago learned to contemplate each other with the wary good humour of Henry Jekyll seeing the face of Edward Hyde in the mirror for the first time. "I was conscious of no repugnance," Dr Jekyll says, "rather of a leap of welcome. This, too, was myself." ❏

ABOVE: students at Edinburgh University, one of the best regarded colleges in Britain.

Masters of the Art of Medicine

I t would be a travesty if Edinburgh's medical reputation rested with the grisly stories of Burke and Hare, the body-snatchers who sold their hellish parcels to surgeons for anatomical dissection. Ever since King James IV of Scotland, himself "weill learnit in the art of mediecein", granted a charter to the Guild of Surgeons and Barbers at Edinburgh in 1506, the city has made much more respectable claims to be one of the world's most important centres of medical science.

As the study and practice of medicine evolved, Edinburgh made conspicuous contributions to the understanding of anatomy, obstetrics, nervous diseases, midwifery, gynaecology, tuberculosis, diphtheria, forensic medicine and public health. In modern times important discoveries and techniques in neurosurgery, organ transplants, ophthalmic surgery and genetics have kept the city in the front line of the battle to cure disease and to alleviate human suffering.

The existence of a medical school in Edinburgh since the 17th century led to (among other things) the foundation of modern chemistry, modern dermatology and modern military medicine, the invention of the Davy Lamp and the respirator, and the first British use of a hypodermic syringe. To earn the right to put M.B.Ch.B(Ed) after one's name still lures students from all over the globe. Even in the middle of the 18th century many came from America and the West Indian colonies. The influence of Edinburgh on the wellbeing of the world is great.

Long before Britain's National Health Service came into being, a caring profession looked after the burghers in an Infirmary which grew from six huts to a network of teaching hospitals served by the University's Faculty of Medicine and the Royal Colleges of Surgeons and Physicians. Not that every student graduated – the standards have always been notorious for their severity – and not every graduate achieved the distinction of the man who was physician to Catherine the Great for 20 years, or the doctor who escorted Louis XVI to the guillotine, or the chief medical officer to the Jacobites at the Battle of Culloden.

Some achieved fame outside medicine, among them Conan Doyle and his mentor Joseph Bell,

whose diagnostic teaching techniques gave Doyle the model for Sherlock Holmes, and Dr Allinson (1858–1918) whose recipe for healthy living is only now getting the response it deserved. He believed in wholemeal so earnestly that he milled it himself and a brand of flour is named after him. On another tack, gardenia, wisteria and poinsettia are named after Dr Alexander Garden, Dr Casper Wistar and Joel R. Poinsett, all of whom studied medicine in Edinburgh at a time when the discipline was inextricably interwoven with botany.

Greatness there was in abundance in the 17th and 18th centuries. In the kirkyard of Greyfriars lie the remains (among other medical innovators) of

the Monros, *primus et secundus*, giants in anatomical research and scientific adventure who straddled the subject from 1697 to 1817.

The story of Edinburgh's medical past is one of legendary figures: Dr Gregory whose mixture of rhubarb, magnesia and ginger was, until recently, the world's most frequently prescribed medication; Syme, described in his day as the Napoleon of surgery; Bright, of Bright's disease; Sophia Jex-Blake, who pioneered the rights of women doctors; Elsie Inglis who did the same for women patients.

As the venerable Royal Infirmary moves to new premises on the outskirts of the city (in 2003), it may not be a gross exaggeration to claim that even now there is no better city in which to be ill. ❑

RIGHT: top-quality treatment.

LITERARY EDINBURGH

Edinburgh has nurtured many great writers, yet most have avoided writing about their own city. What is behind the reluctance?

The Scottish polemical poet Hugh MacDiarmid wrote: "If Edinburgh has not given the creative spirit due place, the creative spirit has not been deluded as to Edinburgh's false position. It is a significant fact that, with all the romance attached to it, it has never been made the subject of any good, let alone any great, poem. It could not have failed to inspire the poets if there had not all along been something wrong with its pretensions – some essential falsity the instincts of their genius could never be deluded by."

Edinburgh has somehow always managed to resist the literary imagination. For MacDiarmid, writing about the city in 1934, the reason was plain: give the imagination short shrift in your civic culture, as Edinburgh had consistently done, and the imagination will quickly pack its bags and move elsewhere. He could never forgive Edinburgh its delusionary "pretensions", nor the fact that the university in Scotland's capital city had never troubled to found a professorial Chair in Scottish literature.

Eluding the limelight

By that time even Glasgow – which in the unwritten national epic plays a dark, commercial Sparta to Edinburgh's enlightened Athens – had enjoyed its share of literary limelight, even if only as "The City of Dreadful Night" in James Thompson's sombre verses of the late 19th century, or the no less gloomy cityscape of his contemporary Alexander Smith's tribute. It is interesting that Smith, a member of the short-lived "Spasmodic" school that briefly flourished in Scotland, began a similar poem dedicated to the capital, but failed to finish it before he died.

If Edinburgh really is one of the great cultural capitals of Europe – as its inhabitants and distinguished visitors insistently maintain –

where is the modern masterpiece that could have done for it what James Joyce's *Ulysses* did for Dublin? And where was its Dickens? Why did its most famous sons – Walter Scott, Robert Louis Stevenson – prefer to retreat into the fantasy worlds of the Middle Ages or the South Seas?

Those who look closely at these things say that Stevenson never managed to shake the dust of Heriot Row from his feet; even when his neighbours were bare-breasted Samoan girls, his models of behaviour were "douce" Edinburgh ladies. Equally, the nightmarish London that forms the backdrop to the decline and fall of the good Dr Jekyll – a man without a fault except that he thought too well of himself and understood too little of the power of the imagination – was based on the Old Town of Edinburgh unmistakably.

MacDiarmid, in that sour essay in *Scottish Scene*, laid the blame for Edinburgh's literary shortcomings at the same door. A city that

LEFT: a Burns memorial forms part of Sir Walter Scott's historical collection at Abbotsford House.
RIGHT: portrait of Hugh MacDiarmid, a harsh critic of Edinburgh's literary shortcomings, by William Menzies.

thought too well of itself was prey to the "hopeless preconceptions which vitiate almost all impressions of it: all the guide-book chatter, all the intellectual rabbit's food of historical tittle-tattle and miscellaneous facts".

The underlying imagination

Edinburgh's great literati were philosophers and historians like David Hume and William Robertson, economists like Adam Smith. They dealt in hard, unromantic facts and appearances. The city's glamour, in the same way, was a matter of glorious architectural frontages and historical anecdotes. What lay behind?

tion. Almost always, the theme it suggests is that old philosophic interplay between imagination and reality: the suffering, passion and violence that underlie the reasonable surface.

Historical set-piece

Perhaps the greatest set-piece, and the one that most closely engages with Scottish history, is the reconstruction of the notorious 1736 Porteous Riots in Scott's *The Heart of Midlothian* (1818), though it is significant that the novel's other great "moment", Jeanie Deans' desperate journey to London, should once again underline the post-1707 dependence on Union that

The point about Glasgow is that its "dark side" lies on the surface. It takes an effort of imagination to find the "dear green place" – the meaning, some say, of its Celtic name "Gles Chu" – and the warm heart under the toughened exterior. By legend, Edinburgh's heart is cold, but with the coldness of reason and intellect rather than cruelty.

MacDiarmid is too pessimistic, expects too much of a place he never really came to understand, even when they did begin to put his poems on the literature curriculum and to offer him honorary degrees. The fact is that Edinburgh has always occupied a very special and complex place in the national literary imagina-

had begun the dismantlement of a separate Scottish culture (and that had been the main cause of the Porteous disturbances).

By and large, though, history in Edinburgh has remained in the physical environment, rarely seeping through into the kind of imaginative writing the city has inspired. Largely, such writing has been private and intense, rather than public and expansive. That, of course, has not been how the city likes to see itself, or how visitors have liked to present it. Joan Lingard's

ABOVE: an artist's portrayal of the possibly apocryphal meeting between Burns and the young Walter Scott.
RIGHT: Robert Louis Stevenson by Count Girolamo Nerli.

1964 novel *The Prevailing Wind* offers an Edinburgh devoid of irony, almost the kind of novel that could have been written by the City Fathers to sustain their own sense of well-being.

The feeling wasn't new to Miss Lingard or even to this century. When the "heaven-taught ploughman" Robert Burns sought literary fame, it seemed inevitable that he should come to his nation's capital: "At Edinburgh I was in a new world," he wrote, "I mingled among many classes of men, but all of them new to me; and I was all attention 'to catch the manners living as they rise'." Sadly, Edinburgh also persuaded Burns that the only poetic manner that mattered was the pompous solemnity of his *Address* to the capital, an inexcusable piece of drivel and thoroughly untypical of his greatest work.

Themes of contrast

Burns was lionised in the drawing rooms and salons of the New Town. A bare half-mile away, across the Castle moat and around the spine of rock that supports the Royal Mile, a different reality awaited, one that had marked out the life and passing of the one Scottish poet that Burns wholeheartedly admired. Robert Fergusson died in the Edinburgh Bedlam (lunatic asylum) in 1774, aged barely 24. His great poem *Auld Reikie* – which just about answers MacDiarmid's accusation – is an astonishing blend of the simple vernacular that Burns was to make his own, with an equally astonishing learning, acquired at the university.

The "Blest place!" he celebrated, though, was also the site of some of Europe's worst slums and Fergusson's life was one of bizarre contrast, ranged between the convivial company of his intellectual peers in taverns and debating rooms, and the grinding poverty and privation which eventually led to his tragically premature death. (Some years later Robert Burns paid for a headstone to mark his grave in the Canongate churchyard. In 1997 the Saltire Society erected a tribute there to the three Roberts: Fergusson, Burns and Stevenson.)

Another writer to perceive the astonishing contrasts of Edinburgh was the "Ettrick Shepherd", James Hogg, a self-taught poet who produced one of the most remarkable novels written in any language, *Private Memoirs and Confessions of a Justified Sinner*. Published in

1824, at a time when religious and political controversy were at their peak in Scotland, it is one of the greatest explorations of the unconscious mind and anticipates many themes in Stevenson's *The Strange Case of Dr Jekyll and Mr Hyde*.

It concerns a pious young man haunted by a mysterious "twin" who goads him to the murder of his brother. Its most famous passages take place in the nightmare slums of the Old Town – alleys Fergusson knew only too well – and, unforgettably, on Arthur's Seat, where George is confronted with the mysterious mountain phenomenon known as "broken spec-

story of a "justified sinner", convinced of her rightness and reinforced in her conviction by the city in which she lives and works. It's as well to be reminded, too, that at least one of "Miss Brodie's girls" goes off to her death. The strain of belonging to "*la crème de la crème*" is often fatal.

A dark side

There is a sombre side to Edinburgh that is every bit as important to its reality as the orderly Athenian skyline. Like every town whose streets and public buildings exude history, its back alleys and the imaginations of its

tre", rationally the projection of a human shadow onto cloud below, but which became in Hogg's account a monstrous threat.

Edinburgh heroine

Such a threat also haunts the world of Edinburgh's most famous heroine, Miss Jean Brodie, and her "prime". It is as well to remember that the doctrine Miss Brodie preaches to her "girls" at Marcia Blaine School – based on the real James Gillespie's School in the city – is Mussolini's Fascism.

The Prime of Miss Jean Brodie (1961) is Muriel Spark's most popular novel; it is also an almost archetypally "Edinburgh" work, the

best writers hide in their deepest reaches human tragedies and dark questions.

In recent years no-one has expressed these more poignantly than Irvine Welsh, best known for his novel *Trainspotting* (1993), a horrifying look at Edinburgh's drug scene which inspired a celebrated film. Almost as dark are the noirish Inspector Rebus stories of crime writer Ian Rankin, set in the city's seedy underworld of gangs, drugs and prostitution, social realities outed from their hiding-place. ❑

LEFT: Muriel Spark, whose Miss Brodie reflected the middle-class city, and **ABOVE:** Irvine Welsh, who has drawn attention to an underclass.

The Bourgeois Hero: Sir Walter Scott

Walter Scott haunts Edinburgh, and in a very real sense he can be said to have invented it. Visitors arrive at Waverley Station – named in honour of his great sequence of novels – and almost the first sight to greet them is George Meikle Kemp's enormous gothic monument to Scott on the south side of Princes Street.

The old Tolbooth is gone, but a stone outline in the High Street pavement marks the Heart of Midlothian, where one of his most powerfully evocative scenes took place. "Scott country" begins 25 miles to the south, in the environs of Abbotsford, the "castle" to which he moved in 1812. Nevertheless, it's impossible to escape his presence in the capital.

He was born in 1771 and was soon ailing from a bout of polio that left him with a lifelong limp. His father was a Writer to the Signet, an important law officer, and as a child Scott imbibed a strong sense of Scotland's independent culture – Scots law had not been affected by the Union with England in 1707 – and the fund of stories of which Scottish history consisted. Apprenticed to his father's office, he quickly learned the workings of that law and history and rose to be one of the clerks of Session and, later, Sheriff of Selkirkshire, the Borders county where Abbotsford was located.

Scott was not the recklessly spontaneous artist demanded by romantic tastes. His first literary interests were mainly scholarly, collecting Border songs and legends. These were published in *The Minstrelsy of the Scottish Borders*, whose success prompted Scott to develop a growing poetic bent. His "first" literary career was as the author of a series of long poems – *The Lay of the Last Minstrel* (1805), *Marmion* (1808), *The Lady of the Lake* (1810) – which were very popular.

However, the economic success of his long poems was almost incidental as most of Scott's energies were poured into his legal and publishing interests. The work for which he is best known is the product of an accident. Like Mark Twain later in the United States, Scott had been quick to see the commercial potential of new printing techniques and had plunged a great deal of his inherited wealth into the Edinburgh publishing and

printing company of Ballantyne. But in 1813 and then, more disastrously, in 1826 the company suffered massive financial collapses. Scott heroically accepted full liability for all his debts and his remaining years, until he died, a broken man, in 1832, are a story of extraordinary perseverance.

By 1812, Scott had realised that the vogue for his poems was over. Byron was the new, racier hero. In 1814, he published anonymously what has been claimed to be the first historical novel in English, *Waverley*. It was a remarkable success and began a long stream of works – including *The Antiquary* and *Old Mortality* (both 1816), *The Heart of Midlothian* (1818), *Redgauntlet* (1824), and

others on medieval and foreign themes – all ascribed to the author of *Waverley*.

It has long been critically unfashionable for a writer to be too successful and Scott's willingness to regard fiction-writing as a trade has denied him a certain snob appeal. Certainly, he is the least read of the great 19th-century writers. Yet most of our suppositions about the Middle Ages come from Scott. So, too, does the whole myth and culture of tartanry, the result of Scott's remarkable stage-managing of King George IV's visit to Scotland in 1822. Scott was a man of his time, close to the heart of its most important movements. It's rare for a writer to wield such influence but it's typical that we should never have forgiven him for it. ❏

RIGHT: portrait of the successful historical novelist by Sir Henry Raeburn.

PUBS AND PERFORMERS

Some of the city's ale houses are bland products of a UK-wide brewery formula;

others have a distinctive flavour, and offer great music and tasty beer

Along oak bar manned by a brassy, middle-aged, bottle blonde or a stern, stocky man, surrounded by toothless old men supping export-strength ale and nursing nips of whisky in a smoky windowless room. This is perhaps a clichéd image of a bygone age of spit-and-sawdust pubs, but they have not totally died away; they remain, clinging to nooks and crannies of the city like barnacles on a boat.

But some of the grimmer aspects of Victorian drinking, including the sodden sawdust that covered many a bar-room floor, have been swept away for good. Edinburgh's pubs are airier and brighter – some even have windows you can look out of – and there are perhaps just enough of the traditional pubs to keep the aficionados happy. The city has seen a flowering of café-bars, where you can eat pretty good food, drink wine, enjoy the company of your children, and order coffee without driving the proprietor and his staff to apoplexy.

Edinburgh, in keeping with the habits of factory shift workers, has for quarter of a century been a place where round-the-clock drinking can be achieved if desired. Certainly, a few places on the 24-hour circuit leave a lot to be desired, but it can be done. The range of drinking establishments in contemporary Edinburgh is much like that in any other thriving, cosmopolitan city in the world: a mix of new and old, providing whet for all whistles in an environment to suit.

Style over content

Over the last decade of the 20th century the major breweries gobbled up most "free houses" left in the city, only to relaunch or repackage them as something else for someone else, often paying little attention to what had made the establishments successful in the past. There is a plethora of "style" bars littering the city where

you can be furnished with the latest brewery-backed alcopop or import bottled beers for a fee. These places often rely on mass consumption to survive. Style over content comes into play with their liberal application of wrought iron, chrome or painted MDF (wood-effect cladding) masquerading as an injection of

sophistication into a pub. The perpetrators of fashion makeovers are often their own worst enemies, as what is "cool" today will usually be "naff" a year or two on.

Brewery-packaged style bars, along with theme bars (currently popular themes are faux-Irish, Latin American or 1970s), are no substitute for the real thing. But, though such premises are increasingly prevalent, there will always be exceptions to the rule, running the gamut from "cattle markets" for young singles, filled with raging hormones, chemical-charged lager and watery cocktails, to vibrant and exciting individualistic pubs that can be appreciated by both young and old.

PRECEDING PAGES: the traditional pint at Bennets Bar in the days before bright modern bars sprang up.
LEFT: pulling a Scottish pint.
ABOVE: Victorian pubs feature stained-glass windows.

The City Café on Blair Street, behind Hunter Square, is one classic example of where style and substance can meet and comfortably coexist. The distinctive "retro" look of the bar is mainly due to the owner's reluctance to change the original fittings and fixtures. Drawing in the young and beautiful as well as all sorts of people who come for a good pint or a well-priced bite to eat, it is one of a number of establishments that can be labelled true melting pots.

Out on a limb

In a such a cosmopolitan environment it is unsurprising that there is a good sprinkling of

gay bars around the city, several of which are situated in Edinburgh's gay district, in and around Broughton Street in the New Town. Planet Out and C.C. Blooms are the most "out and proud" establishments, while others are more subtly "gay friendly" and welcome those of all persuasions with equal enthusiasm.

Those who favour the traditional watering hole are well provided for in Edinburgh. Atmosphere is the key ingredient in places like the Doric Tavern on Market Street, Robbie's Bar on Leith Walk, The King's Wark on The Shore in Leith and the Waverley, off the High Street. They provide a subtle combination of earthy surroundings, quality ales and spirits and local banter that will entertain the curious and satisfy the culture-hungry. Not short on spectacular period decor is the Café Royal on West Register Street (just behind the east end of Princes Street), with exquisite Victorian Doulton tiling, stained-glass windows and an original revolving door providing a gorgeous reminder of the drinking establishments of yesteryear.

Music to the ears

Perhaps some veterans of the Edinburgh drinking scene look back with affection at the days of slops (the dubious practice of emptying beer from tap spillage into fresh pints) and whiskies. Certainly, though the pubs themselves – Victorian decor notwithstanding – were dingy and often unhygienic, the pub scene was in some ways more cultured in the mid-20th century *(see panel below)*, yet one enjoyable aspect of pub culture has blossomed in more recent years and is now stimulatingly diverse and thriving. Pub music goes back to the "good ol' days", but since the freeing up of the licensing hours in the 1970s (reforms in 1976 permitted bars to stay open all day and into the "wee sma' hours" for the first time) there has been a more open-minded attitude towards music.

In the 1950s and 1960s a vibrant jazz music scene had emerged. The early Edinburgh connection with jazz came partly from the Art College, where young painters, often inspired by the fashionable Parisian jazz scene, were especially eager to pick up trumpets, clarinets and trombones and produce a robust musical alternative to the sickly popular music that they heard around them. Many of the early jazz innovators left Edinburgh to find fame, if not fortune, in London. But their disciples clung

ROSE-TINTED AGE OF CULTURE

Older devotees of Edinburgh's pubs will recall the days, in the pre-television, pre-jukebox era, when they were important forums for debate among the "bonny fechters" of the city's animated cultural life. This was especially true of the string of splendid establishments that ran along the length of Rose Street, where, during the 1950s, writers like Hugh MacDiarmid and Norman MacCaig, and jazz musicians like Sandy Brown, held court at the Abbotsford, Paddy's Bar and Milne's Bar. These pubs are still there, and at least one of them, the Abbotsford, is physically much the same as it always was, but today's literati do not seem to congregate in the same way.

on tenaciously at a time when there were few outlets for their music.

Modern jazz

Today, the roots of this scene remain and, while live music has to some extent been edged out thanks to the "pack 'em in" policies of the major breweries, jazz still flourishes. The annual Edinburgh Jazz and Blues Festival (late July to early August) continues to thrive, and, unlike its flashier neighbour in Glasgow, it tends to brings in a small selection of big international names but also devotes much of its programme to showcasing home-grown talent.

wrapped Oriental delicacies and, by night, is transformed into a musical melting pot for every shade of jazz talent, from bebop influenced pianists to bands playing funky freestyle, and from vocalists singing new compositions to the trad jazz standards. Scottish stars perform regularly there as weekly residents or guests.

There are also numerous other residency spots which showcase the talents of traditional jazz outfits, most of them in bars and restaurants around the city. In addition, groups like Fat Sam's Big Band retain the spirit of Basie, Ellington and the other masters of swing with frequent "jumping and jiving" dance nights.

Fusion has been something of a buzzword at the cutting edge of Edinburgh's jazz scene in recent times, and many jazz musicians have collaborated with artists from other musical genres. DJs, dance music producers, and funk and Latin players are as commonplace in a jazz line-up today as the more traditional drums, double bass or brass were in years gone by.

Nowhere can Edinburgh's jazz scene be more keenly observed than at Henry's Jazz Cellar in Morrison Street. This is a unique venture that, by day, is a Chinese *dim sum* bar serving pastry-

LEFT: optics display the range of draught beers.
ABOVE: jazz players on the pub circuit.

Fiddles and fusion

Another long-established gilded star in Edinburgh's crown jewels of pub music is the vibrant folk scene. The banner of folk music is a broad one, under which is collected everything from traditional piping and fiddles to all manner of hybridising between Celtic and other, multinational musical forms. Regular players from all over Scotland, and often from overseas, converge to jam and share songs and stories.

Groups like the Edinburgh Folk Club have helped to bring traditional music forms to the fore. Many young musicians have adopted the notions and habits of old styles that remain popular, and mixed them with newer, international flavours. The bands Salsa Celtica and Shooglenifty provide two examples of this trend; as the name suggests, Salsa Celtica mixes South American rhythms and instrumentation with age-old Celtic practices to create a unique blend of Scottish/Latin folk music.

Ceilidhs, at which traditional Scottish folk music is played and expert and beginner dancers spin a reel together, take place regularly at a handful of venues in the city. They are popular with all sorts, from students to pensioners.

Pop and rock music cannot be ignored, for scores of young bands cut their teeth on the stages of Edinburgh's pub rock venues. Places

respecting pubs can now afford not to install at least one reasonable cask-conditioned ale.

The Malt Shovel on Cockburn Street and the Cask and Barrel on Broughton Street are among those which pride themselves on a vast array of cask ales, while other places, like Maithers on Broughton Street, are known for their impressive selection of single malt whiskies. Though the days of quarter gill houses are past, since European law requires metric measurements, a generous 25 ml or even 35 ml measure will certainly warm the cockles.

A word of warning, however: when asking the advice of locals don't always take people

like the Bongo Club and the Venue book local talent for enthusiastic consumption.

Brewing up a storm

Another change for the better in Edinburgh pubs has been a widespread improvement in the quality of beer offered. As the small brewing companies were gobbled up by their big brothers in the 1950s and 1960s, so the beer range was cut to some half-dozen gassy, canister brands that were indistinguishable from one another. However, an ardent effort by the local Campaign for Real Ale team, led by a man who went on to set up his own brewery to show what could be done, has borne fruit: few self-

at their word, as some Edinburgh folk are fond of a wind-up at the expense of those on unfamiliar territory. One local wag recommended to some first-time visitors a bar where the "best-looking blondes" in town were to be found. Eager to meet these glamorous city dwellers, they sought out the pub only to find that the blondes referred to were pints of "Blond", a particularly tasty, smooth pale beer which was a staple at this bar, The Waverley on St Mary's Street. The female customers may not have been quite up to scratch, but the visitors were not disappointed. ❏

ABOVE: Deacon Brodie's Tavern on the tourist trail.

Scotch Whisky

The variety of malt whiskies on sale in Edinburgh astounds visitors familiar with only a few heavily marketed brands such as Glenfiddich and The Macallan. But is the diversity an illusion fostered by advertising? Isn't the liquid behind the labels pretty much the same? Certainly not, the experienced Scotch drinker will argue. The practised tongue can easily differentiate between Highland malts, Lowland malts, Campbeltown malts and Islay malts, and there's no mistaking the bouquet of a drink such as Laphroaig, which is often described as tasting of iodine or seaweed.

Which is best comes down to individual taste. The one point of agreement is that a whisky made from a good single malt (the product of one distillery) should not be drunk with a mixer such as soda or lemonade, which would destroy the subtle flavour – though ice and water *can* be added. After dinner, malts are best drunk neat, as a liqueur. But blended whisky can be refreshing in hot weather when mixed with soda. The well-known brands of blends (such as Bell's, Teacher's, Dewar's and Johnnie Walker) contain tiny amounts of as many as 30 or 40 malts mixed with grain whisky containing unmalted barley and maize.

In contrast with the upmarket images conferred on Scotch today, the drink's origins were lowly. The first written record dates back to 1494. In the 18th century whisky was drunk as freely as the spring water from which it was made, by peasants and aristocrats alike. It was said that a spoonful was given to new-born babies in the Highlands, and even respectable gentlewomen might start the day with "a wee dram". The poorest crofter could offer his guest a drink, thanks to the ubiquity of home-made stills which manufactured millions of gallons of "mountain dew" in the remote glens of the Highlands. In Edinburgh, no-one needed to go thirsty: excise officers estimated in 1777 that the city had eight licensed stills and 400 illegal ones.

Yet something as easy to make cannot be made authentically outside Scotland. Many have tried, the Japanese having thrown the most modern technology at the problem; but the combination of damp climate and soft water flowing through the peat cannot be replicated elsewhere. Indeed, no-one can agree on what elements create the best whiskies. Is the water better if it runs off granite

through peat, or if it runs through peat on to granite? Does the secret lie in the peat used to dry the malt in a distillery's kiln? Or in the soft air that permeates the wooden casks of whisky as the liquid matures? The arguments are endless, but the prize to Scotland is an annual export business worth more than £2 billion, shared between 100 or so highly automated distilleries.

To make malt whisky, plump dry barley is soaked in large tanks of water for two or three days. It is then spread out on a concrete floor or placed in large cylindrical drums and allowed to germinate for between eight and 12 days. Next it is dried in a kiln, ideally heated by a peat fire. The dried malt is

ground and mixed with hot water in a huge circular vat called a mash tun. A sugary liquid, "wort", is drawn off from the porridge-like result and fed into massive vessels containing up to 45,000 litres of liquid, where living yeast is stirred in to convert the sugar into crude alcohol. After 48 hours, the "wash" (a clear liquid containing weak alcohol) is transferred to onion-shaped copper stills and heated to the point where alcohol turns to vapour.

This vapour rises up the still to be condensed by a cooling plant into distilled alcohol which is then passed through a second still. The trick is to know precisely when it has distilled enough. It is then poured into porous oak casks and left to mellow for at least three years. ❑

RIGHT: enjoying a "wee dram".

THE EDINBURGH FESTIVAL

Art and anarchy collide once a year as some the world's top performers

rub shoulders with bands of ambitious amateurs

The sheer audacity of Edinburgh's decision to launch an international festival of the arts in 1947 is, even in the rosy light of retrospect, breathtaking. It is the kind of chutzpah that Edinburgh folk would expect from Glasgow folk and deny in themselves.

The world was, after all, still reeling from the ravages of a terrible war. The nation was bankrupt. Rationing and the grey pall of austerity prevailed. Yet here was this chilly northern capital, with no reputation as a patron of the arts let alone a fountainhead of culture, blowing trumpets, flying banners, and setting itself up as a unique European platform for the great performers of the world. An international flamenco fiesta in Sheffield would not have seemed less appropriate.

Yet the Edinburgh Festival, now over half a century old, established itself in its first year as one of the red-letter entries in the international calendar of artistic events, and in its scale and variety still has not acquired a rival anywhere in the world. Although the official Festival occupies only three weeks of the city's time and energies every year, the consequences of that audacious gamble in 1947 have had a profound effect on the character of the capital and the lives of its citizens.

The chosen city

Luck courted the Edinburgh Festival from the beginning. By the happiest of chances the idea of such an event, mooted even in the dark days of war, brought the right people together in the right place at the right time.

Rudolf Bing, the general manager of Glyndebourne Opera who became one of the arts world's most influential administrators, had even expressed an interest in Edinburgh's potential as a British equivalent of Salzburg as

PRECEDING PAGES: the free jamboree of Fringe Sunday in Holyrood Park.
LEFT: flamboyant Festival impresario Richard Demarco, pictured outside Donaldson's College.
RIGHT: costume from the souvenir shops.

far back as 1939. At a lunch in London in 1944 he told representatives of the British Council that the United Kingdom should give a lead to the rest of Europe by celebrating peace when it came with a major festival of music and opera.

H. Harvey Wood, the British Council's man in Edinburgh, reminded Bing of the capital's

suitability: it was exactly the right size, it had adequate staging and accommodation facilities for performances and visitors, its scenic beauties and historic associations commanded the admiration of the world, and it was a place with enough pride in itself to welcome strangers. It seemed a compelling argument.

When, eventually, the idea was put to the Lord Provost, Sir John Falconer, he committed Edinburgh up to the neck: "She will surrender herself to the visitors and hopes that they will find in all the performances a sense of peace and inspiration with which to refresh their souls and reaffirm their belief in things other than material."

The first Festival

Perhaps the first Festival's most extraordinary stroke of luck came from an unlikely source: three weeks of blazing August sunshine. The city shimmered under high blue skies. Native reserve melted. Hospitality flowed generously and the city was baked so remorselessly that South American journalists wrote home and complained about the heat. Like their colleagues in a vast Press corps from all over the world, however, they applauded the Festival as an astonishing, heartwarming success.

Everything had not been offered up as a hostage to chance. The legendary maestro

ty when he wrote: "The 1947 Festival, given in a city with no international record for a display of that kind, shortly after years of what human beings themselves condemn as inhuman ferocity ... appeared as an incredibly early demonstration of an unbroken faith in uniting human values and virtues ... This is now shining history."

It was – and remains – a hard act to follow. For a few years, as a shattered Europe began to put itself together again, Edinburgh had the stage to herself and would have been excused a certain amount of freewheeling until other festivals caught up. But Sir John Falconer had

Bruno Walter was reunited with the Vienna Philharmonic Orchestra – a musical triumph and an emotional affirmation of the Festival's wider intentions. Four of the world's greatest virtuosi – Schnabel, Szigeti, Fournier and Primrose – came together as a quartet of stunning radiance. And it was under Walter's baton that the young former telephonist from Blackburn, Kathleen Ferrier – recognised even before her untimely death in 1953 as one of the greatest singers of the century – gave one of the most memorable of all Festival performances in Mahler's *Song of the Earth*.

The great Austrian pianist Artur Schnabel spoke for most of the world's artistic communi-

offered the world "all that is best, year after year" and, with an inspired administrator of Bing's calibre as the Festival's first director, that idealistic promise was in safe keeping.

Maintaining excellence

Over five decades and seven administrators later, the current director, Brian McMaster, shows no signs of being daunted or intimidated by the past pursuit of excellence. The world's great orchestras, instrumentalists, conductors, opera

ABOVE: visual spectacle takes centre-stage in the High Street.
RIGHT: an ensemble dance performance.

and ballet companies – the list reads like a directory of the elite in Western culture – have performed joyfully on Edinburgh's sometimes inadequate platforms. But, says McMaster, "elitist I'm certainly not. Having worked in opera, which suffers from that label, I've always had to break that down. And populist? If it means, patronising, then No."

Of course, the world has become a much more complicated place since 1947. Virtuoso performers have been elevated to expensive megastars. Their engagements are booked years in advance while festival budgets are often allocated only on a year-to-year basis. Moving an opera company – even one small enough to be accommodated in Edinburgh's biggest playhouse – can cost more than the gross takings of its Festival run. The failure rate of commissioned new drama remains too high and too costly for much hope of further adventure, and established companies with a national reputation seem reluctant to leave their bases.

The city transformed

If you live, breathe, and have any kind of sensitivity being in Edinburgh, August is the month when the city vividly demonstrates why Stevenson used its essential duality as a model

STRUGGLE OF THE VISUAL ARTS

The visual arts appeared late on the programme of the International Festival, and lost their place early. After making no provision for them in 1947, the Festival soon began to repair the omission with a series of exhibitions, some of which stand to be counted among its major triumphs. It is a sad fact that their like may never be seen again, anywhere in the world. Rembrandt, Cézanne, Monet, Gauguin, Degas, Renoir, Braque, Soutine, Modigliani, Delacroix, Corot, Rouault and Derain were all celebrated with significant shows before the end of the 1960s.

After that, the Festival had to learn to live in the real world. Private owners became reluctant to part with their masterpieces. The astronomical costs of insurance and security combined with the growing nervousness of other countries to risk the transit of their treasures in the interest of national prestige. The alternative lay in mixed exhibitions – some thematic, others linked with national cultures or artistic styles – and an increasing emphasis on contemporary painting and new work.

Eventually, McMaster decided his resources would be better spent on live art and he dropped the visual art programme altogether. The National Galleries plough valiantly on, as do the city's many independent galleries, but they miss the backing of the "official" Festival.

for Jekyll and Hyde. The transformation is as astonishing as Dr Jekyll's metamorphosis. The staid and sober becomes vulgar and blowsy. That damp hush, settled for centuries up the vennels and closes of the Old Town, explodes into undergraduate babble. Where the town gibbet stood, jazz ricochets off the cobbles. Chaste neo-classical terraces blush with bunting.

As if by Magic

Suddenly, in midsummer, off comes the hodden grey, on goes the motley; a medieval fair splashes over the urban tundra like spilt paint.

The threat of heavy fines is no deterrent to a legion of billposting hucksters. Importuning develops into a form of stylised street theatre.

From the beginning, the Fringe mixed its metaphors by letting its hair down. Word got about that Edinburgh was a good place to be young, and the footloose and fancy-free brought irreverence and anarchy and mischief to the church halls and warehouses which they fitted up as makeshift theatres. If the spirit of the official Festival is the celebration of quintessential excellence in the arts, the spirit of the Fringe is fun, enterprise, improvisation and sheer brass neck.

One wink of watery sunshine and frigid matrons turn into shameless strippers. Police are polite, traffic wardens indulgent. Purple rain would not seem remarkable.

Although the official Festival has lost some of its early stuffiness and generates its own quota of gaiety, it is the unofficial festival, the Fringe, which works the miracle. This impudent parasite, which has been riding piggy-back on the official leviathan for most of its life, is now so renowned in its own right that in Adelaide and San Francisco it is not uncommon to see "straight from the Edinburgh Festival Fringe" posted on a marquee – as if that accolade should be enough to make you part with your money.

Success of the Fringe

In 1959, Dudley Moore – a serious musician in those days – accompanied a baritone in afternoon concerts and played jazz with cutlery and crockery at night. The next year he was part of the Beyond the Fringe quartet which took the official Festival, London and Broadway by storm. In 1964 one future Goodie and three future Pythons played the Fringe in undergraduate revues.

Two generations of new dramatists have used the Fringe as workshop, platform and shop window. Several plays have transferred straight to London's West End. Experiment is expected, innovation assumed. Many talents have sprouted in this fertile seedbed, and, even if you are playing to an audience of only six, two are probably critics and the others are perhaps script editors and casting directors for television companies.

The Fringe has now expanded – with its own headquarters and sophisticated administration – to the extent that in 2001 over 650 companies and individuals presented nearly 1,500 shows in more than 20,000 performances in nearly 200 venues. The annual turnover is well over one million pounds.

These figures bear interesting comparison with the official Festival's most recent statis-

On the bandwagon

To some extent this is also true of other summer festivals and events which have been spawned over the years. The Military Tattoo, which is almost as old as the Festival itself, has been seen on television by billions all over the world and is perhaps the most enduring international image of Edinburgh *en fête*. These nightly glittering pageants, searchlit in the noisy cockpit of the Castle Esplanade, have become folk festivals in their own right. Bagpipes prevail in a tidal wave of tartan fervour, but the additon of Breton bombards and Arabian bugles is not unknown.

tics – where public and private subsidy combine to bridge the gap between £1.9 million worth of ticket sales and the £4.5 million cost of presentation – but it would be foolish to make comparisons or use these statistics to stoke the tiresome argument that either festival is strong enough in its own right to survive without the other. Because they evolved together they continue to nourish each other and each would undoubtedly be immeasurably poorer without the other.

LEFT: the High Street nerve centre of the Fringe.
ABOVE: the home of Edinburgh University Theatre Company is one of nearly 200 Fringe venues.

The Film Festival, which began as an ambitious flicker in 1947, has developed into what professionals in the business regard as the best non-competitive film festival in the world. It champions new work, explores the significance of cinema styles and techniques, and examines the *oeuvres* of important directors in comprehensive retrospective appraisals.

After many years of barely surviving on a shoestring, the Film Festival has grown into a key event in the international movie calendar. Its rivals envy the existence of the Filmhouse, the hub and heart of the festival, whose role as an art cinema for the other 49 weeks of the year generates a committed core audience.

Meanwhile, Charlotte Square's green grass disappears annually under giant marquees which house the Book Festival. Established adult and children's authors from throughout the English-speaking world take part in readings, panels and discussions. The smaller-scale, briefer Jazz and Blues Festival also attracts some performers from abroad and has its devotees *(see Pubs and Performers, page 75).*

On the other hand, the International Television Festival at the end of August – an industry rather than public event – is probably too crowded out by the other arts to reach its full potential in Edinburgh at this time.

The International, Fringe, Film, Jazz and Book festivals, plus the Military Tattoo, all take place, partially overlapping, in August. *(For booking details, see Travel Tips section.)*

Problems no threat

Unlimited funds would solve the major problems of most festivals. Edinburgh, in all its proliferation, is no exception. After that bravely unequivocal declaration of intent in 1947, the City Fathers have wavered more than once and, in their niggardly support grants, seemed intent on enhancing a reputation – justified or not – for civic parsimony. Neither that behaviour nor the constant carping of a voluble minority of the citizenry – who see their town turning into an autumnal haven for limp-wristed wimps, posturing pseuds, and the world's unwashed flotsam – has ever put the Festival at any real hazard. The idea of Edinburgh without its Festival is now, surely, unthinkable.

The opening of The Hub Festival Centre in 1999, in the former Tolbooth Kirk at the head of the Royal Mile, gave the International Festival an attractive new home, quite different in spirit and form from the cramped quarters of its old Market Street premises. The Hub's café proved an instant hit with visitors, while its meeting rooms brought the Festival's expanding educational programme in house. Along with the Edinburgh Festival Theatre on Nicolson Street, with its massive stage and sizeable auditorium, The Hub has finally given the Festival a physical sense of permanence in the heart of the city.

The effect of what Sir Thomas Beecham called "your northern jamboree" on the fabric and texture of Edinburgh life is as incalculable as the millions of pounds it has poured into the pockets of city merchants. Hotels and hostels increase their tariff during the Festival, and every pub, café, restaurant, gift shop, department store, news vendor, taxi driver, hamburger joint and pizza parlour within a mile of the Scott Monument gets a little richer in August. Their increased turnover is tangible.

Elevating exposure

Less tangible is the Festival's enrichment of the human spirit, the elevation of artistic standards, the exposure to new sights and sounds and ideas, frequent demonstrations of an allegedly frigid community's natural bonhomie, and something that may be more important than anything else in conservative Edinburgh – a diminishing tendency to make monuments out of parish pumps.

Festivals are about many things: about hosannas and hallelujahs, about artistic adventure and curiosity, and the constant reiteration of that which has been proved to be special. They are also about people, the linking together of lives and cultures, and they give us the chance to celebrate the best that the best of us can do. ❑

LEFT: straddling the columns of the National Gallery for a fire-eating display on The Mound.

Scottish Cuisine

Edinburgh's fashionable restaurants may differ little from their English counterparts – though steak, fish and game tend to be better north of the River Tweed – but historically the Scots kitchen is no more like the English than the Portuguese is like the Spanish. That expert in Scots gastronomy, F. Marian McNeill, has rightly scolded that expert in the art of French gastronomy, André Simon, for referring to Scottish dishes as "English fare". Many good things come out of England, she admitted, but porridge isn't one of them.

If flour and meat still form the basis of English cookery, meal and fish form the basis of Scottish, along with bakery, which can sometimes be stodgy, heavy and mass-produced but is often delectable. Not too long ago in Scotland there were fewer restaurants than tea-rooms, where people ate afternoon tea or "high tea", consisting perhaps of fish and chips and an array of scones and cakes. Such establishments, sometimes with a piano trio providing gentle music, flourished in Edinburgh until after World War II. Biscuit-making remains an extensive industry, and orange marmalade is a renowned export – though the theory that the name "marmalade" derives from the words *Marie est malade* (referring to the food given to Mary Queen of Scots when she was ill) is still hotly debated.

Of Scottish fish, kippers are a treat. The best are from Loch Fyne or the Achiltibuie smokery in Ross and Cromarty, where their colour remains golden, not dyed repellent red as they are in so many places. Finnan-haddies (*alias* haddock) are a tasty alternative, boiled in milk and butter. Salmon and trout, sadly, are more likely, in all but the top restaurants, to come from a West Coast or northern fish farm as fresh from the river ("wild" salmon is more flavoursome), but the standard remains high. Venison, pheasant, hare and grouse (ritually shot on or around 12 August) are equally established features of the Scottish kitchen, though the last is normally tough and fibrous.

As for haggis – though, like grouse, it is hardly a gourmet delight – it does offer a fascinating experience for brave visitors, and its case has recently been taken up by a celebrity chef in Japan. Scotland's great mystery dish is a sheep's stomach stuffed with its minced heart, liver and lungs, along with suet, onions and oatmeal. After being boiled,

the stomach is sliced open and the contents served piping hot. Butchers today often use a plastic bag instead of a stomach; this has the advantage that it is less likely to burst during the boiling process, ruining the meat.

The tastiest haggis, by acclaim, comes from Macsween's of Edinburgh, who also make a vegetarian haggis. Small portions of haggis are sometimes served as starter courses in fashionable restaurants, though an authentic way to eat it is as a main course with chappit tatties (potatoes), bashed neeps (mashed turnips) and a number of nips (Scotch whisky, preferably malt). This is especially so on Burns Night (25 January), when supper

is ceremonially accompanied by poetry reading, music and Burns's own *Address to the Haggis*; or else on St Andrew's Night (30 November), when haggis is again attacked with considerable gusto.

Other exotic-sounding fare: cock-a-leekie (a soup made from chicken and leeks, but authentic only if it also contains prunes), hugga-muggie (Shetland fried haggis, using a fish stomach), Arbroath smokies (smoked haddock stuffed with butter), crapit heids (haddock heads stuffed with lobster), stovies (potatoes cooked with onion), and cream crowdie (a mixture of oatmeal, sugar and rum). Though the Scots are said to like saltier dishes than the English, they also possess a very sweet tooth, evidenced in their penchant for the fizzy drink Irn-Bru.◻

RIGHT: a traditional Scottish spread.

THE VISUAL ARTS

Art offerings range from international masterpieces to works that document
Edinburgh, mainly housed in a variety of neo-classical edifices

Edinburgh is remarkably well served by a variety of galleries which cater for most tastes. The choice ranges from the National Galleries of Scotland (NGS) to small, privately owned galleries as well as premises owned by the City Council and a number of semi-commercial subsidised spaces.

The NGS occupies four sites in the city: the National Gallery of Scotland, the Scottish National Portrait Gallery, the Scottish Gallery of Modern Art and the Dean Gallery. The most prominent of these is the National Gallery of Scotland, situated on The Mound. This building, by William Playfair, was opened in 1859; its lavish interior decor was planned by Playfair's collaborator, D.R. Hay, who has been described as "the first intellectual house-painter". A late 20th-century refurbishment attempted – with mixed results – to recapture some of the original mood of Hay's scheme.

The Duke of Sutherland Loan and the Maitland Bequest, as well as other major gifts, form the basis of the gallery's collection. Although eclectic, it is particularly strong in French Impressionism and Post-Impression – including works by Monet (such as *Haystacks: Snow Effect*, painted 1891) and Cézanne (*Mont St Victoire*, 1890–95) – and the Italian School. A notable work in the latter category is Botticelli's *The Virgin Adoring the Sleeping Christ Child* (*circa* 1490), which has recently been restored.

Native works

The National Gallery also has an excellent collection of works by Scottish painters. The NGS's assertion that "Scottish painting developed a distinct identity only after the foundation of the Royal Scottish Academy in 1826" has been challenged by recent studies of Scottish art which have demonstrated a historical continuity from a much earlier period, despite the cul-

tural and political ruptures created by the Union of the Crowns and Act of Union (*see pages 26 and 29*). Two of the most interesting examples of Scottish painting in the National Gallery are David Wilkie's *Pitlessie Fair* (1804) and Henry Raeburn's *The Reverend Robert Walker Skating on Duddingston Loch* (1784), reproduced

on *page 30*. Despite doubts about its provenance, the latter has achieved iconic status and is used on NGS promotional material.

Also of note is Allan Ramsay's 1766 portrait of the philosopher Jean Jacques Rousseau; its 'twin', of his contemporary and fellow philosopher David Hume of Edinburgh, is exhibited in the Scottish National Portrait Gallery. The works were commissioned by Hume, although Rousseau was apparently greatly offended by his own image.

Famous faces

The Scottish National Portrait Gallery, established in 1889, occupies a red sandstone *tour-*

PRECEDING PAGES: paintings by Elizabeth Blackadder in the Scottish National Gallery of Modern Art.
LEFT: Botticelli's Virgin and Christ Child.
RIGHT: private viewing at a city gallery.

de-force in the gothic revival style on Queen Street. As an institution, it seeks to "collect and display images of distinguished, celebrated or even infamous Scots" in a wide variety of media. This policy has continued to evolve as recent exhibitions and commissions have shown the lives of "ordinary" people in Scotland. Portraits range from an anonymous depiction (dated 1578) of Mary, Queen of Scots to a portrait by the photographer Gunnie Moberg of the living novelists Duncan McLean and Irvine Welsh.

The Portrait Gallery also houses a considerable photographic archive, including the work of the pioneers of the "calotype" photograph,

David Octavius Hill and Robert Adamson. Their portfolio contains a fascinating group of studies collectively known as the *The Fishermen and Women of the Firth of Forth*, which anticipates modern documentary photography.

Modern adaptations

The Scottish National Gallery of Modern Art, along with The Dean Gallery (both in Belford Road; *see page 188*), houses a collection of 20th-century and contemporary art. The former was founded in 1959 and 40 years later the Dean opened to provide extra space for large-scale touring exhibitions and to house three major donations – the Paolozzi Gift, the Roland Penrose Collection and the Keiller Bequest. This gallery has been imaginatively adapted from its original use as an orphanage to suit its present purpose. Some eyebrows have been raised at the dedication of such a large amount of space to a living artist (Sir Eduardo Paolozzi), but there is no doubt that the Dean has a collection of Surrealist art of international import, with significant works by Miró, Man Ray, Ernst, Duchamps and many others.

By contrast – though it is perhaps unfair to criticise it given the short time in which it has been developed and the limited display space – the scope of the National Gallery of Modern Art collection is, by international standards, at best average. Its policy on acquisitions attempts to be all things to all people by acquiring art of international quality and at the same time trying to build up a representative selection of work by Scottish artists, and on both counts it has only been partially successful. Proposals for a national gallery of Scottish art have been torpedoed by vested

---

ART DURING THE ENLIGHTENMENT

In any era, but particularly during the Enlightenment, there are many interesting examples of various other cultural and intellectual disciplines having a direct influence on visual art. Allan Ramsay's portraits of Hume and Rousseau are a case in point. In 1754 Hume, along with Adam Smith and Ramsay, founded the Select Society, a forum for intellectual debate in Edinburgh. In both portraits, Ramsay concentrates our attention on the faces of the sitters with a strongly focused light, suggesting that these thinkers were themselves illuminating human understanding.

Sir Henry Raeburn was deeply indebted to the work of Ramsay, and he followed in his footsteps by going to study

in Italy. Coincidentally, Raeburn established his practice in Edinburgh in the year of Ramsay's death. A list of Raeburn's portraits reads like a roll-call of society figures, one of the most famous being his portrayal of the fiddler Neil Gow (in the National Portrait Gallery), who was in demand all over Scotland for his spirited renditions of strathspeys and reels.

In the early 19th century David Wilkie's paintings (such as *Mr and Mrs Chalmers-Bethune and their daughter Isabella* in the National Gallery) and his studies of the face owe much to the contemporary surgeon and anatomist Charles Bell. Wilkie, in turn, contributed illustrations to Bell's *The Anatomy of Expression in Painting*, published in 1806.

interests and factions in the the art establishment, and it is pertinent to note that Scotland lacks a modern purpose-built art museum which could stand alongside the likes of the Guggenheim in Bilbao or Louisiana in Denmark.

Exhibition hosts

Adjacent to the National Gallery of Scotland on The Mound is the Royal Scottish Academy (closed until summer 2003; *see page 142*), completed in 1822 and originally called the Royal Institution. Its construction is shown in a famous painting by Alexander Nasmyth in the National Gallery of Scotland. The building acts

Turning to newer galleries (*see also Travel Tips: Culture*), the Fruitmarket Gallery on Market Street was refurbished and structurally improved in 1993 by the Edinburgh-based architect Richard Murphy. It runs a programme of international and Scottish exhibitions of varying quality, many of them consisting of conceptual work. Opposite is the City Art Centre, which has a growing collection of Scottish art that it displays in part at any one time, on a rolling basis, as well as hosting touring exhibitions (again of varying quality) and the occasional "blockbuster". In nearby Cockburn Street, two galleries cater for younger *avant-*

as the Royal Scottish Academy (RSA) headquarters and also hosts the annual exhibitions of the members of the Academy, the Society of Scottish Artists (SSA), Visual Arts Scotland and the Royal Society of Painters in Watercolours (RSW). They are primarily social events (particularly that of the RSA), when the great and the good turn out on the opening night accompanied by the Academicians themselves in their robes. The most dynamic of these organisations is the SSA, which exists to promote innovative work and encourage new talent.

LEFT: the sculpture park of the Gallery of Modern Art.
ABOVE: inside the National Gallery of Scotland.

garde tastes. The Collective Gallery, as its name implies, is run for and by artists, while Stills combines a contemporary photography gallery with a bookshop, café and darkroom premises.

Much of the ground work for institutions such as the Collective and the Fruitmarket was done by Professor Richard Demarco (pictured on *page 80*), a maverick impresario who, since the mid-1960s, has done more than any other individual to internationalise the visual arts in Edinburgh and Scotland as a whole. Demarco's achievements are legion, and by inviting artists of the calibre of Tadeusz Kantor, Joseph Beuys and Gerhard Richter to show in the city in the 1970s and 1980s he succeeded in jolting the ultra-conservative Edinburgh art world from its complacency. Although Demarco no longer runs a gallery in the conventional sense, his remarkable photographic archive numbering over 500,000 items can be viewed by appointment (tel: 0131-557 0707).

More small spaces

The Talbot Rice Gallery at Edinburgh University's Old College *(see page 122)* is worth a look, particularly the Torrie Collection which contains several important works including Giambologna's late 16th-century *Anatomical Figure of a Horse* (showing the anatomy of the animal in the *écorché* or flayed form). The gallery also has a rolling programme of exhibitions usually focusing on established Scottish artists. Inverleith House in the Royal Botanic Garden *(see page 212)* leans towards conceptual work these days, but also puts on shows of occasional interest to a wider public.

A relative newcomer to the Edinburgh scene is the Ingleby Gallery, established in 1998. Set in an elegant Georgian townhouse overlooking Arthur's Seat, it steers a fine course between couthy Scottishness, vapid decorativeness, crafty worthiness and fashionable conceptualism. The work of artists such as Howard Hodgkin, Emily Young and Felim Egan combine modern beauty and quality.

A number of foreign cultural organisations operate visual arts programmes, including the French, Italian and Danish Institutes. Edinburgh Printmakers in Union Street runs workshops and courses as well as featuring work by local and international artists. Arts venues and cafés throughout the city often have temporary exhibitions of variable quality.

In Dundas Street there is a clutch of commercial galleries, each with its own niche. These include the Dundas Street Gallery, Bourne Fine Art and The Scottish Gallery. The last is a long-established concern concentrating on contemporary Scottish work and crafts, jewellery and furniture. Nearby, The Open Eye Gallery pursues a similar policy, with some success, and has recently opened Eye Two which specialises in 20th-century American and European printmaking – exhibitions to date have included Hockney, Warhol, Picasso and Matisse. ❏

RIGHT: meeting of minds at a diploma show.

PLACES

A detailed guide to the city and surroundings, with main sites cross-referenced by number to the maps

Where else does a slightly ramshackle medieval town glower down on such Georgian elegance? What other comparable urban centre contains such huge chunks of sheer wilderness within its boundaries? Does any other city in Europe have so many solid Victorian suburbs surrounded by such bleak housing estates? The Edinburgh author Robert Louis Stevenson summed it up: "Few places, if any, offer a more barbaric display of contrasts to the eye."

The Old Town probably packs more historic buildings into a square mile or so than anywhere else in Britain. Its spine, the Royal Mile, is a wide thoroughfare which runs from the Castle to the Palace of Holyroodhouse. Thanks to Scotland's young upwardly-mobile professionals, who have discovered the convenience of living in the centre of a city, many of the old, run-down tenements are being given a much-needed facelift.

The New Town, one of Europe's urban success stories, won Edinburgh its sobriquet "Athens of the North". Some saw its urbane classicism as regimentation, but it remains a memorial to the genius of the Scottish Enlightenment. This fact was recognised internationally in 1995 when both the Old and New Towns, together with other nooks and crannies such as Dean Village, were awarded the rare honour of being declared a UNESCO World Heritage Site.

What helps make Edinburgh so civilised is the fact that its centre is not a business area that dies after the offices close. The tenemented inner suburbs, a fascinating urban landscape, enable many of its citizens to live right in the heart of the city. And, when they feel the need to fill their lungs, it's a short journey to harbours such as Leith and Newhaven, to riverside walks by the Water of Leith, to the variety of parks within the city limits or to the top of one of the seven hills on which Edinburgh stands.

Such is the scale of Scotland that, using Edinburgh as a base, you can comfortably take day trips to such historically rich locations as North Berwick, Dunbar, Haddington, Melrose and Abbotsford, Linlithgow, Dunfermline and Lochleven Castle. What's more, it's less than an hour by rail or road to Glasgow, Scotland's other great city. Not that anyone in Edinburgh could imagine why you would possibly want to visit Glasgow. They're in no doubt at all that Edinburgh is the best place in the world – and, for much of the time, it's perfectly possible to agree with them. ❑

PRECEDING PAGES: the view from Arthur's Seat; Edinburgh Castle during the Military Tattoo; North Bridge memorial to the city's regiments who helped build the British Empire.
LEFT: Grosvenor and Lansdowne Crescents and St Mary's Episcopal Cathedral.

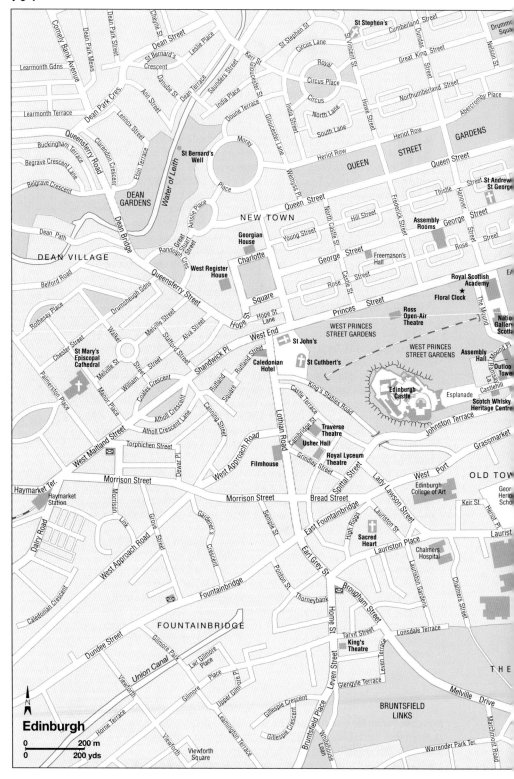

Edinburgh

| 0 | 200 m |
| 0 | 200 yds |

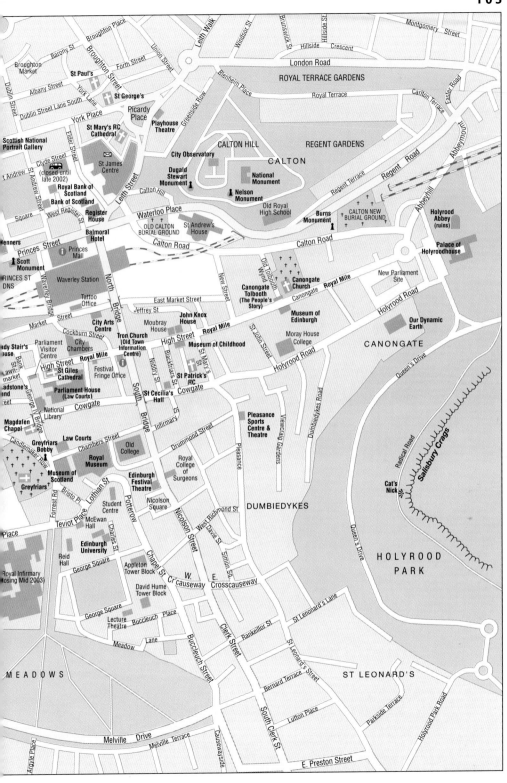

THE OLD TOWN

*This mile-long picturesque heart of the city has often been called
a museum piece tracing 500 years of Scottish history,
but many of its oldest buildings are still lived in*

Map
on pages
108–9

E dinburgh's medieval Old Town packs more historic buildings into a square mile or so than anywhere in Britain. Native novelist Robert Louis Stevenson suggested the reason: "It [the Old Town] grew, under the law that regulates the growth of walled cities in precarious situation, not in extent, but in height and density. Public buildings were forced, whenever there was room for them, into the midst of thoroughfares; thoroughfares were diminished into lanes; houses sprang up storey after storey, neighbour mounting upon neighbour's shoulders, as in some Black Hole of Calcutta, until the population slept fourteen to fifteen deep in a vertical direction." For an impression of what it was like to live in this "black hole" in the 18th and 19th centuries, *see page 37.*

The population of the Old Town peaked at more than 40,000 in 1851, after which the overcrowding led to its progressive abandonment – the rich and influential had mostly departed at the turn of the 19th century, and half a century later the middle and artisanal classes began leaving too. The first wave of departures was called "the Great Flitting", and crowds would gather to watch all the fine furniture, crockery and paintings being loaded into carts for the journey down the newly-created "earthen mound" (now called The Mound) to the neoclassical New Town. The population reached its nadir in 1981 when it sank to less than 3,000, then it began steadily to climb again.

But, despite the Old Town's partial reclamation for residential or mixed use, the Royal Mile and surrounding streets continue to rely heavily on tourism and the network of often tacky businesses that cater to the tourists *(see The Heritage Industry, page 112).*

In the 19th century the former, fine homes of the well-off were inherited by the poor and the feckless, an anomaly that is nicely drawn by James Bone in *The Perambulator in Edinburgh* (1911). This unpleasant irony may, from the point of view of architectural preservation, have been a blessing. Most of the people who took over were simply too hard up to make any "improvements", and many beautiful painted ceilings, elaborate plasterwork and carved fireplaces in places like Chessel's Court and James's Court have survived. The Old Town was also fortunate in that Edinburgh's 19th-century architects respected the ancient street patterns when they set about "slum clearance" projects. Although in the rebuilding of the Canongate 28 closes were wiped out, and over the years many more have gone, more than 100 of these alleyways and courtyards survive in the Old Town.

LEFT: the rampant lion and Castle, emblems of Scotland and its capital.
BELOW: the Heart of Midlothian on the site of the old prison (Tolbooth) near St Giles' Kirk.

The Royal Mile

The "backbone" of the Old Town is the Royal Mile, the city's oldest thoroughfare extending just over a mile, which starts at Edinburgh Castle and runs down the hill to the Palace of Holyroodhouse. There are four sections: Castlehill (nearest the Castle), the Lawnmarket, the High Street and the Canongate (which was a separate burgh until 1856, and in medieval times had been physically separated from Edinburgh proper by the gate of the Netherbow). The English author Daniel Defoe, writing in the 1720s, described the Royal Mile as "perhaps the largest, longest and finest street for buildings and number of inhabitants in the world."

Edinburgh Castle ❶ (open daily; entrance fee) is Scotland's most popular tourist attraction, though it is most impressive when looked up at as an entirety atop the volcanic Castle Rock from the lower levels to the north, west and south. (A "crag-and-tail" geological formation has created a gentler downward slope along the Royal Mile.) From inside the castle complex and from the Castle Esplanade there are good views over the city. Although the original castle was Edinburgh's first recorded building, much of the present-day complex dates from the 18th and 19th centuries, when the royal castle was transformed into a garrison fortress with barracks and modern defences.

The kings' fortress

In many ways the Castle – which probably has most to offer the visitor interested in military history – has an odd character. As well as admitting tourists en masse it is still heavily used by the British Army as headquarters and barracks (though the main garrison left in 1923), and it stages one of the world's great showbiz events, the annual Edinburgh Military Tattoo. Over the centuries the Castle has also been used as a royal residence, a prisoner-of-war camp, an ordnance factory and a records office. With its steep, easily defended sides, natural springs

TIP

Lively and informative historical walking tours of the Old Town (daytime or evening) are offered by several companies, usually with themes such as infamous ghosts or the underground city. *See Guided Tours section of Travel Tips.*

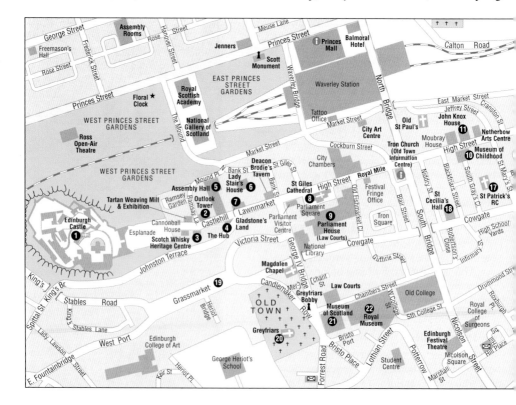

and excellent vantage points, the Castle Rock was squabbled over for thousands of years, by Picts, Scots, Britons and Angles, and by their successors. The first documented castle on the site was built by Malcolm III in the late 11th century *(see Beginnings, page 21)*. The stronghold has been taken by the English and retaken by the Scots more than once, and in the course of conflicts its fabric has been destroyed and rebuilt time and again.

By the time Mary, Queen of Scots ascended the throne in 1542, it was Scotland's principal royal castle, but after the "Lang Siege" by Mary's enemies in 1571–73 priority was given to strengthening the fortifications rather than repairing the living quarters. It was never much favoured as a residence and thereafter was hardly used as such. In 1618 the English poet John Taylor wrote that Edinburgh Castle "is so strongly grounded, bounded and founded, that by force of man it can never be confounded". Several decades later Oliver Cromwell put an army presence permanently in the Castle, yet after the Restoration the Stuart faction was unable to repel the forces of William of Orange in 1690. The Castle last saw action in 1745 when besieged by Bonnie Prince Charlie's Highland/ Irish army, which failed to breach its defences. In fact, the citizens of Edinburgh begged the Prince to lift the siege because the Castle garrison was wrecking the city with cannon fire.

Inside the Castle gates

Most visitors to the Castle tour it with an audio guide (extra charge) and in some parts of the complex there is little labelling. On crossing the drawbridge notice the statues of King Robert the Bruce and Sir William Wallace, heroes in battles against the English. Following the route around the edge of the complex you will

Plan on page 110

The Castle guard is changed when the Queen is in residence at Holyrood Palace.

BELOW: the Palace and Crown Square inside the Castle.

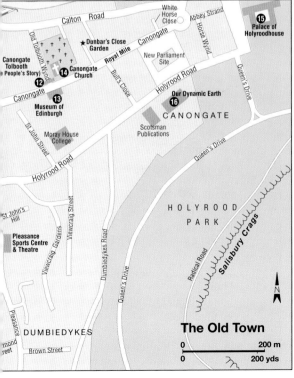

The Old Town

Above the Castle entrance is the coat of arms of Regent Morton, who rebuilt it after the Lang Siege of 1571–73.

RIGHT: armour on display in the wood-panelled Great Hall.

come to the Mills Mount Restaurant and, on the ramparts beside it, the **One O'Clock Gun ⓐ** which has been fired at 1pm daily (except Sunday) since 1861. There is also a café at the top of the castle in Crown Square. Continue down to Museum Square and the **National War Museum of Scotland ⓑ** in the old ordnance storehouse and hospital, which charts 400 years of military history. Displays explore themes including the individual's experience of military life and the Highland soldier. Past the Governor's House you can continue onward to the **Castle Vaults ⓒ**, used in the 18th century as a prison of war.

Through the gateway to the Upper Ward you come to the church-like **Scottish National War Memorial ⓓ**, converted from the North Barracks in the 1920s by Robert Lorimer to commemorate Scots killed in World War I. (It now remembers those killed in both World Wars.) Tucked behind it, occupying the highest point on the Castle Rock, is the Castle's oldest building, **St Margaret's Chapel ⓔ**, a tiny Romanesque chapel dedicated to the saintly wife of King Malcolm III. Army officers from Scottish regiments like to get married here. The huge cannon outside the Chapel is "Mons Meg", forged in Flanders in the 15th century and perhaps used at the siege of Norham Castle on the River Tweed in 1497.

On the other side of the War Memorial are another military museum, the **Great Hall ⓕ**, with its decorated hammer-beam roof (uncovered and "restored" in the late 19th century), and the **Palace ⓖ**. There are some original painted panels in Mary, Queen of Scots' chamber where she gave birth to James VI, but the Laich Hall's wall and ceiling decoration has been recently recreated. Upstairs the **Crown Room** houses the Honours of Scotland (crown jewels) which were locked away after the Treaty of Union with England in 1707 and forgotten about. In fact, no one was quite sure where they were until a commission set up

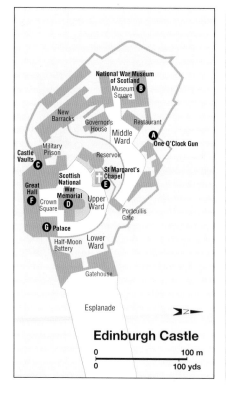

Edinburgh Castle map

National War Museum of Scotland
Museum Square ⓑ

New Barracks

Governor's House

Restaurant

Middle Ward

One O'Clock Gun ⓐ

Military Prison

Reservoir

Castle Vaults ⓒ

St Margaret's Chapel ⓔ

Scottish National War Memorial ⓓ

Great Hall ⓕ

Crown Square

Upper Ward

Palace ⓖ

Portcullis Gate

Half-Moon Battery

Lower Ward

Gatehouse

Esplanade

Edinburgh Castle

0   100 m
0   100 yds

by Sir Walter Scott in 1818 traced them to a locked chest in a locked room in the Castle. In 1997 they were joined by the Stone of Destiny, Scotland's symbolic coronation seat which, in 1296, had been carried off to London's Westminster Abbey to sit beneath the throne of England for 700 years. A colourful and informative introduction to the jewels includes a line-up of all the Scottish monarchs and tableaux recreating important events.

Maps on 108–9 and 110

Views, tartan and whisky

Back outside on the Esplanade are several military graves and statues. Immediately below the Esplanade on **Castlehill** stands an iron fountain marking the spot where Edinburgh used to burn its witches. Beyond this is a picturesque cluster of tenements called **Ramsay Garden**, designed by the late 19th-century planning genius Patrick Geddes, on a site once owned by the poet Allan Ramsay.

Back on Castlehill the Castlehill Reservoir building is occupied by the **Tartan Weaving Mill and Exhibition**: behind the shop is the Edinburgh Old Town Weaving Company's functional mill with an exhibition illustrating how tartan is woven, where you can have a go yourself (open daily; entrance fee). The **Outlook Tower ❷** houses Patrick Geddes' **Camera Obscura** (open daily; entrance fee). Holograms, pinhole photography and a "magic gallery" lead up to the regular show of live panoramic and close-up images of the city, which provides a good introduction to Edinburgh.

Across the road are **Cannonball House**, a 16th-century house which gets its name from the cannonball half-buried in the wall, and the **Scotch Whisky Heritage Centre ❸** (open daily; entrance fee) occupying former school premises. This venture sets out to explain how Scotch whisky is made, with an audio-

The Ramsay Garden flats were built to house students, but they now rank among the most sought-after homes in Scotland – especially the ones with stunning views over Princes Street and the Firth of Forth.

BELOW:
looking down the Royal Mile from the Castle.

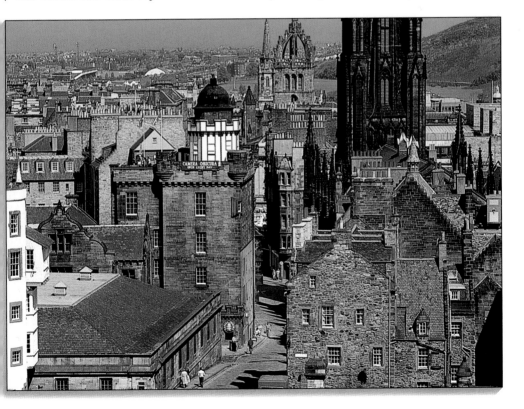

The Writers' Museum sits adjacent to peaceful, residential James's Court, where Burns resided when visiting the city.

BELOW: Robert Louis Stevenson's printing press in the Writers' Museum.

visual show and a journey in a whisky barrel through 300 years of history. There's also a shop (more expensive than other nearby whisky outlets). A few yards further down, the imposing 19th-century gothic bulk of the Tolbooth St John's Church – where Edinburgh's Gaelic-speaking population worshipped until 1984 – has been transformed into **The Hub ❹** (Edinburgh's Festival Centre: open daily) offering information and ticket sales (and a café/restaurant).

Closes off the Lawnmarket

On the north side, across from The Hub, is a narrow passageway to Milne's Court and the public entrance to the Scottish Parliament's debating chamber in the **Assembly Hall ❺** (which fronts on Mound Place). This gloomy building is actually owned by the Church of Scotland and is where the annual General Assembly of the Kirk takes place. Also off the **Lawnmarket** is Lady Stair's Close leading to **Lady Stair's House ❻**, a handsome 17th-century pile which serves as the **Writers' Museum** (open Mon–Sat; Sun pm during Festival; free) dedicated to Scotland's three world-famous writers: Robert Burns, Sir Walter Scott and Robert Louis Stevenson. Lady Stair was, in fact, one of the later inhabitants; the house was built by William Gray of Pittendrum in 1622.

The displays are interesting in a low-key way. Paintings, etchings, engravings and busts of the Big Three proliferate, along with such memorabilia as locks of hair, bibles, pipes, pocket books and walking sticks. The short-lived enthusiasm of the Edinburgh *literati* for Burns is nicely caught in an engraving showing the ploughman-poet declaiming in front of Adam Ferguson, Dugald Stewart and the High Court judge Lord Monboddo. Temporary exhibitions feature other Scottish writers too.

THE HERITAGE INDUSTRY

The Scotsman's propensity for nostalgia is long-standing. As Sir Walter Scott noted in *Weir of Hermiston:* "For that is the mark of the Scot of all classes: that he stands in an attitude towards the past unthinkable to Englishmen, and remembers and cherishes the memory of his forebears, good or bad." In Edinburgh pride in the past has come close to suffocating the city, as those in the tourist trade have been sucked into relying heavily on tacky "heritage centres" and souvenir shops crowded along the Royal Mile.

In the early years of the 21st century, Edinburgh has a lot going for it, and some new attractions are higher quality, but countless shops still bank on the appeal of clan ancestry and shortbread packaged with the face of Bonnie Prince Charlie to eager foreigners (the fashion for Highland trappings having been begun by Scott himself; *see page 36*). The story of one of Scotland's most successful industries is slickly packaged for the whole family at the Scotch Whisky Heritage Centre. Away from the tourist district local children are perhaps the target market for Shaping a Nation, an interactive exhibition opened in the West End in 2000, which drums up national pride by focusing on a parade of influential and inventive Scots (Fountainpark, Dundee Street; open daily; entrance fee).

The merchant's house

Back on the Lawnmarket, immediately to your right is **Gladstone's Land** ❼ (open Apr–Oct: Mon–Sat and Sun pm; entrance fee), a 17th-century house and shop which has been restored by the National Trust for Scotland. The house is well worth a visit, and gives some insight into 17th-century Edinburgh life – dirty, difficult and malodorous. Built in 1621 and called after the original owner, Thomas Gledstanes, a prosperous merchant, the interior is stuffed with period oak furniture, long-case clocks, Dutch paintings (no masterpieces) and domestic bric-a-brac and kitchen utensils. The bedchamber features a wooden beamed ceiling painted with fruit and flora, and contains an elaborately carved four-poster bed probably made in Aberdeen.

Nearby **Deacon Brodie's Tavern** takes its name from an 18th-century villain called William Brodie – the model for Robert Louis Stevenson's *The Strange Case of Dr Jekyll and Mr Hyde* – who was a highly respected master carpenter by day and an unscrupulous burglar by night. If you are interested in the workings of the Scottish Parliament you may wish to drop in at the **Parliament Visitor Centre** across the road, on the corner of George IV Bridge and the top of the High Street (entrance on George IV Bridge; open Mon–Fri; Sat in Aug and early Sept; free), which has an information desk and displays including plans and an architect's model of the new Parliament building at Holyrood (*see page 119*).

The beggar's troubled church

Now continue downhill on the middle section of the Royal Mile, called the **High Street**, whose dominant feature is **St Giles' Cathedral** or "High Kirk" ❽ (open daily; free). This great gothic church with its distinctive crown-shaped

Map on pages 108–9

Gladstone's Land incorporates a 17th-century shop booth with replica goods – and livestock.

LEFT: tartan cloth for sale.
BELOW: hat trick on the Royal Mile.

Arms of the National Library of Scotland, on George IV Bridge.

BELOW: ceiling of the Thistle Chapel. **RIGHT:** St Giles' Cathedral framed by a modern statue of David Hume.

steeple is where the reformer John Knox once preached, and it remains the focal point of the established Church of Scotland. A church has stood on the site since the 9th century and parts of the existing building date back to around 1120. It was dedicated to St Giles, the patron saint of beggars and cripples, in 1243, and has been knocked about a bit. It was burnt down by the English in 1385, rebuilt and extended in the following century; parts were restored in 1830 and it was then remodelled and "refaced" between 1872 and 1873. Work is ongoing to stop the fabric of the church falling apart.

Through the centuries St Giles' has been enmeshed in Scotland's religious turbulence. The Roman Catholic bishops and their trappings were ejected by Knox and the reformers in 1560, only to reappear in Anglican form in 1633 when Charles I tried to impose Episcopacy on Scotland. (It was then that the church was redesignated a cathedral, and the name has stuck despite its reversion to Presbyterianism). After the National Covenant was signed in 1638 bishops were again ejected, but they returned in 1660 at the Restoration of Charles I – and remained until 1689.

Most of the stained glass in St Giles' is mid- to late-19th century, as the Church of Scotland had previously taken a sour view of such embellishments. One of the windows was installed in 1985 and is dedicated to the poet Robert Burns. The ornate **Thistle Chapel** in the southeast corner was completed in 1911; it was designed by Robert Lorimer for The Most Ancient and Most Noble Order of the Thistle, an order of chivalry founded in the 17th century (Scotland's equivalent of England's Order of the Garter) and features carved-oak knights' stalls and a wealth of heraldic symbols. There is an agreeable café/restaurant in the basement, much used by lawyers from the courts on the

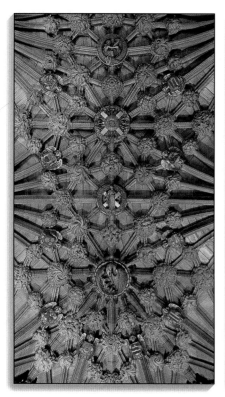

other side of Parliament Square, a grand neo-classical affair behind St Giles' (notice the rooftop sphinxes).

The courts in **Parliament House** ❾ are themselves worth a visit, particularly Parliament Hall (open Mon–Fri; enter by No. 11; free) with its great hammer-beam roof of Danish oak under which the Scottish Parliament used to meet. Nowadays it is where the "Writers" (solicitors) and advocates foregather to discuss cases, usually while walking up and down. "The ritual is to march in pairs," noted James Bone in 1911, "facing towards one another at the turn like officers on board ship." Parliament Hall is lined with some handsome paintings and sculpture by artists including Raeburn, Roubiliac and Steell.

Haunts from the past

On the east side of St Giles' is the **Mercat Cross** (topped by a unicorn, pictured) from which kings and queens are still proclaimed, and where a ghostly herald is said to have read the names of the men about to die at the Battle of Flodden in 1513. It was here that the Marquis of Montrose was hanged in 1650, dressed in a new suit "of pure cloth all laid with rich lace". This fierce 17th-century warrior, whose military prowess rattled the Scottish establishment to its foundations, died with his "speech full of composure, and his carriage as sweet as ever". Across the High Street are the **City Chambers**, headquarters of the City of Edinburgh Council, which were built as an "exchange" (office block) in the late 18th century. Running underneath the City Chambers is an old street called Mary King's Close which was devastated by fire in 1750, and where, it is said, strange chills are apt to descend on visitors and even stranger scratching noises can be heard.

Past the Festival Fringe office on the right, the nerve centre of the annual event, is the former Tron Church, built to serve the Presbyterian congregation ousted from St Giles' in the 17th century. It is now the **Old Town Information Centre** (open mid-June–Sept: daily), also containing a free exhibition consisting of panels on the history and attractions of the Old Town ranged around extensive excavated remains of one of the city's earliest streets, which archaeologists discovered under the floor.

The **Museum of Childhood** ❿ (open Mon–Sat; Sun pm in July and Aug; free), across North Bridge, claims to be the oldest museum in the world of its kind; it contains a splendid collection of games, puzzles, models, teddy-bears, china dolls and much besides, which children usually find hard to get near because of crowds of wistful adults. Opposite is **Moubray House**, probably the oldest inhabited house in Edinburgh, built *circa* 1472, where Daniel Defoe lived during his posting in the city as an English spy. Adjacent is the equally historic (built *circa* 1490) **John Knox House** ⓫ (open Mon–Sat; Sun pm in July and Aug; entrance fee), run as a museum by the Church of Scotland and dedicated to the great 16th-century Protestant reformer. There is little evidence that Knox ever lived there, but the Church tries to remind the world that the Reformation in Scotland was a lot less bloody than it was in England, and that

Map on pages 108–9

The present, 19th-century Mercat Cross replaced the 16th-century original.

BELOW:
John Knox House.

One bronze John Knox stands on the site of his grave near St Giles' Cathedral (above), while another guards the Church of Scotland's Assembly Hall.

BELOW: outside the Museum of Edinburgh.

John Knox, far from being a crazed fanatic, was in many ways an advanced, liberal thinker. The adjoining **Netherbow Arts Centre**, comprising a small theatre, galleries and restaurant (box office in John Knox House), is named after the east gate to the city (marked by plaques) which was demolished in 1764.

Social and civic history

The **Canongate** (the canons' "gait" or road from Edinburgh to Holyrood Abbey), the street which forms the bottom part of the Royal Mile, is particularly rich in 16th- and 17th-century buildings and was for long the smart residential quarter of aristocracy eager to be close to Holyrood Palace. The **Canongate Tolbooth** ⓬, which served as an administrative centre and prison, is readily recognised by its clock projecting from towers and turrets dating from 1591. Today the Tolbooth houses **The People's Story** (open Mon–Sat; Sun pm during Festival; free), a fascinating museum – originally conceived as a repository of Labour Party and trade union history – which traces, with tableaux, sounds and smells, the lives, work and pastimes of the city's ordinary citizens from the late 18th century to the present.

Across the road is the **Museum of Edinburgh** ⓭ (open Mon–Sat; Sun pm during Festival; free) devoted to the history of Edinburgh. This restored amalgamation of several 16th-century houses is packed with remarkable Edinburgh-made artefacts and has intriguing collections of Edinburgh police cudgels and three-dimensional shop signs made for hatters, tobacconists and instrument makers. Also on display is the original National Covenant of 1638 *(see page 27)*.

Back on the north side of the street is the **Canongate Church** ⓮, begun in 1688 for the congregation which was driven out of Holyrood Abbey to make

way for King James VII's newly created Knights of the Thistle. The Canongate Church is a handsome building, but no more intriguing than its churchyard. Here lie the philosopher Dugald Stewart, the poet Robert Fergusson (whose headstone was paid for by Robert Burns), the visionary Lord Provost George Drummond, artists Alexander and John Runciman, and economist Adam Smith.

Just below the churchyard is the little known **Dunbar's Close Garden**, a small walled plot laid out in the 17th-century style with gravel paths, stone seats and box hedges. The Canongate once featured many such small gardens, and in the 18th century a "physic plot" would have been the only source of medicinal plants. Below the garden is **White Horse Close**, once one of Edinburgh's most important coaching inns and now an attractive courtyard of whitewashed houses.

Holy seat of the court

The **Palace of Holyroodhouse** ⓑ (usually open daily, but closes occasionally; Nov–Mar: last admission 3.45pm; entrance fee) began life as an Augustinian abbey founded by David I in 1128 (according to legend, after he found a remnant of the "holy rood", or cross, in a stag's antlers) and grew into a royal palace in the early 16th century to provide a more comfortable alternative to the Castle. It was much added to in the late 17th century by Sir William Bruce for Charles II but the king never set foot in the place (although his father Charles I was crowned in the Abbey Church in 1633).

Holyrood ceased to be a working abbey in 1610; the church's conversion to a Catholic chapel was later damaged by a mob and royal tombs desecrated. In 1650 Cromwell's troops almost burnt the palace to the ground (by mistake) and then botched the restoration work.

Map on pages 108–9

Insignia on the façade of Canongate Church.

BELOW: the Palace of Holyroodhouse.

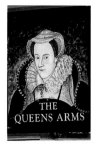

*The tragic reign of
Mary, Queen of
Scots, the Palace's
most famous occu-
pant, is remembered
in a pub sign.*

BELOW: the Morning
Drawing Room
of Holyroodhouse.

The history of the palace's occupancy is long and often grisly. It was here that Mary, Queen of Scots witnessed the butchery of her Italian favourite David Rizzio, and the scattered remains of the executed Marquis of Montrose were reassembled and laid in state here prior to being given a decent burial in St Giles' in 1661 *(see page 28)*. Bonnie Prince Charlie held court at Holyrood in 1745 during his short-lived triumph, and the palace was used by George IV during his hilarious state visit to Edinburgh in 1822. The portly Hanoverian stalked the palace wearing flesh-coloured tights under an exceedingly brief Royal Stewart tartan kilt. "As he is to be here so short a time," remarked one waggish Edinburgh lady, "the more we see of him the better." An identical outfit was also worn by the Lord Mayor of London, a biscuit-maker from Wapping and one of the king's drinking pals. George IV nevertheless set a precedent which the British royals have been following ever since. Queen Victoria and Prince Albert favoured Holyrood as a stop-over on their way to and from Balmoral, and the present Queen is usually in residence here for part of June.

Like Hampton Court in London, Holyrood is rather an odd mixture, in this case of 16th- and 17th-century buildings, the former being more interesting from a historical viewpoint. Those parts of the interior open to the public (on a 40-minute guided tour) include Mary, Queen of Scots' apartments, lavishly decorated 17th-century State Rooms with magnificent plasterwork ceilings, and the long Picture Gallery which features 111 mostly mythical Scottish kings and queens all painted in quick succession (rather badly) by a Dutchman, Jacob De Wit, in the late 17th century. It was discovered in 2000 that their sequenced numbers may later have been changed, so some real kings of long ago are wrongly identified.

All new in the Old Town

A large former brewery plot on the south side of the Canongate, stretching to **Holyrood Road**, will remain a building site until at least the middle of 2003, the controversial **new Parliament** project having been delayed after estimates of building costs spiralled. However, if the plans of Catalan architect Enric Miralles are fully realised, the Scottish Parliament will have a magnificent showpiece with state-of-the-art facilities (which will, incidentally, incorporate historic Queensberry House, previously a private hospital). Meanwhile, developments along the rest of Holyrood Road, which runs parallel to the lower Royal Mile, are injecting new life into the bottom end of the Old Town.

Turn into Holyrood Road from Horse Wynd and immediately on your left is the first significant Holyrood development to have been completed, **Our Dynamic Earth ⑯** (open Apr–Oct: daily; Nov–Mar: Wed–Sun; entrance fee). Opened in 1999, this amazing tentlike structure offers a "journey of discovery" through 11 galleries which explore the formation and evolution of the planet, as well as climatic zones from the polar zone to tropical rainforest. It's full of dramatic effects and is great for children, but don't expect a lot of in-depth information. Next door are the gleaming new offices of *The Scotsman* newspaper. Also part of the area's transformation are new hotels, including the luxurious Mac-Donald Holyrood Hotel opposite, offices, flats and retail space, but there are no plans to demolish the ugly 1960s towers of the Dumbiedykes housing estate which mar the otherwise wonderful view of **Salisbury Crags** (the view being a consolation for residents of flats facing Holyrood Park and the crags).

Holyrood Road continues for nearly two-thirds of a mile (1 km) before turning into the more historically interesting, but very gloomy, **Cowgate** (reached

Map on pages 108–9

The heraldic beasts on the Palace gateposts echo the Mercat Cross unicorn.

BELOW: the foyer of Our Dynamic Earth.

from the High Street via St Mary's Street). At the point where the Cowgate meets St Mary's Street, there is a restored fragment of the **Flodden Wall**, part of the defences built to keep out the English after the ruin of the Scottish army at Flodden in Northumberland in 1513.

The Irish quarter

The Cowgate – which runs under South Bridge and George IV Bridge – was known as the "Irish quarter" right into the 20th century after the thousands of immigrants who swarmed into the area, particularly after the 1846 Great Famine. Although most of its teeming population was "decanted" into the peripheral housing estates in the 1950s and 1960s, most names on tenement doors around the Cowgate are Irish and the Irish Catholic influence is exemplified by the huge bulk of **St Patrick's** Roman Catholic church ⓱ (affectionately known as "Saint Paddy's"). St Patrick's was originally built for a late 18th-century Episcopalian (Anglican) congregation, then in the 19th century the building fell into the hands of Presbyterians before its acquisition by the Catholics in 1856.

A little further along is **St Cecilia's Hall** ⓲ which now belongs to Edinburgh University, but which was built by the Edinburgh Musical Society in 1762 as a fashionable concert hall modelled on the Opera House at Parma. Despite an ugly exterior, St Cecilia's Hall has a stunning oval-shaped interior noted for its excellent acoustics. It is still used for chamber concerts and recitals, and it contains the university's magnificent collection of early keyboard instruments (open Wed pm and Sat pm; Mon–Sat am during Festival; entrance fee).

At the west end of the Cowgate (visible from George IV Bridge above) is the 16th-century **Magdalen Chapel** (open Mon–Fri), one of few buildings in Scot-

BELOW:
the ruined church of Holyrood Abbey, which inspired Mendelssohn's Scottish Symphony.

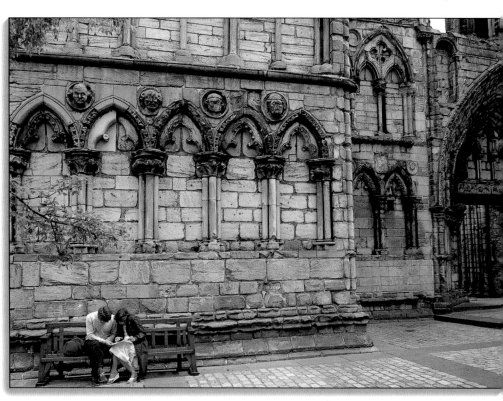

land with pre-Reformation stained glass. It is now the headquarters of the Scottish Reformation Society which has been involved in restoring the building. The bodies of Protestants who were hanged in the Grassmarket in the late 17th century – when the Stuart kings Charles II and James VII tried to root out Presbyterianism – are buried in the chapel. On the the Grassmarket itself is a 20th-century memorial to these religious martyrs, enclosed within railings on the site of the old gallows.

Map on pages 108–9

The hangman's marketplace

The Cowgate opens up into the semi-pedestrianised **Grassmarket** ⓳, which gets its name from its former function as a marketplace for Lothian farmers selling hay, corn and seed, which lasted from medieval times until 1911. But the Grassmarket was also one of Edinburgh's more important execution venues (along with Castlehill, the Mercat Cross, and the Gallowlees) and huge crowds used to flock into the street to watch convicted felons dancing at the end of the hangman's rope. A national centre for dance (Dancebase) opened in the Grassmarket in 2001, adding to the existing mix of a hotel, small trendy shops and pubs.

The ornate West Bow well (1674) by the Grassmarket recalls a bygone age.

Candlemaker Row, at the southeast end of the Grassmarket, leads up to the entrance to **Greyfriars Kirk** ⓴. The church building is unremarkable, having been damaged and repaired many times over the years, but its graveyard contains some of the most spectacular funerary sculpture in Britain *(see page 166)*, many of the key figures in Edinburgh's history having been buried here. And it was here that the National Covenant was signed by those who pledged to defend their native religion in the face of Stuart attempts to impose Episcopalianism on Scotland. Most famously, however, Greyfriars contains the grave of the West

BELOW: view of the Grassmarket from a Victoria Street antique lace shop.

Map on pages 108–9

Greyfriars Bobby, the much photographed statue at the top of Candlemaker Row.

BELOW: words of a man trapped under a collapsed house, carved at Paisley Close's entrance.

Highland terrier "Greyfriars Bobby" (immortalised by Walt Disney). So devoted was the little dog to its master, John Gray, a policeman who died in 1858, that it kept vigil over his grave for 14 years.

Scotland and beyond

You can return to the High Street from the top of Candlemaker Row by turning left, past the National Library, or cross George IV Bridge to visit, on Chambers Street, two important national museums. The dramatic modern sandstone building on the corner is the **Museum of Scotland ㉑** (open Mon–Sat and Sun pm; Tues till 8pm; free). It covers the history of Scotland from the earliest times to the present day *(see pages 124–25)* and offers panoramic views from the roof terrace and a useful museum shop.

Linked to the new building (you can pass freely between them), is the 19th-century **Royal Museum ㉒** (open as Museum of Scotland). Its central hall, with soaring, slender, steel pillars and glass roof, is a superb piece of architecture. Exhibits of varying but mostly high quality include natural history (there's a room full of amazing stuffed animals), science, technology and extensive decorative arts collections, not only Scottish but also from abroad, especially China, Japan and Korea. Special exhibitions are normally showing and lectures are held frequently.

On the other side of the Royal Museum (fronting on South Bridge) is Edinburgh University's imposing **Old College**, designed by Robert Adam and completed by William Playfair. Buildings of note further south along South Bridge are the glass-fronted **Edinburgh Festival Theatre** – with an extended stage area larger than that of the Royal Opera House in London – and, opposite, the hall of the **Royal College of Surgeons**, again the work of William Playfair. ❏

Triumph of the Traverse Theatre

The beginnings of things become more difficult to pin down as time shrouds truth in rosy veils. So you will hear at least a dozen different stories about the origins of the Traverse Theatre, that world-renowned cockpit of avant-garde drama, which opened on 2 January 1963.

Just after Hogmanay (New Year) celebrations, most things in Scotland are unable to move, let alone open. Yet there they were, a brave band of dedicated idealists, greeting their first audience in the tiny 60-seat theatre they had fashioned with their own hands out of a former brothel and doss-house in James's Court, just down the hill from the Castle. For the record, the play was Jean-Paul Sartre's *Huis Clos*, the theme of which seeks to demonstrate that "hell is other people". The sourness of public squabbles would certainly dog the Traverse.

The need for a new theatre was summed up in a witty early 1960s Festival revue song:

You can talk of Ionesco,
You can talk of Harold Pinter,
But if you think this town
Is culture's crown
You should come here in the winter.

Edinburgh exasperated its intelligentsia with its double standards: for the three weeks of the Festival the city leapt to life and became the core of the artistic universe; then the lights went out for another year. By creating a small club dedicated to presenting the best of world drama, the Traverse hoped to burnish the cultural lamp and keep it burning.

Its director, Terry Lane, succeeded beyond all expectations by producing a programme which in the first year included a world premiere and eight British premieres, and aired the work of Arrabal and Ionesco, Jarry, Grabbe and Betti. Membership, which rose to around 2,000, implied a whiff of daring. By the mid-1960s, with Jim Haynes – arguably the theatre's founder father and certainly its spiritual guru – nearing the end of his tempestuous term as artistic director, the theatre was attracting two kinds of headlines. The tabloid press rejoiced in scandals over nudity, foul language and internecine punch-ups. Critics in the serious newspapers, such as Kenneth Tynan and Harold Hobson, held the Traverse up to the cultural world as a shining example of courageous experimental theatre.

In 1969 the Traverse moved to the Grassmarket, where for 22 years it produced inspiring work under a succession of young directors including Max Stafford-Clark, Michael Rudman and Mike Ockrent, all of whom went on to do notable work in London. In 1991 it moved to the new Saltire Court office block, where the glorious main auditorium has an extremely flexible stage. It has been called "Britain's first purpose-built theatre for new writing since Shakespeare's Globe".

Under the auspices of Philip Howard, the artistic director since 1996, the Traverse has continued to be innovative, willing to take a risk, and committed to new writing: over 400 new plays have been mounted in four decades. World, British and Scottish premieres all attract a dedicated aurdience.❏

RIGHT: bright lights of the Traverse.

THE MUSEUM OF SCOTLAND

Situated in the heart of the Old Town, one of Edinburgh's newest museums is now its premier treasure house, presenting Scotland to the world

After nearly half a century of prevarication, Scotland's most important national museum was opened in 1998 on the day of the nation's patron saint, St Andrew. It brings under one roof the core of the Scottish Collection which had previously been scattered. This comprises more than 10,000 precious artefacts, from a hoard of Roman silverware found in East Lothian to a drinking cup commemorating Robert the Bruce's victory against the English at the Battle of Bannockburn.

STORY OF A NATION

The historical narrative starts in the basement with Beginnings, including a stunning diorama of Highland and Lowland forests prior to human intervention, and Early Peoples, a large area containing archaeological finds from Pictish gravestones to part of a Viking boat. On the ground floor, The Kingdom of the Scots charts Scotland's development as a unified nation from AD 900 to the Union in 1707; then the story continues upstairs with three floors devoted to exhibits on trade and industry, society, the Church, science and the arts in the 18th and 19th centuries. Finally, on the top floor are objects deemed to define the 20th century *(see right)*.

▷ **SHOWING THEIR COLOURS**
The cult of Jacobitism is a key theme of "Scotland Transformed", as exemplified by this tartan suit, made for a supporter of the Stuarts.

▷ **MODERNIST LANDMARK**
Although Prince Charles opposed the radical design, by Benson and Forsyth, the Museum of Scotland is acclaimed architecturally as well as for its contents.

△ **RARE JEWEL**
An exquisitely crafted brooch, *circa* 800 AD, found in Ayrshire, exudes high status and may have been gifted from one regional ruler to another.

△ **JAWS OF DEATH**
This stone carving of a lioness devouring her human prey is a recent archaeological find from a Roman site at Cramond on the outskirts of Edinburgh.

WORKSHOP OF THE WORLD

One major focus of the Museum of Scotland is on the industries (such as glass-making, above) that became the bedrock of Scotland's economy in the 18th and 19th centuries, and the innovations which contributed to its success as one of the world's leading industrial regions. Dominating level 4 is the Ellesmere locomotive, built in 1861, which remained in service until 1957; also on display is the world's first successful rotary printing press, designed by Thomas Nelson. Shipbuilding displays include an 1830 model of a Leith shipyard showing wooden ships under construction.

Scottish exports made their way across the British Empire, and manufacturing benefited from seams of coal and ironstone close at hand, while transport of raw materials and products was revolutionised by pioneering developments in railway engineering, canals and shipbuilding (Clyde-built ships becoming known as the world's best). One display case charts the success of Scotch whisky, which is attributed to the failure of grape harvests, allowing whisky to succeed brandy as a favourite tipple.

◁ **HANDS-ON EDUCATION**
The Discovery Centre enables children to learn about Scotland's history by investigating the backgrounds of objects in the museum.

▷ **CONTINENTAL CULTURE**
The classical emblems and vibrant colours of a painted wood panel from Dean House, Edinburgh, show the influence of the Renaissance after the Reformation of 1560.

◁ **NORTHERN KNIGHTS**
The 12th-century Lewis chesspieces, found on the Hebridean isle, show the cultural legacy of Viking invaders. They have become well known and much copied.

▽ **CONTEMPORARY ICONS**
Objects in the 20th-century gallery, from a *Braveheart* film poster to the Bic biro, were chosen by the Scottish public, labelled with their own reasons for their selections.

THE FIRST NEW TOWN

*The elegant planned town was once separated from the Old Town
by the Nor' Loch and is now kept apart by Princes Street Gardens.
It contains some of Britain's finest streets and squares*

Map on page 130

A line by the Scots poet Hugh MacDiarmid – "Edinburgh is a mad god's dream" – will make sense to anyone who crosses the North Bridge from the Old Town to the New, particularly after having sampled a few drams. The bridge crosses a deep gorge, with a railway that tunnels under Grecian temples. High up to the left is the romantic skyline of the Old Town, rising to the Castle's massive silhouette. To the right there is a soaring monument resembling a gothic space-probe and a long, straight street of shops, department stores and hotels overlooking gardens in the valley.

The view is beautiful, yet topographically and architecturally insane. No sane human would devise a city with a fault-line through its heart, with buildings clinging to volcanic cliffs and streets that straddle canyons. It is only the east wind, blowing down the Firth of Forth, that restores common sense. This is in fact the most rational of British cities, a product of enlightened self-interest. And the key to understanding its divided character lies in the North Bridge.

Birth pangs

The New Town is a separate city, although the offspring of the Old. By the middle of the 18th century, Edinburgh was in a sad condition. Although still Scotland's largest city and a centre of law and learning, it had, since suspension of the Scottish Parliament in 1707, lost its purpose as a capital. Ambitious Scots, heading south to further their careers in London, were abandoning a city that failed to meet the needs of a new age. Edinburgh was overcrowded and impoverished, its ancient buildings crumbling with decrepitude. Even the social fabric was chaotic, with the highest and the lowest living cheek by jowl in a labyrinth of dark medieval alleys, sharing the same taverns and emptying their slops into the street from the windows of their tenements.

In the Age of Reason, old Edinburgh remained a gross affront to the dignity of Scotland. Yet, despite this, or quite possibly because of it, the city was a powerhouse of intellect and commerce, buoyed up by the promise of prosperity and in thrall to current fashions for "improvement". Scotland was now North Britain, part of the richest and most powerful nation in the world. If London was to play the role of Rome within this new world order, then Edinburgh could at least be the new Athens, a city famed for intellect and beauty.

There had been several schemes over the years to expand the city northwards, but such dreams had always foundered in the murky waters of the Nor' Loch. Filling the deep valley now occupied by Princes Street Gardens, the loch had for centuries formed part

PRECEDING PAGES: the Charlotte Square residence of Scotland's First Minister. **LEFT:** National Trust restorers. **BELOW:** view of the eastern New Town from the Castle.

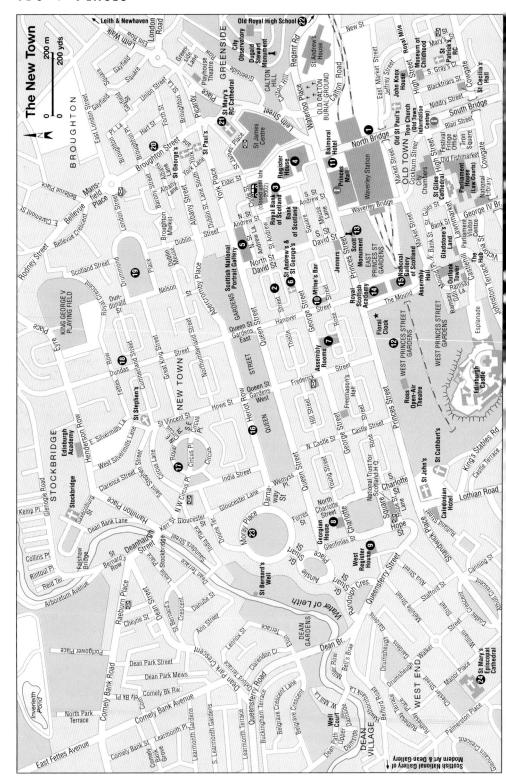

Map opposite

of Edinburgh's defences, besides providing its upright citizens with suitably foul waters in which to duck witches and "loose women". But, now that peace was settled and justice firmly in the hands of lawyers, it had become an inconvenience that confined the city to its overcrowded ridge.

In 1752 the possibility of getting rid of this barrier was raised once more in a pamphlet entitled *Proposals for carrying on certain public works in the city of Edinburgh*. It was a brilliant piece of propaganda: touching on a nerve of civic shame, appealing to financial prudence, even greed, yet inspiring in its vision of a new, enlightened age. It also had the full support of George Drummond, the city's charismatic Lord Provost. The timing was immaculate and official backing guaranteed. The *Proposals* led directly to the New Town's birth.

First stage is bridged

The loch took 60 years to drain. This might seem excessive, but allowance must be made both for its situation and for Scotland's climate. In the meantime it remained essential to bridge its valley before a new town could be built. The **North Bridge** ❶ was completed in 1772 (it was replaced by the present steel-arched version in 1895). With views that place a thousand years of human history against a backdrop of extinct volcanoes, it is a thought-provoking structure. Each morning it is crowded with students hurrying towards the university, their eyes glued to the pavement as they worry about essays on geology, philosophy or architecture. Strangely, it is only tourists who stop to look over the parapet.

Construction of the bridge coincided with the birth pangs of the New Town that it was designed to serve. This remarkable development now forms part of the core of Edinburgh, an inner-city landscape that remains unparalleled in

"[New Town architecture] is nearly always more three-dimensional [than in Ireland, Italy or France] ... even if you're being Greek you usually carry the design round all sides."

– SIR JOHN BETJEMAN

BELOW:
North Bridge, connecting the Old and New Towns.

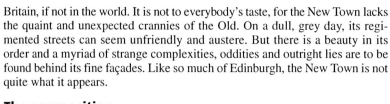

Britain, if not in the world. It is not to everybody's taste, for the New Town lacks the quaint and unexpected crannies of the Old. On a dull, grey day, its regimented streets can seem unfriendly and austere. But there is a beauty in its order and a myriad of strange complexities, oddities and outright lies are to be found behind its fine façades. Like so much of Edinburgh, the New Town is not quite what it appears.

The composition

The layout of the first New Town development was the product of an architectural competition held in 1763, with a medal and the freedom of the city as the prize. The winner was James Craig, an unknown architect aged 22. His plan, as drawn on paper, looks neither original nor interesting; a rigid grid of streets with squares at either end that any pretentious young sophisticate might have devised. What made the New Town special was its setting. The main thoroughfare, George Street, was to be built along a ridge, with views down side-streets, south to the Castle and north to the distant hills of Fife. It was, and still remains, entirely possible to check the progress of the harvest from a pavement in the city centre.

The Melville Column in St Andrew Square remembers the man who governed Scotland 1782–1805.

Houses along Princes Street faced the Old Town across the slowly draining Nor' Loch, while their equivalents on Queen Street, the northernmost thoroughfare, were fronted by a sweep of steeply sloping gardens with the Firth of Forth as a dramatic backdrop. Human, geometrical perfection was balanced against nature in the spirit of the age. Whether Craig himself, or indeed the judges, were consciously aware of this is a matter for some doubt but, more than two centuries later, the New Town is still regarded as a triumph of mid-Georgian artistic composition.

BELOW: welcome to the George Hotel.

Plain beginnings

George Drummond died in 1766, so never lived to see his dream take shape. The first house to be completed, in 1768, was at the eastern end of **Thistle Street ②**, a narrow lane running between and parallel to George and Queen streets, that Craig intended for the homes of artisans and shopkeepers. (From North Bridge, turn left into Princes Street then cross over and walk up St David Street, turning left into Thistle Street just beyond George Street.) **No. 1 Thistle Court** is an attractive yet entirely unpretentious little house with walls of undressed stone, lacking any hint of the formal grandeur normally associated with the New Town.

Just around the corner, on the north side of **St Andrew Square**, there are other early houses that, although considerably larger, are almost as plain. (Their impressive porticoes were added later, when classical embellishments came into vogue.) During the first years of its development the New Town was, in fact, neither strictly classical nor uniformly planned. Desperate to recoup on its considerable investment (the North Bridge alone had cost £16,000), the Town Council allowed individual householders considerable freedom of design and on occasion turned a blind eye to gross infringements of the plan.

Craig had intended that a pair of fine churches should terminate the vistas along George Street but, in thoroughly suspicious circumstances, it was actually the mansion of a millionaire rather than a house of God that came to occupy the prime position on St Andrew Square.

The Dundas mansion

It may be that Sir Laurence Dundas saw little fault in bribery (he had acquired his massive fortune while Commissary-General, in charge of military supplies), or perhaps the Town Council was a little over-eager to encourage him to build the New Town's first great house. At any rate, when they sold him "an area in the East Square" in 1767 they failed to take a note of its exact position. The Dundas mansion – now the **Royal Bank of Scotland ❸** – was designed by Sir William Chambers and is still one of the most splendid buildings in the city. Elegantly classical and set back behind its railed-off forecourt, it somehow manages to be both ostentatious and restrained. Just next door, and lacking any such restraint, the rival **Bank of Scotland** dates from 1846. With its statues set on columns high above the street, it is a celebration of Victorian extravagance – classicism on an epic scale in the style of Cecil B. de Mille.

Chambers' reputation as Britain's leading architect in the later 18th century was rivalled only by that of a fellow Scot, Robert Adam. In 1772, as the Dundas mansion neared completion and the North Bridge opened, the British government approved plans by Adam for the first great public building to be sited in the New Town. **Register House ❹**, fronting on Princes Street, is a repository of Scottish legal and historical records dating back to 1855, together with some parish records that date back to the 16th century. The search room, in

Map on page 130

TIP

The east side of St Andrew Square is in the midst of a transformation, with the arrival of the upmarket department store, Harvey Nichols, and a new shopping street linked to the St James Centre and refurbished bus station.

BELOW: the Royal Bank in St Andrew Square was originally a grand private home.

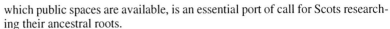

The statue of the Duke of Wellington outside Register House is known as "the Iron Duke in bronze by Steell".

BELOW: exterior statuary of the Scottish National Portrait Gallery.

which public spaces are available, is an essential port of call for Scots researching their ancestral roots.

Although the two banks and Register House are now overshadowed by the brutal 1960s monstrosity of New St Andrews House, part of the **St James Centre** (a shopping mall dominated by a branch of John Lewis), they have behind them charming lanes and gardens overhung with cherry trees. Two pubs on West Register Street, the **Guildford Arms** and the **Café Royal**, have retained late-Victorian interiors. The latter, containing tiled panels depicting great inventors, is particularly worth visiting. Its oyster bar, set behind a mirrored screen, is even more dramatic in its decor.

Scottish portraits

Queen Street, on the north side of St Andrew Square, formed the northern limit of Craig's New Town and, unlike Princes Street, still retains much of its original appearance. Unfortunately it is now a major traffic artery and, since its gardens are not open to the public (nearby residents hold keys for their own use), there is little pleasure to be had from strolling its considerable length. At its east end just above St Andrew Square, the **Scottish National Portrait Gallery ❺** (open Mon–Sat and Sun pm; free except special exhibitions) is, however, well worth visiting.

The building, a Venetian-Gothic "palace" designed by Rowand Anderson in 1885, has some splendid murals in its entrance hall depicting the Victorian, romantic view of Scotland's history, whilst the portraits on display suggest a rather different reality with a cast of hopeless monarchs and their courtiers, many of whom were beheaded. In the gallery devoted to the 20th century, figures from the arts, politics and commerce huddle in their separate groups like guests invited to a party at which no-one knows the host. A Paolozzi bronze stands duty as a waiter, while Conservative politician Sir Alec Douglas-Home, who was briefly British prime minister in 1963, gazes quizzically across the room at left-wing nationalist Hugh MacDiarmid and friends, plotting poetry and revolution while enjoying a free drink.

Exclusive refinements

George Street, leading westward from St Andrew Square, parallel to Queen Street, was designed to be the New Town's most important thoroughfare, a title that it still lays claim to, having the city's greatest concentration of exclusive shops, smart auction houses and fashionable bars. Its most important building is **St Andrew's and St George's** church ❻, built in 1781–83 after Sir Laurence Dundas had appropriated its intended site on St Andrew Square. Behind a dignified classical façade is the finest church interior in Edinburgh, consisting of a simple oval with a gallery and exquisite plaster ceiling. Remarkably, it is not the work of a well-known architect. The Council held a contest for the best design and the winner was an amateur, Captain Andrew Frazer of the Royal Engineers, who received 10 guineas (£10.50) as a prize.

Map on page 130

Almost opposite the church, and as grand as a cathedral in comparison, **The Dome** is a former bank that is now one of the city's fashionable bars. The central hall, with its coffered dome, marbled columns and mosaic floor, is breathtaking in the scale of its extravagance. Like many of the New Town's grandest buildings it is, despite its classical appearance, Victorian, and it reflects the wealth that Edinburgh acquired as a financial centre in the 19th century.

Further down the street, the **Assembly Rooms ❼** were opened in 1787 for concerts and other suitably refined entertainments that contrasted with more raucous pleasures in the Old Town. Sadly, the magnificently decorated rooms are now little used through much of the year, but they come into their own in August as one of the largest and liveliest of venues for the Festival Fringe.

New Town gets finer

Edinburgh is not a city that embraces change with great enthusiasm and its citizens were only slowly tempted to the New Town's spacious modern homes. Nonetheless, in the 1780s the plan was taking shape and proving a success. Wealth, as the *Proposals* had predicted, was increasing and there was a new sense of civic pride in constructing Britain's finest city. Regulations were tightened up, ensuring higher building standards and greater unity of style. As the streets marched westwards they were given names that emphasised the unity of Britain under the long rule of George III. **Hanover Street** and **Frederick Street** (named after Prince Frederick) crossed George Street from Princes Street to Queen Street. Subsidiary to these were Rose Street, for England's emblem, and Thistle Street (equal in its status but a little shorter) for the Scots, although the leek of Wales and shamrock of Ireland were ignored.

TIP

George Street is Edinburgh's premier street for designer clothes shops, including Karen Millen and Jaeger – with more outlets opening all the time.

BELOW: the Georgian House on Charlotte Square.

Bute House is the centrepiece of Adam's classical design for the north side of Charlotte Square.

In 1791 Robert Adam was commissioned to design **Charlotte Square**, the westernmost culmination of Craig's plan which was by this time almost 30 years old. By then, the "Great Flitting" from the Old Town was under way, with medieval mansions off the Royal Mile degenerating into slum housing for economic refugees from the Highlands and Ireland. The New Town, meanwhile, had become the apogee of stylish sophistication and Charlotte Square is undoubtedly one of the most elegant urban residential spaces ever built in Britain. The **Georgian House** ❽ at No. 7 (open end Jan to 24 Dec: Mon–*Sun; entrance fee) gives some idea of the style in which its wealthy residents once lived. Here, the National Trust for Scotland (NTS) has used its historical expertise, together with appropriate furniture and artworks, to recreate the house as it might have looked just after 1796, when John Lamont, 18th chief of Clan Lamont, paid £1,800 (the equivalent of some £200,000 today) for the new-built property.

Georgian interiors

The house's character is spacious, civilised and formal, although the sideboard in the dining room contains a chamber pot which the gentlemen would have used when the ladies had retired up to the drawing room and the better claret had been opened. The basement kitchens are another world, once staffed by Highland maids who may have come down to the capital never having been inside a house with windows or learnt a single word of English. Lamont himself, although a Highland chief, would not, of course, have ever been inside a "black-house" or understood a word of Gaelic.

The NTS also owns several other properties in Charlotte Square, including No. 6, **Bute House**, the official residence of Scotland's First Minister (not open

to the public). The **National Trust for Scotland Headquarters** (No. 28) contains a gallery of paintings by Scottish Colourists such as Peploe and Cadell, who introduced Edinburgh to Post-Impressionism in the 1920s, and a fine collection of Regency furniture acquired by the modernist architect Sir James Stirling (open Mon–Sat and Sun pm; free).

The most striking building in Charlotte Square is **West Register House ❾** with its massive dome that dominates the vista from George Street. This was formerly St George's church, designed by Robert Reid and completed in 1815. It was the last essential piece in Craig's jigsaw plan for the New Town which had taken almost half a century to complete. The building now houses public records and there are usually displays of maps and documents in the foyer.

Continuity and change

Two hundred years ago the New Town was remarkable for its modern architecture and the logic of its layout. It was a city of the future that took no account of sentiment or Scottish architectural traditions. Now it is remarkable for having kept so much of its Georgian character in the face of changing fashions and the whims of city planners. The Victorians tended to go classical when building in the New Town, there were revivals of the style in the 1900s and the 1930s, and even late 20th-century architects, with some unfortunate exceptions, have refrained from excessive use of concrete and glass. Side streets between Princes Street and Queen Street remain largely Georgian, while George Street has acquired some dignified and noble buildings for its businesses and institutions.

Equally unspoilt but with a very different character, **Rose Street** is a traffic-free back route between Charlotte Square and St Andrew Square, lined with

The Edinburgh World Heritage Trust, which can provide information on New and Old Town heritage and conservation, has offices with periodic exhibitions at No. 5 Charlotte Square (open Mon–Fri; free).

BELOW: shopping in the rain on Princes Street.

NEW TOWN STONE

Now that "Auld Reekie" has shed its overcoat of soot from smoking chimneys, the New Town is showing its true colours. Pale grey beneath cloudy skies, with a hint of biscuit gold in the sun, they are the weathered hues of Craigleith sandstone, the raw material of Georgian Edinburgh. Hard, fine-grained and non-porous, yet susceptible to detailed carving, it was considered one of the finest building stones on earth and its source was just a mile or so to the west of the city centre. Robert Adam used it to advantage in Charlotte Square and for Register House; Thomas Hamilton and William Playfair employed it as a national equivalent to the Parthenon's Pentelic marble for their Grecian temples *(see pages 152 and 221)*. Most of the New Town wears the same distinctive uniform.

Railway transport in the later 19th century allowed builders greater choice of raw materials, such as pink Dumfriesshire sandstone, Portland stone and granite, all of which may be spotted in the New Town, but Craigleith quarry remained in use until the 1890s, by which time it was itself a city landmark, a hole 200 ft (60 metres) deep. (It was filled in during the 1960s and is now the site of a supermarket.) When New Town buildings are restored, stone is imported from quarries in Northumberland.

BELOW: Princes
Street is at its
liveliest where it
meets The Mound.

modest houses, quirky little shops, restaurants and innumerable pubs. At the eastern end, **Milne's Bar** ⓰ is definitely worth a visit. Half a century ago, this was the heart of Edinburgh's bohemia where Hugh MacDiarmid and friends wove intoxicating arguments and wrote poems about Scotland's fractious character and the promise of a socialist new age. (They used a cosy room off the downstairs bar which was referred to as their "little Kremlin".) Although the poets have departed and a juke-box drowns out any rhetoric, the pub itself remains remarkably unaltered, reflecting a quite different city to the trendy bars on George Street, just a hundred yards away.

The fashionable frontier

Princes Street, the broad southern frontier of the New Town, was originally entirely residential, a boulevard of tenements and houses with views across an open valley to the Castle and the Old Town. It was only in the 19th century that its character began to change as shops and hotels spread westward from North Bridge. The shops grew into department stores, while the coming of the railway brought hotels constructed on the scale of palaces. Unlike its New Town hinterland, Princes Street abandoned architectural restraint for an extravaganza of Victorian romanticism, Renaissance, gothic and baronial styles, that mirrored the eclectic skyline of the older city. By 1900 Princes Street had become Scotland's most fashionable shopping street and, with its stunning situation and fine modern buildings, it was considered the most beautiful in the world.

Its situation is still stunning, but in some respects Princes Street has suffered a sad fate. Many of its finest buildings were demolished in the 1960s when Victorian architecture was despised. Their bland, cheap modernist replacements

Map on page 130

do not inspire much admiration and neither does the street's wholesale surrender to commercialism. High rents and rates have driven out many of the independent businesses that formerly gave the street its character. In their place are the chain stores, bargain bookshops and fast-food joints that can be found in any high street. Judging by the crowds, this may be what the public wants, but older residents of Edinburgh will tell you that Princes Street has lost its soul.

But fortunately this is Edinburgh, where nothing is as simple or straightforward as it might at first appear. Despite the tat, the traffic and the crowds, Princes Street still offers more in terms of culture, self-indulgence and sheer peculiarity than the majority of Britain's city centres can provide in their entirety.

Grand railway hotels

In deference to the New Town's logic, one should start, once again, at the junction with North Bridge. This where the A1, once known as the Great North Road, starts its tortuous 407-mile (655-km) route down to London. Travellers arriving here by stagecoach after an exhausting four-day journey could, from 1796, stay at Fortunes Tontine Tavern, Edinburgh's first respectable hotel. Then in 1846 the North British Railway arrived, cutting travel time from London down to half a day and bringing a new breed of visitor, the tourist. Now the site of the old coaching tavern is occupied by the vast bulk of the **Balmoral Hotel ⓫**, which opened in 1902 to provide the most luxurious lodging in the capital.

The hotel (formerly the North British Hotel) had its own lift from the station, bathrooms and electric light, although the management prudently arranged the wiring so that no more than a single lamp could be switched on in any room and coal fires cost an extra 1s 6d (7½p) to be lit. Such meanness, which wealthy visitors from Glasgow considered typical of Edinburgh, has long been abandoned, but at least one old tradition is retained: the hotel clock, which can be read from half a mile away, is still set three minutes fast to discourage travellers with trains to catch from slackening their pace.

The Balmoral's long-term rival is the **Caledonian Hilton Hotel**, at the other end of Princes Street, which is equally grand. The relationship between the two venerable hotels is typical of the generally harmless but snobbish little rivalries for which Edinburgh is well known, and which can also be found among clubs, schools and places to be seen. Next door to the Balmoral, the Tourist Information Centre (open daily; *see Travel Tips: Planning the Trip*) above **Princes Mall** has geared up to the age of cyber-travel with computer terminals providing access to a database of useful information. Princes Mall, formerly Waverley Market, is an indoor shopping centre which is discreetly tucked away below the level of the street.

Civilised survivors

While the majority of shops in Princes Street are at best unmemorable, there are a few exceptions. **Jenners**, on the corner of St David Street, has been an Edinburgh institution since 1838, although the present building dates from 1893. Architecturally intriguing, proud of its high quality and staffed with gentle

BELOW: the landmark Balmoral Hotel.

TIP

Take some bird
peanuts to feed the
squirrels in Princes
Street Gardens.

charm, it is one of Britain's most civilised department stores, although its labyrinth of galleries and stairs are notoriously challenging to the navigation skills of customers. However, Princes Street has not achieved its world renown on account of its shops. It is the view over **Princes Street Gardens** ⑫ that makes the thoroughfare unique and that gives it a sense of space and dignity.

The survival of this lush green valley in the centre of the city can be traced back to a bitter wrangle that may well qualify as having been the world's first conservation battle. Craig's plan for the New Town allowed for open outlooks, not only to the north, across open fields to Leith, but also to the south, where the Nor' Loch was to be tamed as a canal in ornamental gardens. But, with the loch proving stubbornly resistant, the plan for a canal was quietly shelved, no doubt on the grounds of cost, and in 1770 some enterprising property developers named Home, Young and Trotter proposed to build a line of houses to the south of Princes Street, where Princes Mall now stands. At once the residents were up in arms and a long legal battle ensued. Some houses, which were completed in 1796, while the dispute was still going on, were allowed to stay, since their roof-lines were below the street, but no further building was allowed. Finally, in 1816, the whole length of the valley was protected by an Act of Parliament.

Garden monument

BELOW:
Princes Street
Gardens in spring.

Ironically, the most striking feature of the gardens is a truly massive building. The **Scott Monument** ⑬ (open daily; entrance fee) is a 200-ft (60-metre) high gothic ornament inaugurated in 1846 to commemorate the nation's most celebrated writer. Although it was restored in the late 1990s it still presents a some-

what mottled look, since the project's multi-million pound budget apparently did not include the cleaning of its stonework. Inside its upper levels there are exhibhitions on famous Scots and from balconies there are good views that some would say are all the better for the fact that the monument itself cannot be seen; but, as visitors will soon discover, Edinburgh is not a city that suffers from a shortage of either good viewpoints or steps to climb (this monument's narrow winding staircase being particularly tricky).

The gardens are well used and well maintained, crowded with sunbathers on hot summer days, and are curiously romantic on misty autumn afternoons when the city skyline disappears behind a "haar" (mist). This is a proper, old-fashioned city park with bedding plants and terraced walks, war memorials and statues to forgotten dignitaries, benches with commemorative plaques, ice-cream stalls and a carousel. At the **Ross Open-Air Theatre** a few people may be listening to a band or watching a display of Highland dancing.

Art on the causeway

Dividing the East Gardens from the West and climbing up into the Old Town, **The Mound** is an artificial causeway that provides a striking setting for some suitably impressive architecture. As the New Town slowly grew, vast quantities of soil were excavated in a search for firm foundations, and dumped into the muddy valley to provide a second, unofficial route of access to the High Street. The Royal Scottish Academy and the National Gallery of Scotland were built on The Mound to designs by William Playfair between 1822 and 1854, their Grecian style reflecting Edinburgh's aspiration to be thought of as the "Athens of the North".

Map on page 130

The Floral Clock, tucked below The Mound, has ticked away the summer hours since 1903 and is replanted with a new theme every spring. A cuckoo pops out of its chalet every 15 minutes.

LEFT: fun beneath the Castle. **BELOW:** Scott seated underneath his monument.

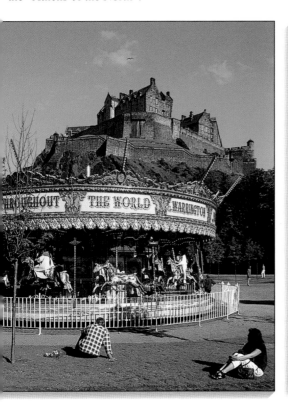

Map on page 130

The lavish interior of the National Gallery of Scotland.

BELOW: the steep climb to the Old Town from the National Gallery.

Due to building works, including a new link between the galleries within the bowels of The Mound, the **Royal Scottish Academy** ⓮ will be closed until the summer of 2003, when it will reopen with a major Monet exhibition. The **National Gallery of Scotland** ⓯, which will remain open during building works (open Mon–Sat and Sun pm; free except special exhibitions), houses a magnificent collection that is particularly strong on European baroque art, Dutch Masters, French Impressionists and, of course, Scottish painters *(see page 91)*. Being of relatively modest size, it does not overwhelm the visitor and is seldom overcrowded, yet it includes some masterpieces, including Rembrandt's sad and gentle *Self-Portrait*, Frans Hals' exuberant *Portrait of Verdonck* and the sinister *Fábula* by El Greco, which rank among these artists' finest works.

The place to be

When the New Town was conceived, James Craig could not have envisioned that his residential suburb would mature into the city centre of today. With its galleries and shops, banks and company headquarters, restaurants and hotels, the New Town fulfills an ever more important role. Yet, remarkably, it still retains a human scale and is notorious for its provincial sociability. Those who pull the nation's strings in almost any field are still likely to be found exchanging gossip in the New Club in Princes Street, eating oysters in the Café Royal or being ushered from a chauffeured car in Charlotte Square. Some of their faces are well known, others wield more subtle power, but within the New Town's small exclusive world they all know each other well. More than 200 years after the New Town's creation it is still the place to meet and be seen for anyone who aspires to be a somebody in the affairs of the Scottish capital. ❑

The Money Men of Charlotte Square

One of the most remarkable facts about Edinburgh is that, despite its modest size and GDP (Scotland as a whole accounts for less than 10 percent of the UK's GDP), its finance companies look after over £250 billion worth of equity capital funds. Indeed it is the fourth largest equity management centre in Europe after London, Paris and Frankfurt. Although Glasgow is also doing rather well as a finance centre these days, the sector is contributing to a huge expansion of the capital's economy at the turn of the 21st century, boosting employment and bringing an influx of highly qualified workers from outside the city and south of the border.

The booming finance sector has led to job creation in other sectors, too. Naturally, Edinburgh's bankers, investment fund managers, stockbrokers, corporate lawyers, accountants, insurance executives and unit-trust operators have to be "serviced". This means nice business for the city's glossier public relations firms, advertising agencies, design studios and photographers – not to mention restaurants, wine bars and auction houses like Sotheby's, Phillips and Christie's.

Just as "the City" is shorthand for London's financial community, so Edinburgh's used to be known as "Charlotte Square". But the industry's growing requirements for office space in the late 20th century could not be met within its traditional territory comprising this elegant New Town square and the "George Street corridor" to St Andrew Square. As a result two new financial districts have grown up: Edinburgh Park in the Gyle, 5 miles (3 km) west of the city centre; and, closer to the centre, "The Exchange" in the West End, where many of the biggest players have relocated. The development of the latter is continuing apace, dominated by the imposing Standard Life HQ in Lothian Road, the Edinburgh International Conference Centre and the city's tallest building, Exchange Tower.

Edinburgh's star role in the financial world can be traced back to the enthusiasm of the Scots for making and then keeping money. They have always been among the modern world's best and canniest bankers. This is why the Scottish clearing banks have a statutory right (dating from 1845) to print their own distinctive banknotes – a right the English banks were stripped of following a series of 19th-century bank failures. The Scottish banks have retained much of their historic clout, as illustrated by the Royal Bank of Scotland's takeover of one of the big four English banks, National Westminster, in 2000.

However, the biggest fish in Edinburgh's financial pond are the giant insurance companies, the most important being Standard Life, founded in 1825, which is Europe's biggest "mutual fund". Some rivals, such as the Scottish Widows Fund, are even more venerable. Yet traditional investment trusts are increasingly sidelined by high-tech investments concentrated on the "Silicon Glen" between Edinburgh and Glasgow. Scotland is an innovator in technology-based financial services and Edinburgh's telecommunications structure is said to be the best in Europe. ❑

RIGHT: Saltire Court in the West End.

Locked gardens, reserved for the use of key-holding nearby residents, lie largely undisturbed behind wrought-iron railings.

Robert Louis Stevenson lived at 17 Heriot Row from childhood until he married at the age of 30. The street has been one of the smartest of New Town addresses ever since its construction in the first years of the 19th century. Over the next 20 years the city slowly spread down the hillside towards Canonmills and Stockbridge, but this later New Town has a different character to the 18th-century development. In place of Presbyterian simplicity there is exuberance. The architecture is far richer, more varied and romantic.

Unique hierarchy

Royal Circus ⑰ looks a perfect, formal circle on the map. In fact it is constructed on a steeply sloping site with its ring of stately houses set back from public view behind laburnum trees and cobbled crescents. From here **Great King Street** strikes off to the east as the northern New Town's central avenue. The architecture is palatial, with lengthy terraces that mimic the façades of huge impressive mansions. These "palace fronts", a common feature of the New Town, mask a complex hierarchy of interior arrangements.

The central ranges are composed of individual houses, although they are now likely to be sub-divided. The pavilion wings, a storey higher, were purpose-built as tenements, a form of property unique to urban Scotland, that allowed the city's architects to be uncompromising in their love of grandeur. The ground floor is a "main-door flat", self-contained behind its own front door and often with a basement and a garden. A second doorway provides access to a common stair that serves the flats above. While such stairs are rather dark and grim, the flats themselves are often magnificent. Drawing rooms are up to 30 ft (9 metres) long, with 14-ft (4-metre) high ceilings decorated with fine mouldings.

BELOW: exclusive Heriot Row.

Shops, galleries and gardens

As might be expected, the New Town has some very stylish shops, which are found along the cross streets running down the hill. **Dundas Street** ⓲ is particularly interesting with its art galleries, antique shops and antiquarian booksellers. The range is broad: from paintings priced at tens of thousands of pounds in Bourne Fine Art to rummage boxes filled with broken toys and brassware in dusty basement junk shops. The Thrie Estaits (No. 49) is never lacking in intriguing oddities, while **The Scottish Gallery** (No. 16) is one of the longest established, showing contemporary Scottish work in various mediums. The street is at its liveliest on Saturdays when it is generally possible to gain entrance to a private view and discuss the finer points of Scottish art with the New Town's glitterati over a glass of wine.

Dublin Street, east of and parallel to Dundas Street, has fewer shops, perhaps owing to the fact that it is mountainously steep. A bench on its summit, at the junction with York Place, bears a small brass plate that is inscribed "Remembering J.C.H. who was often tired". The views are stunning and the street itself is very picturesque, with handsome Georgian houses and original shop fronts. At the bottom of the hill **Drummond Place** ⓳ is a private green oasis, its wooded gardens locked away behind high railings. Occasionally calls are made for such gardens, of which there are many in the New Town, to be taken over by the City Council and opened to the public. In time, a compromise may be reached concerning better-known examples such as Charlotte Square, but Drummond Place and other enclaves off the beaten track are likely to remain securely locked for many years to come. Key-holders, who pay up to £100 (US$150) a year, are defensive of their rights, pointing out that the gardens are maintained at no cost

Map on page 130

TIP

Visitors wishing to buy high-quality contemporary design should peruse The Scottish Gallery and The Open Eye Gallery nearby (75–79 Cumberland Street), which showcase cutting-edge crafts, jewellery and furniture.

BELOW: the light touch in a National Trust workshop.

The New Town is now almost universally admired, but it did not appeal to 19th-century advocates of Romanticism: John Ruskin thought the streets too regimented and Lord Cockburn complained of "every house being an exact duplicate of its neighbour".

BELOW: fanlights feature above the doors of many New Town properties.

to rate-payers and that Edinburgh has ample public parks and open hills available for all to use. Their real fear, of course, is that, were the gardens opened to all and sundry, "undesirables" would soon destroy their air of peaceful seclusion.

Such seclusion is, for many of its residents, an essential aspect of the New Town's character. Even late at night, there is no edge of danger in the air, making it a pleasure to wander through the quiet streets, soaking up an atmosphere that can seem more redolent of a romantic costume drama than of real life. Old street lights mimic the effect of oil lamps, glowing softly in the darkness and reflecting off the cobblestones. Owls hoot in the gardens and music wafts out of opened upstairs windows; sometimes comfortable furniture and pictures or a bookcase can be glimpsed through parted curtains, and perhaps someone reading or writing at a desk.

The unconventional east

The northern New Town was developed in an ordered manner and its boundaries were clear. In the 1820s houses on its outer limits, from Royal Circus through to **Mansfield Place**, overlooked open fields without any hint of a transition between the city and the country. Things were somewhat less clear-cut, however, to the east, where the New Town hit the winding lane from Edinburgh through Broughton village. In the 18th century **Broughton** was notorious for wizardry and witchcraft. When the New Town's monumental terraces began to flatten its old cottages, a hidden labyrinth of medieval homes somehow managed to survive behind the new imposing new houses, uncharted even on official maps. Sadly, city planning was eventually triumphant and the labyrinth has gone, but this part of the New Town is still distinctly unconventional. In the 1960s it was

on the frontier of respectability and, like Stockbridge *(see page 199)*, it attracted those in search of an alternative yet comfortable lifestyle. Now, like all the New Town, it is expensive to live in, but it has remained true to its cultural roots.

Broughton Street  begins the old winding route to the valley. It has been the heart of Edinburgh's gay community for many years, focused on the Blue Moon Café, basement clubs and boutiques selling costumes that would not be appreciated at a Holyrood garden party. It also has off-beat junk shops, organic food shops and continental-style cafés, restaurants and bars, the latter ranging from the cosily traditional, such as the Barony, to the ultra-trendy Baroque.

Leith Street, which links Broughton Street to the North Bridge, is the only corner of the New Town to have suffered the effects of post-war city planning. Georgian terraces and squares that had degenerated into slums were demolished in the 1960s to make way for the **St James Centre**, and the vandalism was continued in the 1970s to accommodate an Inner Ring Road that was never finished. Only now, 30 years later, is the planners' vision of a modern New Town nearing fulfilment, with the construction of an entertainment complex on **Greenside**, under Calton Hill. The only building of architectural interest in this urban wasteland is **St Mary's Roman Catholic Cathedral**  beside the Picardy Place roundabout. Behind the early 19th-century façade it features an extraordinary nave, dating from the 1930s, with huge Art Deco angels as corbels.

Grand ambition

As the New Town grew, schemes for its development became ever more ambitious. From the top of Leith Street, at the junction with North Bridge, **Waterloo Place**, flanked by Georgian buildings, appears unremarkable. The fact that

Map on page 130

Sculptures by Eduardo Paolozzi in front of St Mary's R.C. Cathedral are symbolic of the role of Italian immigrants in Edinburgh society.

BELOW: Broughton Street curios.

THE RESTORED NEW TOWN

In the 1960s the New Town was in a sorry state. Streets were black with soot, façades were crumbling and falling roof slates were a constant hazard during winter gales. Worse still, as houses were converted into offices or flats, old doors, fine plasterwork and even Adam fireplaces were ripped out, to be replaced by modern styles.

The turning point came in 1970 with the setting up of the New Town Conservation Committee (NTCC), which provided both advice and grants for restoration projects. Soon scaffolding and portakabins became features of the city landscape and each year previously dingy tenements emerged fresh and elegant from under plastic sheets. Meanwhile, home-owners scoured reclamation yards and junk shops in search of the antique details that were required by the new fashion for period design.

Today the successor of the NTCC, the Edinburgh World Heritage Trust, still hands out grants for conservation and repair, while almost every building in the New Town is accorded listed status. As some new owners find out to their cost, even putting in an extra bathroom requires prolonged negotiation with the authorities. The New Town is now entirely safe from desecration; indeed some fear that it is in danger of becoming an architectural museum.

TIP

The renowned choir of
*St Mary's Episcopal
Cathedral sings at
5.30pm Mon–Fri (not
Wed) and 10.30am
and 3.30pm Sun;
recordings may be
purchased on site.

the street is a bridge spanning a considerable chasm only becomes apparent when you approach its open section above Calton Road. Begun in 1815, the Regent Bridge took seven years to build, cost £250,000 and almost bankrupted the city. But it allowed the New Town to spread out to the east at a time when British confidence, buoyed up by Napoleon's defeat, demanded ambitious projects to reflect national prestige.

A huge development was planned, spreading from **Calton Hill** towards Leith, while the hill itself *(see page 220)* was to become Edinburgh's Acropolis, surmounted by a monumental copy of the Parthenon. The vision remained unfulfilled owing to a lack of funds, but the fragments that were built reflect the grandeur of the dream. Thomas Hamilton's **Old Royal High School** ㉒ – on the south side of the hill on Regent Road, the continuation of Waterloo Place – is one of Britain's finest Greek revival buildings, modelled on the Propylae in Athens. It was proposed as a possible seat for Scotland's parliament and various proposals for its future use have been put forward, including a Scottish National Photography Centre. Past the old school William Playfair's stately terraces curve around the hillside, picturesquely following the subtle undulations of the land and taking full advantage of the panoramic views. **Royal Terrace**, on the north side of the hill, is particularly imposing. It was once favoured as a residential address by rich shipping merchants who could watch the ships pass along the Firth of Forth from the windows of their drawing rooms.

BELOW:
burning leaves in
Randolph Crescent.

Western drama

As Playfair's terraces were spreading around Calton Hill, there were equally dramatic changes taking place at the New Town's western fringe, namely on the

Earl of Moray's erstwhile country estate above the Dean Valley, which was developed in the 1820s. The elegant streets are laid out in the manner of a suite of ceremonial apartments, with **Randolph Crescent** as the entrance hall, **Ainslie Place** as an ante-room and **Moray Place ㉓** as the great 12-sided inner sanctum. While a circuit of this architectural parade is impressive in itself, the natural drama of the setting can only be appreciated from **Dean Bridge**, which arches over the Water of Leith to the west of Randolph Crescent. From here the back walls of the houses are revealed, clinging to the edge of a ravine more than 100 ft (30 metres) deep. This is just one example of the many achievements of the New Town that are the product of a shot-gun marriage between architecture and topography.

The **West End**, south of Queensferry Street, was the last part of the New Town to be built according to the neo-classical ideal and, despite having some attractive backwaters such as **William Street**, with its boutiques, pubs and pretty Georgian shop fronts, the district's character is formal and a little dull. The sheer scale of boulevards such as **Shandwick Place** and **Manor Place** only serves to emphasise their lack of life.

At the head of Melville Street, **St Mary's Episcopal Cathedral ㉔** is the largest church built in Scotland since the Reformation. Designed in the gothic style by George Gilbert Scott and completed in 1917, it was paid for by the Walker family, who had made their enormous fortune from developing the West End. Though it is not (arguably) a beautiful cathedral, its twin spires – named Barbara and Mary after the Walker sisters – are a landmark feature of the city skyline and contribute greatly to the spiritual aura of sunsets viewed from the North Bridge. ❑

Map on page 130

The ornate altar of St Mary's Episcopal Cathedral.

BELOW: the graceful curve of Moray Place.

THE TENEMENT LANDSCAPE

Map on page 158

The suburbs to the immediate south of the Old Town, notable for Scottish baronial housing for the "respectable" middle classes, offer up many a tale of enterprise and philanthropy

Not many people know this, but the cartoonist Ronald Searle's fictitious centre of mayhem and chaos, St Trinian's School for Young Ladies, sprang from the south Edinburgh suburb of Marchmont. Between 1922 and 1946 an Edinburgh schoolteacher called Miss C. Fraser Lee ran an establishment there called St Trinnean's School for Girls (motto: "Light and Joy") along the lines of the liberal "Dalton" system of education. In some straight-laced Edinburgh circles this was seen as anarchy, and Miss C. Fraser Lee's college for middle-class young ladies acquired a totally unjustified reputation as an educational free-for-all.

Searle learned all about St Trinnean's School from two of Miss C. Fraser Lee's pupils when he was posted to Scotland as an army engineer in 1941. The combination of female gentility and utter chaos was a notion that appealed to him hugely, and he immediately dashed off a cartoon to the magazine *Punch*. When the war was over, Searle returned to the subject of St Trinian's with a vengeance. The rest, as they say, is history.

This is, somehow, typical of the respectable suburbs of inner Edinburgh. Nothing is quite what it seems. The well-crafted tenements of Marchmont, Bruntsfield, Morningside and Merchiston throw up many contradictions and surprises. Another fictional monster from the inner suburbs of Edinburgh is Miss Jean Brodie, Muriel Spark's demure schoolteacher with advanced ideas, who taught her *crème de la crème* to thrill to the iron hand of the Italian dictator Mussolini.

PRECEDING PAGES: baronial-style tenements. **LEFT:** the street as playground. **BELOW:** Dalry in the southwest, looking towards the Castle.

Living high

The tenemented inner suburbs of Edinburgh are a fascinating landscape. They were built for, and are still largely inhabited by, hard-working, reasonably well-off schoolteachers, bank clerks, insurance under-managers and shopkeepers. The bigger flats contained enough rooms to house a servant or two. It is probably from these suburban tenements that Edinburgh acquired its reputation for gentility and sniffishness *(see page 58)*.

In some parts of Britain the word "tenement" is synonymous with poverty and hard times. Not in Edinburgh. The citizens of Edinburgh have long been used to living high. In the Old Town the "quality" and hoi-polloi lived cheek-by-jowl in narrow tenements, rubbing shoulders on the common stairs. And even when the Scottish gentry moved north into the purpose-built elegance of the New Town, most of them continued to live in flats.

The enthusiasm of Edinburgh's middling classes for suburban villas with gardens front and rear is a recently acquired taste. This is why Edinburgh's inner

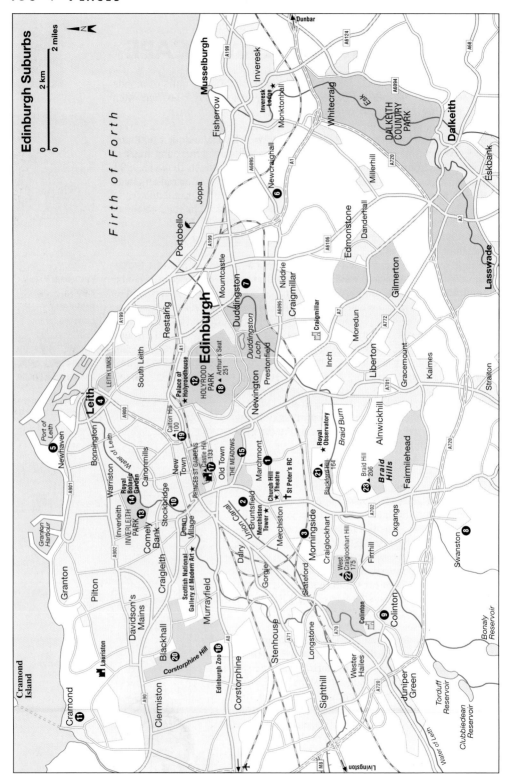

Edinburgh Suburbs

N

0 — 2 km
0 — 2 miles

Firth of Forth

Cramond Island

Cramond **①**

Lauriston

Granton

Pilton

Davidson's Mains

Clermiston

Blackhall

Corstorphine

Corstorphine Hill

Edinburgh Zoo **①**

② Scottish National Gallery of Modern Art ★

Murrayfield

Stenhouse

Sighthill

Wester Hailes

Longstone

Gorgie

Dalry

Slateford

Craiglockhart

West Craiglockhart Hill 175 ▲
㉒

Firrhill

Oxgangs

Colinton

Colinton **⑨**

Juniper Green

Torduff Reservoir

Clubbiedean Reservoir

Water of Leith

Livingston

M8

Granton Harbour

Craigleith

Comely Bank

Inverleith

INVERLEITH PARK

Stockbridge

Dean Village

Port of Leith

Newhaven **⑤**

Bonnington

Warriston

Water of Leith

Leith ④

LEITH LINKS

South Leith

Restalrig

Royal Botanic Garden **⑭**

⑬

⑩

New Town

PRINCES ST GARDENS

Castle Hill 133 **⑰**

Old Town

THE MEADOWS

Bruntsfield

Merchiston Tower ★

Merchiston

Marchmont

Church Hill Theatre ★ **①**

②

③

Morningside

Calton Hill 100 **⑲**

Edinburgh

Palace of Holyroodhouse ★ **⑫**

HOLYROOD PARK

⑱ ▲ Arthur's Seat 251

Newington

St Peter's RC ✝

⑮

Prestonfield

Duddingston Loch

Duddingston **⑦**

Mountcastle

Portobello

Joppa

Fisherrow

Musselburgh

Inveresk

Inveresk Lodge ★

Monktonhall

Newcraighall **⑥**

Niddrie

Craigmillar

Craigmillar 🏛

Inch

Liberton

Gracemount

Kaimes

Straiton

Moredun

Edmonstone

Danderhall

Gilmerton

Whitecraig

ESK

DALKEITH COUNTRY PARK

Dalkeith

Eskbank

Millerhill

Lasswade

Alnwickhill

Fairmilehead

Braid Burn

Royal Observatory ▲ **②**

Blackford Hill 164 ▲

㉑

Braid Hill 206 ▲ **㉓**

Braid Hills

Swanston

Bonaly Reservoir

A90, A8, A71, A70, A702, A703, A720, A68, A1, A199, A900, A901, A902, A6124, A6095, A6106, A701, A772, A7, M8

Dunbar

suburbs – unlike the inner suburbs of, say, London, Liverpool or Manchester – are overwhelmingly a landscape of stone-built tenements. The long rows of three-up two-down houses which characterise so many English cities hardly appear in Edinburgh. Much of the inner city consists of great cliffs of blonde (and sometimes red) sandstone, usually four or five storeys high, and often elaborately modelled.

The quality and style of the tenements vary, depending on who they were built for. Those built to house Edinburgh's working classes (at Tollcross, Leith, Tynecastle and Fountainbridge) tend to be flat-fronted, unadorned, and about as interesting as cold porridge. They contain pokey flats which have precious little in the way of embellishment. On the other hand, the Edwardian buildings run up for the middle classes (such as at Spottiswoode, Comely Bank and Goldenacre) tend to be restrained but handsome, with bay windows, ceramic-clad common stairways and excellent plasterwork and joinery.

Baronial inner suburbs

By far the best are the tenements built in the exuberant "Scottish baronial" style of the late 19th century. These are some of the city's unsung splendours. Inner suburbs like Marchmont, Bruntsfield, Morningside, Polwarth and Merchiston (and, to a lesser extent, Abbeyhill, Leith and London Road) are crammed with elaborately modelled tenement blocks, most of them bristling with spires, corner turrets, crow-stepped gables, mock cannons, skewputts and mock gargoyles, all topped with wrought-iron roof ridges, fancy lightning conductors and weather vanes.

It all forms, in the view of architectural historian-critic Colin McWilliam, "large-scale splendour that can speak from a distance, with carefully composed elevations and majestic corner towers". For aficionados of architectural detail, inner-city Edinburgh is a veritable paradise. The city owes this fantasy-land to a handful of energetic practitioners like John Pyper, George Wilson, Edward Calvert, John C. Hay and the resoundingly named Hippolyte Jean Blanc (who was born and bred in Edinburgh of a French father and an Irish mother).

Baronial Edinburgh is probably at its finest in the district of **Marchmont** ❶, which is situated about a mile south of the High Street, on the edge of the handsome public park known as **The Meadows**. Marchmont owes its existence to the commercial shrewdness of Sir George Warrender of Lochend, whose family had owned the land around the area since 1695. When Warrender realised, in the middle of the 19th century, that he could get a lot more money by "feuing" (leasing) his land out for housing instead of renting it out for grazing, he hired a clutch of experts (among them the architect David Bryce) to put together a development plan for the area.

By 1869 the first of the Marchmont feu plans was drawn up. But Warrender laid down conditions. All the street names (Marchmont, Warrender, Arden, Lauderdale, Thirlestane and Alvanley) were to be called after the various branches of his family and all the tenements were to be designed on flamboyant

Map opposite

City-dwellers have lived in buildings up to six storeys deep for many centuries.

BELOW: languid afternoon in London Road.

Scottish baronial principles. Elevations were to be approved by Warrender himself. And to maintain the respectability of the area – not to mention the property values – none of the shops in Marchmont were to be rented to purveyors of hard liquor. Although that last condition has long since lapsed, there are still remarkably few pubs.

Great men of Marchmont

The construction of Marchmont between 1869 and 1914 was a huge building programme. But it produced the greatest concentration of baronial tenements anywhere in Scotland. Streets like Warrender Park Road and Marchmont Road positively bristle with turrets, spires, candle-snuffer roofs, ogee-shaped domes and other architectural features. Probably the best – or at least the most vigorous of the designs – were Edward Calvert's, who was responsible for most of the astonishing **Warrender Park Terrace** facing The Meadows.

The whole development was a great success. Edinburgh's expanding middle classes fell over themselves to buy the roomy flats of Marchmont. Sir George Warrender and his family became even richer, and continued to live in the 16th- and 17th-century splendour of Bruntsfield House, which is now a part of **James Gillespie's High School** (entrance on Lauderdale Street). And to educate Marchmont's booming child population, the Edinburgh School Board founded James Gillespie's Primary School next door to the High School, among whose alumni are TV comedian Ronnie Corbett, the late film actor Alistair Sim and former Liberal Party leader David Steel. (Gillespie himself was an 18th-century mill-owner and snuff merchant turned philanthropist, whose homely bust can be seen in the Merchants' Halls in Hanover Street.)

Many of Marchmont's architects, and some builders, left their mark in fancy plaques bearing their initials: EC is Edward Calvert, ABC is the Argyle Building Company, JP is John Pyper, and so on.

BELOW: the Victorians didn't stint on chimneys.

Bruntsfield and Merchiston

The district of **Bruntsfield** ❷ lies to the west on the other side of the **Bruntsfield Links**, which is about all that is left of the "burgh muir" (town's land) where James IV assembled the huge Scots army which he marched to ruin and dreadful defeat at Flodden in the north of England in 1513. Many of Edinburgh's plague victims were also buried on the "burgh muir", and human remains used to turn up regularly in suburban gardens all over south Edinburgh.

Although the sandstone tenements of Bruntsfield are generally less flamboyant than those in Marchmont, there are handsome examples by architects such as MacGibbon & Ross (Bruntsfield Crescent) and Hippolyte J. Blanc (Bruntsfield Terrace). The great sandstone cliffs march down the hill to Polwarth to the north and Merchiston in the west. Good-looking tenements abound, especially in **Viewforth Square,** but public buildings are few, although some are worth searching out. One such is Edward Carfrae's **Boroughmuir School** (1911) in Viewforth.

Where Bruntsfield blends into **Merchiston** at the top of Bruntsfield Place, Colinton Road leads a short distance to another building well worth a look. **Merchiston Tower**, or Napier Tower, is a restored 16th-century tower house now surrounded by the uninspired 1960s modernity of one of the campuses of Napier University. (Elevated from a college to a university in 1992, it is one of Scotland's largest higher educational institutions with some 12,500 students.) This is the family home of John Napier of Merchiston (1550–1617), the Presbyterian theologian and mathematical genius (and favourite of James VI) who not only devised logarithms and cooked up the idea of the decimal point but also published a paper entitled "Secrette Inventionis" which gave the world the

Map on page 158

The 16th-century home of John Napier, the "Wizard of Merchiston", is now part of Napier University.

BELOW: sketching in the open air on Bruntsfield Links.

notion of the armoured tank and the military submarine. Napier was one of the world's great original mathematicians, who ranks with Newton, Copernicus and Kepler, but local people regarded him as some kind of necromancer who was adept in the black arts.

A plethora of churches

Church Hill (or "holy corner") is so called because of the assortment of churches which stand at the four corners of the crossroads at Bruntsfield Road, Colinton Road, Morningside Road and Chamberlain Road. None of the churches is of any particular architectural or historical interest, except perhaps Hippolyte J. Blanc's exercise in elaborate French-style gothic at **Christ Church** (Episcopal) on Bruntsfield Place, where Blanc was a member of the congregation. The church was built between 1875 and 1878.

A much more interesting history is attached to the Italianate **St Peter's** Roman Catholic church, situated about 500 yards to the south in Falcon Avenue. St Peter's is a product of that bizarre conjunction of circumstances which seems to underpin so much Edinburgh history. The church was set up in 1907 in one of the most staunchly Protestant parts of Edinburgh by Canon John Gray, an English-born priest. It was funded by his friend Andre Raffalovitch, a wealthy Russian-born Jew who had fallen in love with the city. The building was designed by Sir Robert Lorimer, who was probably the most important Scots architect of his time.

Another building in this area with some ecclesiastical resonance is the **Church Hill Theatre** near the top of Morningside Road. Built in 1892 to a design by Hippolyte Blanc, this was the last church occupied by the Morning-

In a setting sun against a blue sky, the tenement cliffs of Edinburgh can be stunning; under grey clouds in a drizzle, the streets can seem like dank canyons.

BELOW: a fine day in Logie Green Road.

side Free Church congregation, one of whose ministers (until his death in 1847) was the great Thomas Chalmers. A brilliant theologian, orator and mathematician, Chalmers was the leading light of the 1843 "Disruption" which split the Church of Scotland *(see page 40)*.

One of the many buildings the itinerant Free Church congregation used before they found a home was the tiny schoolhouse on the opposite side of Morningside Road. For most of its working life this handsome little building (1823) was known as the "cuddy school" after the number of country children who travelled to the school on their "cuddies" (the Scots word for horses and ponies). The animals were tethered in the lane beside the school which is still known as Cuddy Lane.

Map on page 158

Morningside characters

Morningside ❸ has had its share of remarkable residents, permanent and temporary. Jane Welsh Carlyle was one; another was David Deuchar, the jeweller who discovered the genius of the painter Henry Raeburn. George Meikle Kemp, the architect/builder who designed the Scott Monument in Princes Street, lived in Morningside, as did Susan Ferrier, the 19th-century novelist who was regarded as "Scotland's Jane Austen". Morningside House (now replaced by a supermarket) was home to the eccentric High Court judge Lord Gardenstone, a man who "increased the mirth of the company" and who liked to warm his bed with piglets and to ride into town with a servant dressed in full Highland dress trotting behind him.

Further down Morningside Road, on the opposite side, is Morningside's liveliest and most famous hostelry, which used officially to be called The

Near the top of Morningside Road, on the left facing south, is a grey stone which is claimed (without evidence) to be the "bore stone" on which James IV raised his banner before the Battle of Flodden.

LEFT: picnic in a communal back garden, Bruntsfield. **BELOW:** Morningside Road at dusk.

Map
on page
158

*The grandiose
former asylum,
Craighouse.*

BELOW: the civic
design of Tollcross
is apparent
from the air.

Volunteer Arms, but has always been known as **The Canny Man's**. The pub owes its former official title to the fact it was used by the Edinburgh Volunteers (the local militia) on their way to and from the musket range at Blackford Hill. The title "Canny Man's" is ascribed to James Kerr who bought the pub in 1871 and used to instruct his hard-drinking customers to "ca' canny" (take it easy). The Canny Man's is worth a visit for its large selection of old clocks, pictures, posters, bridles and hunting horns – indeed, anything that can be hung – which bedeck the walls. James Kerr himself is still remembered by the old folk of Morningside as a generous man and a great attender of funerals at the Morningside Cemetery.

Morningside also has a long connection with poverty and madness. It was the site of Edinburgh's poorhouse and still contains the **Royal Edinburgh Hospital** (one of the biggest mental hospitals in Scotland, off Morningside Road). At the beginning of the 19th century the notorious Edinburgh Bedlam at Darien House (where the poet Robert Fergusson died) was closed down and replaced, in 1813, with this much more progressive public asylum set up by a doctor called Andrew Duncan, who gave his name to one of the Royal Edinburgh Hospital's clinics. The original building by Robert Reid, known as "The East House", is on the corner of Millar Crescent and Morningside Terrace.

The enlightened tradition established by Duncan was continued by Thomas Clouston, who set up the Craighouse hospital nearby in 1894. In Clouston's view "nothing we can do for the comfort of our patients is too much to atone for the cruelty of past ages". **Craighouse**, on the hill southwest of the Royal Hospital, is now part of Napier University. Designed by Sydney Mitchell, it has palatial public rooms and sits in its beautiful grounds like a French château. ❏

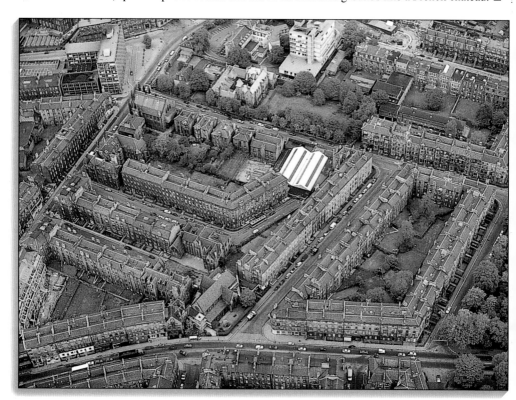

Scoring Schools

Myth and reality are always hard to tease apart in Scotland, and nowhere more than in education. The myth is, first, that Scottish schooling is of universal excellence and, second, that it is an instrument of meritocratic social mobility, enabling the "lad o'pairts" (man of mettle) to rise above humble origins. Yet one of the first questions Scots ask in trying to measure one another up is: "Which school did you go to?"

In Edinburgh this question is social, and it works at two levels. First, were you educated in the private (fee-paying) sector, or the public? Second, at what rank within that sector were you educated? In recent years, government has published performance indicators for Scotland's schools. These are arranged by the media into league tables which everyone professes to disregard but reads avidly. Yet their correlation with the social status of Edinburgh schools is pretty tangential, particularly in the private sector.

By and large, the greatest social cachet applies to those schools which have the least connection with the Scottish education system that everyone likes to believe is a world-beater. Schools like Fettes (where British prime minister Tony Blair was educated), Loretto and Merchiston Castle are, to all intents, imperial outposts of the English "public" school system which, despite its name, is the most prestigious stratum of *private* education. Their pupils are mostly boarders, and they sit English examinations with a purposeful eye on Oxford or Cambridge universities.

The next stratum is much more Scottish and, though there are parallels in other cities, closely associated with the capital. It consists of the great Edinburgh day schools. The best known are George Watson's, George Heriot's, Stewart's & Melville, Edinburgh Academy and, for girls, St George's. Most were founded by mercantile philanthropists as "hospitals" in the 17th and 18th centuries: George Watson was a banker, George "Jinglin' Geordie" Heriot a financier. Formerly supported by government grants, they are now purely private and charge hefty fees. They are big schools, but with small class sizes, excellent facilities and a strong academic record, with university entry in the 75–85 percent range. A cynic would say that their prime purpose is to turn the children of Edinburgh professionals into the next generation of Edinburgh professionals.

Schools run by Edinburgh City Council all have a comprehensive entry policy, yet those with a selective past – such as Gillespie's (the model for Muriel Spark's Marcia Blaine), Boroughmuir, Trinity and the Royal High School (Edinburgh's oldest school, founded in the 12th century) – are still much sought after. School catchment areas are, in consequence, a contributing factor to property prices.

Does the colour of one's old school tie still count? At one level it does, because parents still believe it does. But the designation of new universities has undermined the selective schools' dominance of higher education access, and municipal decentralisation has enabled talented head teachers to transform the performance of schools of previously poor reputation. The reality is fast changing. The myths may take longer. ❏

RIGHT: tools of the learning trade.

THE TESTAMENT OF GRAVEYARDS

Exploring Edinburgh's graveyards is a fascinating way of learning about the often extraordinary lives of the people buried or remembered in them

Dozens of Edinburgh's luminaries and members of the Establishment, from the Reformation onwards, have gravestones in the city's principal burial sites. Some are notable, too, for their architectural distinction or the tales they tell. The main pre-Reformation graveyard was at St Giles', which closed in 1585 and is now built over, while outlying areas were served by St Cuthbert's, at the west end of Princes Street Gardens.

WHERE THE FAMOUS LIE

Most of the oldest surviving gravestones, however, are in the churchyard of the Greyfriars *(see page 121)*, begun in the 1560s when a Franciscan friary stood on the site. It contains around 500 stones including very early ones in remarkably good condition, and the notorious Covenanters' Enclosure, where 1,200 religious martyrs were imprisoned in cruel conditions in 1679 – ironically in the same place where the National Covenant was signed just over 40 years earlier.

The geniuses of the Enlightenment period are mostly buried in the Canongate churchyard or Old Calton Burial Ground beneath Calton Hill, worth visiting for its spectacular situation alone. Churchyards in the old villages around Edinburgh, now its suburbs, are also interesting *(see pages 175, 198 and 204).*

▷ **IMMODEST SUBURB**
In Dean Village, the garden cemetery, laid out by a private company in 1845, contains some grandiose illustrations of Victorian self-regard.

▽ **FALLEN COURTIER**
George Buchanan, lying in Greyfriars churchyard, was an adviser to Mary, Queen of Scots, executed for his role in the murder of Darnley.

▷ **FREEDOM FIGHTERS**
Abraham Lincoln with a kneeling slave is the emotive image of Old Calton's Emancipation Monument, which honours Scots who died in the American Civil War.

◁ PRESTIGIOUS SITE
Canongate churchyard, off the Royal Mile, contains the graves of poet Robert Fergusson, visionary Lord Provost George Drummond and economist Adam Smith.

△ TRAITOR'S TOMB
This gloriously ornate tomb, in a side chapel of St Giles' Cathedral, contains the Marquess of Argyll, villain of the film *Rob Roy*. His enemy, Montrose, is interred nearby.

THE GHOULISH CORPSE TRADE

In the early 19th century Edinburgh's graveyards were famous for being infamous. As cemetery watchtowers testify, they became the hunting grounds of "resurrectionists", or body-snatchers, who plundered fresh graves for corpses to sell to physicians at the city's medical school for anatomical study.

During the winter of 1828–29 two Irish immigrant labourers, William Burke and William Hare (pictured above), cut corners by assisting the specimens of Robert Knox, Fellow of the Royal College of Surgeons, into the condition required for his popular lectures. When it was discovered that they had murdered at least 16 people, and sold their bodies to Knox, the anatomist's reputation was permanently tarnished. A mob attacked his house and burned his effigy and his colleagues indicted him for the zeal which made him indifferent to the source of his corpses, but he was nevertheless able to continue in his profession. Hare escaped the gallows by testifying against his accomplice, who was publicly hanged.

△ SENTIMENTAL SLABS
Within the walls of Edinburgh Castle, in a semi-circular enclave, are the wee gravestones of army officers' dogs.

◁ THE ACADEMICIAN
Medallion of painter David Allan, Old Calton.

▷ TALL AND PROUD
The 90-ft (27-metre) obelisk dwarfing all else on the small Old Calton site honours five political martyrs.

LEITH AND NEWHAVEN

On Edinburgh's northern shore are fascinating, discrete maritime communities, foremost among them the fashionable Port of Leith, once a separate town and hub of trade and industry

Maps on pages 158 & 172

Although Edinburgh has a powerfully etched world image, up until the end of the 20th century this image consistently omitted the city's harbour on the Firth of Forth. Yet **Leith ❹**, which lies only a couple of miles north of Princes Street, has a fascinating history as long as that of its larger neighbour, and it was for several centuries one of Scotland's most important shipping terminals. Well before Leith was absorbed into Edinburgh it played a crucial role in the city's economic and strategic well-being. In some ways the Port of Leith has been treated poorly in return, and since the decline of its maritime industry it has fared badly, but the arrival of the Royal Yacht *Britannia* in the port may prove to be the catalyst required to kick-start Leith's economy and help turn around its self-image as well as making it known to the outside world.

Neighbouring **Newhaven ❺** is also a very old part of Edinburgh, which developed as a fishing village. As with Leith, its traditional industry has all but disappeared and its history and local interests have been somewhat swept aside in the schemes of the City of Edinburgh Council. It is now a quiet backwater which attracts a few visitors to its picturesque harbour and local history museum.

PRECEDING PAGES: the Waterfront Wine Bar by Rennie's Lock. **LEFT:** music aboard ship during the Jazz Festival. **BELOW:** freshening up in port.

Squeezed out and sacked

Leith's turbulent relations with Edinburgh date back to medieval times when only Scotland's "royal burghs" (like Edinburgh) had the right to trade abroad. As Leith was not a royal burgh, the "traffickers" (merchants) of Leith were supposed to stand back and let the merchants of Edinburgh do all the lucrative foreign trading with the Baltic, France, the Low Countries, Scandinavia and England. It was a monopoly that Edinburgh relished and Leith bitterly resented. And it was a law that was much ignored; the Leith men preferred to risk the wrath of the kings rather than let Edinburgh take all the business. Leith's resistance to Edinburgh's overweening ways irritated the Edinburgh mercantile establishment so much that in 1510 it tried, with some success, to turn Leith's flank by buying the nearby fishing/shipbuilding village of Newhaven from King James IV. It was an ominous start to what was a very nasty century for Leith.

In 1544 an English fleet led by the Earl of Hertford ploughed up the Forth with specific instructions from Henry VIII to "Sack Leith, and burn and subvert it ...". This the English troopers proceeded to do with great enthusiasm, and returned three years later (in 1547) for a repeat performance. In 1560 the English army was back – this time to help the Protestant Scots, "Lords of the Congregation", winkle out a French army which had dug itself into Leith at the behest of the Catholic Regent Mary of Guise (mother of Mary,

The coat of arms of the Port of Leith.

Queen of Scots). After a protracted siege and artillery duel, which did the fabric of Leith no good at all, the French surrendered and were shipped home.

Status and identity

If the 16th century was something of a disaster for Leith, the 17th century was not much better. In 1603 King James VI of Scotland (James I of England) confirmed Edinburgh's grip on the trade coming through Leith, in 1645 the port was hit by an outbreak of bubonic plague which wiped out two-thirds of the population, and in the l650s Leith was occupied by Cromwell's army (who built a citadel in Leith to house their troops). But in the l8th century the affairs of Leith – like the affairs of the rest of Scotland – began to improve (despite the Jacobite insurrections of 1715 and 1745). By the tail-end of the 18th century, Leith had become not only Scotland's major port but also an important centre for ship-building, ship-repairing, glass making, sugar refining, rope making, brick making, tanning and whisky distilling.

Edinburgh's grip – some say stranglehold – on Leith was loosened in 1833 when Parliament passed an act setting up the port as an independent burgh. Proudly, Leith set up all the trappings of a municipality: a town hall, burgh court, police office and police force. Edinburgh, however, refused to transfer the income from Leith's customs dues. Halfway up Leith Walk there is a pub called the Boundary Bar through which the Edinburgh/Leith border used to run. As the two municipalities had different drinking hours, customers could extend their happiness by moving from one end of the bar to the other. This was only one of many anomalies which used to irritate the burghers of Edinburgh and delight the imbibers.

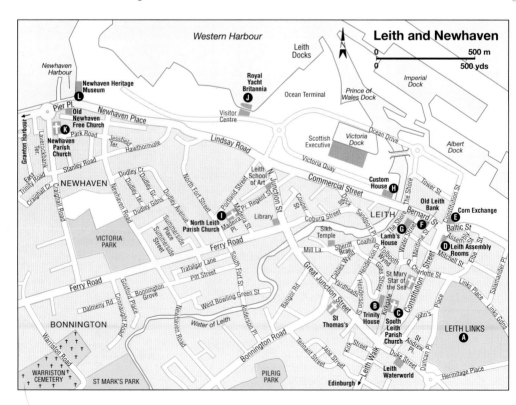

Prosperity through commerce

Meanwhile, throughout the 19th century Leith expanded as dock after dock was built: the Victoria Dock in 1851; the Albert Dock in 1881; the Imperial Dock in 1903. Ships from Leith exported coal, salt, fish, paper, leather and Scots ale, and returned with (among much else) grain, timber, wine, foreign foods and Italian marble. They traded with Hamburg, Bremen, Amsterdam, Antwerp, Copenhagen, Gothenburg, occasionally North America and Australia, and did a brisk coastal business with ports in eastern England.

Ship-building and ship-repair firms flourished too: Ramage & Ferguson; James G. Man & Son; Menzies & Co; Crann & Somerville; Hawthorns (which also made railway engines); and latterly Henry Robb Ltd, which dominated the market, building 500 mostly specialised vessels over 65 years. Around the docks and shipyard grew up a complex infrastructure of shipping agents, marine engineering shops, cooperages, marine insurance firms, grain and coal merchants, and ships' chandleries (not to mention pubs, flophouses, bookies and whores).

It is therefore unsurprising that by the end of the 19th century Edinburgh was plotting to resume its grip on the increasingly prosperous Port of Leith. It finally achieved its aim in 1920, despite a resounding defeat of the proposal in a plebiscite held by the anti-union Leith Town Council. Subsequently the port lapsed into its role as one of Edinburgh's most intriguing northern suburbs, though as recently as the 1960s Leith was still a tough, vigorous dockland, brimming with mildly dangerous pubs, seamen's flophouses, bookies and brothels. Fishing loomed large, too. Until the mid-1960s four fleets of deep-sea trawlers plied out of Leith and the nearby harbour of Granton. The 2-mile (3-km) stretch of shore between Leith and Granton used to be littered with ship-

Map opposite

Saying "Leith Police" aloud used to be a test of sobriety, but when Leith was subsumed into Edinburgh in 1920 the force became a division of the city police force, and the Leith Town Hall became a concert venue.

BELOW: a fisherman comes into harbour.

yards, ship-repair yards, a ship-breaking yard, a dry dock, a ropeworks, a wireworks and a networks. Many of local women earned extra money by making fishing nets at home with the aid of hooks attached to the backs of cupboard doors.

The fall and rise

All that has changed. Like most British ports (such as London, Liverpool, Glasgow and Bristol) the Port of Leith is a shadow of its former self. Most of the ships have gone, and gone with them is the old character of Leith. The few cargoes that do come through the harbour mouth are in giant containers and are disposed of by a handful of men, and Leith's ancient tradition of ship-building ground to a halt when British Shipbuilders closed the Robb Caledon yard in 1984.

Since then the area around the mouth of the Water of Leith has been redeveloped to attract middle-class newcomers: namely young business people, civil servants from the Scottish Executive (formerly the Scottish Office) and those who run the increasing number of upmarket bars and restaurants that cater for more affluent residents, office workers and (now) tourists. Old warehouses, maritime offices and at least one cooperage have been converted into luxury flats, and delapidated old buildings have been demolished to make way for the new. But people who have lived in Leith for generations are not, on the whole, participants in the new Leith, and the majority occupy poor-quality housing and lack opportunities.

Leisure then and now

A good place to start a tour of historic Leith is **Leith Links** , at the eastern edge of the district. Now a pleasant tree-edged park, Leith Links was one of the

TIP

The high-class Restaurant Martin Wishart on The Shore has quickly acquired a reputation as one of the best restaurants in Edinburgh, serving top-quality seafood, game and poultry (tel: 0131-553 3557).

BELOW: the Water of Leith estuary and The Shore.

world's first golf courses (dating from the 15th century), older by at least 13 years than anything St Andrews can claim, and where kings including Charles I played. The "Gentlemen Golfers of Leith" did, however, have to share the Links with linen-bleachers, horse-riders and grazing cattle (although after a cow attacked a woman in 1862 grazing was stopped). Along the sea edge of the golf course was Leith Sands, the venue for notoriously violent horse races for several centuries until the land was swallowed up by the docks. At the northeast corner of the Links is the former **Seafield Baths**, a neo-classical bathhouse built in 1813 as one of Edinburgh's most fashionable venues.

Map on page 172

Off Duke Street, near the southwest corner of the Links, is **Leith Water-world**, the baths' modern equivalent and the best leisure facility in Leith (there's also plenty of parking here). The major crossroads nearby was once a rather more important centre of activity than it is today, for on its north side was the Kirkgate (gateway to the kirk of St Mary, now South Leith), which was up until the 1960s the commercial and social heart of Leith. Leithers still mourn its passing. When Leith went into decline after World War II and the Kirkgate became run-down, the City Council simply demolished it and built flats and the soulless **Newkirkgate** shopping precinct in its stead.

The high-toned Honourable Company of Edinburgh Golfers began their playing days on Leith Links before quitting for the quieter pastures of Musselburgh and then Muirfield.

Distinguished survivors

However, behind Newkirkgate two historic buildings have survived. The neo-classical **Trinity House** ❸ (built 1816), on the left, was a maritime museum and still contains an important collection of maritime memorabilia; open by arrangement only for guided tours, tel: 554 3289. **South Leith Parish Church** ❸ has a fascinating history, for, though the late 15th-century building was extensively

BELOW: the former Seamen's Mission building, now the Malmaison Hotel.

THE WHALING PORT

One of the reasons that Edinburgh Zoo has such a fine collection of penguins is that Leith was one of the world's most important whaling ports – and the whales were hunted in the penguins' home territory. This unfortunately went on for much longer than is generally realised. In 1615 James VI granted Sir George Hay and Sir Thomas Murray a monopoly on the Greenland (Arctic) whale fishing, to be operated out of Leith. In the 1750s the Edinburgh Whale Fishing Company picked up where Hay and Murray left off, and began to kill the Greenland whales in a much more systematic and efficient way, from much bigger boats.

At the end of the 19th century, the Scots-Norwegian firm of Christian Salvesen & Co of Leith began large-scale whaling in the waters of the Antarctic. In 1908 a Leith Harbour was established on the bleak coastline of South Georgia, and generations of Leith and Edinburgh seamen spent their working lives risking life and limb on whale-catchers in the Antarctic, or as "flensers" hacking evil-smelling fat and blubber from the corpses of the giant beasts. "When one of Salvesen's factory ships put into Leith," remembers one old seaman, "you could smell the bloody thing from Princes Street."

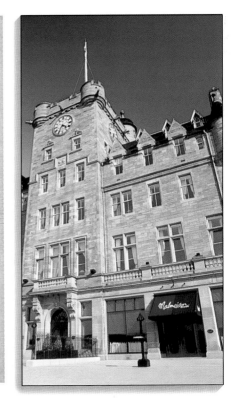

remodelled in the 19th century, the array of graves in the kirkyard and the church records (it claims to have the most complete records in Scotland) together effectively tell the history of the parish.

Originally controlled by the trade guilds, who built a series of chapels off the nave, it was perhaps as large as St Giles' Cathedral until the chancel was destroyed during the Siege of Leith in 1560. Inside there is an old map of the Siege, as well as a fine Victorian hammer-beam roof and oak screen with heraldic crests. If the gates are locked, enquire at the church hall at 6 Henderson Street. Local historian John Arthur conducts tours (contact the church hall, tel: 0131-554 2578) of particular interest to those who have family connections with Leith or an interest in the history of Christianity in Scotland.

Further up Constitution Street is **St Mary Star of the Sea** Roman Catholic church, built in 1854 to the designs of Edward Pugin and Joseph Hansom after Catholic Emancipation. At the top of the road the 18th-century **Leith Assembly Rooms ❿** (linked to the Exchange Building added in 1809) are now used as private offices. Across the road, to the north, the old **Corn Exchange ❺** (built 1860), with a stone frieze depicting cupids engaged in grain production, is also in private hands.

Large sums of public money were spent on cleaning and repairing Leith's principal buildings during the 1980s, but few of them are currently put to appropriate use, and according to some local observers restoration efforts have been mostly superficial.

Many Leithers are cynical about Edinburgh Council interventions and claim that decisions are made without consulting local people. The culture of Leith has indeed taken a beating, but Leith Initiative for Tourism (LIFT) is determined

The narrow Kirkgate used to house the Gaiety Theatre (venue for music hall greats like Will Fyfe, Harry Gordon and Lex Mclean), Sam Ret's huge fish and chip shop, and other businesses such as Hendry's the offal butcher and the Maypole Dairy.

BELOW: serving bubbly at one of Leith's smart restaurants.

that locally owned businesses and communities will at least benefit from the district's emergence on the tourist map.

Fashionable dockland

Bernard Street retains a faint semblance of the old town, with a statue of Robert Burns, who visited Leith, and, halfway down on the left, the curved neo-classical façade of the **Old Leith Bank** – now offices – which minted its own coins. However, it is **The Shore**, running alongside the river to the docklands, that is the focus of modern-day Leith (though it is probably its oldest street). It is peppered with fashionable watering holes and bistros with nautical-sounding names, several of which serve good seafood. Just off The Shore (left after exiting from Bernard Street and left again into Burgess Street) is **Lamb's House** , a 17th-century merchant's house, now run as an old people's centre, where Mary, Queen of Scots allegedly dined when she alighted at Leith in 1561 upon her return from exile in France.

Across the Bernard Street Bridge over the Water of Leith is the grand **Custom House** , built to Robert Reid's design in 1810. Owned by the National Museums of Scotland, it is used for storage, and there is no public access. Back on The Shore, proceeding towards the docks, look up to see the **Signal Tower** above the Fishers bistro. It was built in 1685 as a windmill and the battlements were added during the Napoleonic War. Beyond are Tower Place and the very tasteful **Malmaison Hotel**, which occupies a former "sailor's home" (1883) run by the Seamen's Mission to accommodate men whose ships were in port.

Further along the riverside a bridge leads to new-built apartments on Rennie's

Map on page 172

This 18th-century pub on The Shore occupies the site of one of Leith's earliest multi-use tenements, dating from 1438.

BELOW: Burns in Bernard Street.

TIP

Lothian Regional
Transport bus service
No.22 takes you to the
Royal Yacht Britannia
from Princes Street,
tel: 555 6363.

Isle (which are fetching high prices despite the less than pristine state of the water on their doorstep). If you cross and walk past these you will come to the huge modern **Scottish Executive** building. (From here, it's possible to glimpse the Ocean Terminal and flags of the Royal Yacht – *see below*). Turning left at the near side of the government building, you can walk across the bridge at Rennie's Lock to the conservatory at the back of the pleasant Waterfront Wine Bar and Bistro. Facing the Scottish Executive across a broad paved expanse is a strip of stylish restaurants in converted warehouses on Commercial Quay.

Places of god and royalty

There are several more interesting churches in Leith which some visitors may wish to visit, but it is not especially pleasant to stroll around the rest of the district. At No. 25 North Junction Street the small but renowned **Leith School of Art** occupies a former Norwegian seamen's church. **North Leith Parish Church ①** in Madeira Street, off Ferry Road, is an elegant neo-classical church built in 1816 to a design by William Burn. Another classical essay is **St Thomas's** in Great Junction Street, which took the former name of the Victorian gothic church at the end of Mill Lane (founded by the father of Prime Minister William Gladstone in 1843), itself now a **Sikh temple** and the focal point of Leith's large Sikh community.

Situated in the landmark **Ocean Terminal** leisure complex and cruise ship welcome point (designed by Sir Terence Conran and opened in autumn 2001) the decommissioned **Royal Yacht** *Britannia* ① (open daily; closes at 5pm Oct–Mar, 6pm Apr–Sep, last admission 90 mins before closing; entrance fee) is a unique and fascinating tourist attraction. Launched in 1953, the 412-ft (125-

BELOW: Leith's maritime tradition is acknowledged in the names of bars.

metre) three-masted "yacht" travelled all over the world in the service of the British Royal Family before coming to rest at Leith (which it had visited once before) in 1998. A visitor centre introduces the yacht, its naval crew and royal patrons, and on board you can see the royal apartments (designed by Sir Hugh Casson in the style of an English country house), grand dining room, Admiral's quarters and engine room. Insights are offered into the living and working conditions of the 240 seamen who operated the yacht and the Royal Family on and off duty (including Charles and Diana on honeymoon).

It is hoped that the Terminal will attract a big increase in the currently modest business from cruise ships berthing in the port, thereby making Leith Edinburgh's window on the world once more – and perhaps even the first port of call for monarchs, as it was in its former heyday.

The new Newhaven

While the centre of Leith has suffered from 1960s planning, the adjacent fishing village of Newhaven has, to a great extent, been ruined by conservation. Known since medieval times as "Our Lady's Port of Grace", Newhaven in the 1960s was a brisk if grubby little community, with a useful fishing harbour (pier by Robert Stevenson) and a busy fishmarket. There was a High Street and Main Street, both of which were lined with shops, pubs and small businesses through which tram-cars and later buses used to trundle. Newhaveners disliked Leithers, and the boundary between Leith and Newhaven was the scene of many a scuffle. A familiar sight on the streets of Edinburgh was the Newhaven "fishwife" who went from door to door selling fish from a creel (basket) on her back.

But time moves on; the picturesque fisherfolk's houses have been "restored"

Map on page 172

Flying the flag: the Britannia at sea, on a state visit to Iceland.

BELOW: tales of the sea beside Newhaven Harbour.

Map on page 172

TIP

Harry Ramsden's 175-seat restaurant beside Newhaven harbour is the doyen of the city's traditional fish and chips diners (tel: 0131-551 5566).

BELOW: new blends with old in Newhaven Main Street.
RIGHT: a bracing walk around the harbour.

by the City of Edinburgh for wealthier folk, there are far fewer shops (the once-crowded **Main Street** is a ghostly dead end) and the harbour is occupied by just a few pleasure boats and the odd fishing vessel. The Ancient Society of Free Fishermen, a trade guild founded in 1572, still exists, but it lists precious few fishermen among its members. On the other hand, the harbour area is quite lively on summer weekends, and Newhaven remains one of Edinburgh's most interesting corners.

Ship-building and fishing

The village was (probably) founded in the late 1400s by James IV to build the *Great Michael*, then the biggest warship on earth and designed to be the flagship of the Scottish navy. It is said that James IV cut down most of the oaks in Fife and Lothian to build the monster. But, like many such grandiose schemes, the *Great Michael* was not a success. After the ruin of the Scots army and the death of James IV at Flodden, the great ship was sold to the French, who left her to rot in Brest harbour. Newhaven never became much of a ship-building centre but did well enough from cod, haddock, whiting and herring. But the famous Newhaven oyster fishery was almost wiped out in the 19th century when the Edinburgh City Council (which had the rights over the oyster beds) got greedy and leased the fishery to an Englishman, George Clark, for the huge sum of £600 a year for 10 years. To recoup his cash, he brought in a fleet of 60 oyster dredgers from England, but they overfished the beds and ruined the fishery.

Newhaven sports little in the way of public buildings, apart from the handsome **Newhaven Parish Church ꓘ** (built 1836) in Craighall Road, **Old Newhaven Free Church** in Pier Place (built in 1855 and now an indoor climbing centre) and, at the harbourside opposite (next door to Harry Ramsden's fish and chip restaurant), the **Newhaven Heritage Museum ꓘ** (open daily noon–5pm; free) which occupies a former school building and remembers times past in the village. On the plateau above Newhaven are a number of handsome Victorian and Georgian villas, many of them built for prosperous sea captains.

Half a mile to the west is the **Old Chain Pier Bar**, once the site of a pier built in 1820, which became the terminus of the Edinburgh & Trinity Railway. For many years the bar was owned by a decidedly eccentric lady called Bet Moss who used to keep order among her sea-going clientele with a naval cutlass.

Further west lies **Granton Harbour**, built to a plan by Robert Stevenson in 1834–44. There used to be a train ferry from Granton across the Firth of Forth to Burntisland in Fife, and until the 1980s the harbour was host to a large fleet of trawlers, esparto grass boats and oil tankers. Today it is the home of the Royal Forth Yacht Club. Most of the West Harbour has been clumsily reclaimed from the sea and covered in huge retail warehouses, but a major regeneration of the Granton and Newhaven waterfront area is under way, comprising mainly new residential developments. It remains to be seen whether this will prove to be a Good Thing. ❑

THE WATER OF LEITH

Map on page 186

In the age of water-powered mills, villages grew up along the banks of the river which winds through Edinburgh to Leith – lying, now, on the route of a quiet, leafy walkway

Critics of Edinburgh (and there are a few) have said that all great cities should have a river – something which Edinburgh lacks. They don't count the Forth estuary, which belongs more properly to the port of Leith and to the old fishing villages of Granton and Newhaven; and they tend to laugh derisively when the Water of Leith is mentioned.

True, Edinburgh's "river" is no mighty flood. It is an often meagre stream which only achieves any decent volume when it debouches into the Forth at Leith, and which has found such a furtive channel through the city's gorges that it sometimes seems to disappear altogether. Yet this humble waterway, which rises in the peaty moorlands of the Pentland Hills above East Colzium, was critical to the economy of 18th-century Edinburgh.

Harnessed with the aid of dams, weirs and lades (flumes), it supplied power and water to bleach works, dye works and tanneries, and became the energy source for paper (including Bank of Scotland notes), snuff, flour and timber mills. By the end of the 18th century, 71 mills lined the banks of the 22-mile (35-km) river. One or two remain today (although no longer powered by water) and the residue of many others can be traced. In the 19th century *Chalmers Caledonia* described the river as "perhaps the most useful of any [river]… in all Scotland".

PRECEDING PAGES: Dean Village in summer. **LEFT:** the Water of Leith at Dean Bridge. **BELOW:** the signed walkway.

Path beside the river

Inevitably, as steam power took over, the river's industrial role declined, and at the same time so did the physical appearance of much of its immediate environment – so much so that, for most of the 20th century, the Water of Leith was casually associated with derelict buildings, choked undergrowth, old car tyres, rusting scrap and all the other sleazy detritus of water-borne litter. But in the 1970s Edinburgh District Council addressed the issue and, deciding to make a virtue of the river's industrial past and – in some areas – attractive dells and woodland, began building the **Water of Leith Walkway**.

Most of the riverside between Balerno, at the southwest edge of the city, and the Water's outlet at Leith is now accessible to walkers. Funding from the City Council and several other public bodies, as well as a Millennium Commission grant, has allowed the creation and upgrading of paths by the Water of Leith Conservation Trust to continue in recent years, such that the project is virtually complete and the leafy, traffic-free walkway to follows the channel all the way along its winding course through Edinburgh, a distance of 13 miles (25km).

For part of the length of the walkway, a route had already existed along the courses of, first, the recycled

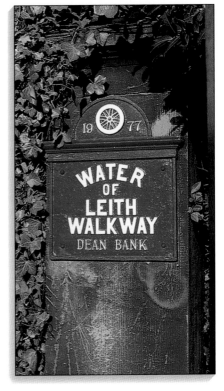

BELOW: old yew
trees in Malleny
Garden, Balerno.

former Balerno Branch Railway, which was built using the valley for much of its length, and, second, the Union Canal towpath at Slateford. Here, more than anywhere, can be seen the importance of the river valley as a communication route for people and goods. Many bridges and retaining walls of the Balerno Branch Railway – built in the 19th century – still remain, although passenger services were discontinued in 1943 and goods traffic in 1968.

River communities

The Water of Leith Walkway thus begins just north of **Balerno**, by the High School, and immediately adopts the path of the old railway line. It continues along the south side of the river, past **Currie**, but remains essentially in the countryside, removed from the southwest outskirts of Edinburgh until it approaches the A720 city bypass.

The path then skirts the romantically named village of **Juniper Green** Ⓐ, which is believed to take its name from the juniper bushes that once covered the lower slopes of the Pentlands. Like all the "villages" to its north along the Water of Leith, it's now part of Edinburgh, one of the city's more characterful suburbs. Juniper Green is first mentioned in records in 1707 and developed as the industrial use of the river grew.

The section of the walkway between Juniper Green and Slateford employs a former railway tunnel to bypass the village of **Colinton** (*see Villages, page 198*). The prosperous Colinton area was a centre of the milling industries in the 18th and 19th centuries, although Colinton was settled much earlier. The remains of **Colinton Castle**, built in the 16th and 17th centuries, can still be

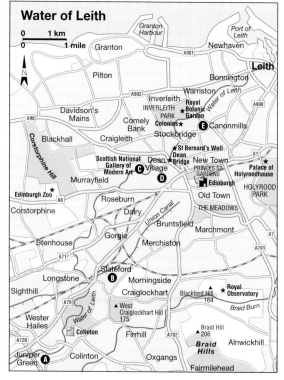

Water of Leith

seen in the grounds of Merchiston Castle School, situated close to the east bank of the river above Colinton village. In the 19th century Robert Louis Stevenson would come to Colinton to visit his grandfather, who was minister there.

The Water of Leith was for long a tricky crossing at the village of **Slateford ❽**, which takes its name both from the local stone and its function as ford. The crossing was actually a mill dam and consquently, as historical records state, it "was extremely difficult and dangerous and thereby occasioned several unlucky accidents and even some melancholy instances of persons who have lost their lives". But such tragedies were avoided after the building of a road bridge, which now converges with the Union Canal Viaduct and the Caledonian Railway Viaduct at Slateford. The **Union Canal** was opened in 1822 and had its own port, Stoneyport, at Slateford where rags and coal for the mills were offloaded and stone from local quarries taken on board. When the railways took over, traffic on the canal dwindled to nothing, although lunch and dinner cruises departing from the Bridge Inn on the waterside in Ratho, West Lothian, may still be enjoyed (tel: 0131-333 1320). The canal is now a semi-natural habitat for birds, beasts, fish, walkers, anglers and boatmen.

Nature and art

The **Water of Leith Visitor Centre** which opened in 2000 at Slateford (24 Lanark Road; open Apr–Sept: daily; Oct–Mar: Wed–Sun; entrance fee) educates schoolchildren and the public about the work of the Conservation Trust in conserving the river habitat, and about the Water of Leith's former economic importance in powering water mills and its natural history. The Trust stocks the river with native brown trout, employs scientists to monitor water quality

Map opposite

BELOW: the Water of Leith at Colinton.

(currently good along most stretches) and organises volunteers in clearing rubbish which is, unfortunately, still dumped in the river by vandals.

From Slateford the river wanders across the flat beds of two drained lochs – **Gogar** and **Corstorphine** – before reaching Dean Village by way of Roseburn. One of the most dramatic sections of the walkway, this was one of the last to be completed as it involved major engineering works to enable the path to run under both the canal acquaduct and the railway viaduct.

On the approach to Dean, just before you reach Belford Bridge, it is possible to scramble up the bank from the waterside footpath to the **Scottish National Gallery of Modern Art** (open Mon–Sat and Sun pm; free), which is well worth visiting. Walk around to the front to enter and appreciate the neo-classical architecture (designed by William Burn in 1825) and the Henry Moore and Eduardo Paolozzi sculptures (among others) which adorn the grounds. The gallery was founded in 1959 and moved to its present splendid home in 1984. The collection dates from 1900 and includes works by Picasso, Matisse, Freud, Hockney and Scottish artists such as John Bellany. There's also a good self-service restaurant on site with an outdoor terrace. The **Dean Gallery** (open Mon–Sat and Sun pm; free), in an similarly grand 19th-century building across the road (opened 1998), now houses the national collection of Dada and Surrealist art and sculpture gifted by Edinburgh-born Paolozzi. Both galleries hold interesting temporary exhibitions (usually an entrance fee).

Water of Leith Village

Dean Village – the crow-stepped huddle of russet buildings in a leafy gorge below Dean Bridge – was once known as Water of Leith Village. "Dean" itself

TIP

The Caledonian Brewery, at 42 Slateford Road, gives visitors fascinating tours (Mon–Fri at 11am, 12.30pm and 2.30pm; entrance fee) and a free glass of one of its award-winning traditional ales.

BELOW:
Belford Bridge, the start of the Dean Bank footpath.

is an old word for gorge or deep valley, and the original Village of Dean was a small – now defunct – community to the north of the river, on the western lip of the valley. Its inhabitants worked either at Craigleith Quarry or Dean Farm; but when this village surrendered to redevelopment in about 1880 its name somehow got transferred to the village beside the river.

The Water of Leith used to be its namesake village's *raison d'être*. There were mills and granaries beside the river as early as the 12th century, although the commercial and industrial heyday of the village was in the 18th and 19th centuries, when it was dominated by the Ancient Incorporation of Baxters (or bakers) and the Incorporation of Weavers. There were 11 mills on the short stretch of water which flows through the valley, but towards the end of the 19th century other industries, including distilleries and tanneries, began to replace the dwindling activities of the baxters and weavers.

Baxters' emblems

However, it is the influence and memory of the flour millers (who had supplied much of Edinburgh's bread) which persists most strongly today in Dean Village. The Baxters' arms, sculpted on a stone panel salvaged from the ruins of mill buildings, can now be seen on the façade of an old house at the top of Bell's Brae. The arms include the Biblical injunction: "In the sweat of thy face shalt thou eat bread." Other emblems of the bakers (for example, sheafs of corn and the two wooden paddles which manoeuvred the bread into hot ovens) are recorded on stone elsewhere in the village – in streets like Miller Row and buildings like the Old Tolbooth, where the Baxters would meet to decide the level of wages and prices.

Map on page 186

Many flora inhabit the riverbank, as do birds such as grey herons and dippers.

BELOW: Well Court, Dean Village.

In the midst of the largely vernacular architecture is a burst of designer Victoriana at **Well Court**. This was the product of an experiment in model housing for working people conceived by John Ritchie Findlay, the philanthropic owner of *The Scotsman*.

From giddy heights

Most visitors to the city get their first astonished glimpse of the Christmas-card community of Dean from Thomas Telford's **Dean Bridge** to the east, whose four arches magnificently straddle the Dean Valley from a height of 106 ft (32 metres). This narrow bridge (built in 1832) was commissioned by John Learmonth, then Lord Provost of Edinburgh, who wished to develop the Dean area and needed a better link with the city centre. Dean Bridge is still one of Edinburgh's main arteries and is only a few minutes walk from the West End of Princes Street. However, a 19th-century doggerel warned of the perils of the bridge's steep sides:

The Dean Bridge is terribly tall / Please take care that you do not fall
Down into the Water of Leith / Far below, as it flows beneath.

Indeed, Telford's masterpiece quickly acquired a gloomy reputation. As a sombre poem written by Robert McCandless in 1887 laments, it became a place:

Where many a man / Alas has ran / There in an evil hour
And cast away / His life that day / Beyond all human pow'r.

To discourage suicides, the stone parapet was eventually heightened. That slowed the rate but didn't – and doesn't – deter the most determined.

Passers-by must now crane their necks to look down into the valley, where they see cobbled streets and courtyards, red pantiles and turreted mews, and old mill buildings which now have the huffed and tidied look of desirably converted apartment blocks. The Water of Leith rushes through them all with unusual energy and the great, overhanging cliffs of New Town tenements add their dimensions to the valley, making this ancient settlement seem more than ever a secluded, secretive place which time has by-passed. In fact, present times have been very busy down in Dean, restoring, renovating and even building harmonious new housing.

Healing waters

The short walk from Dean to Stockbridge, below the great, viaduct-style arches of Telford's bridge and the soaring domestic ramparts of the New Town, is one of the most unusual in Edinburgh. It also takes you past the territory of one of the city's more fanciful legends, which claims that St Bernard of Clairvaux, the founder of the Cistercian Order, visited Scotland in the 12th century while raising soldiers for the Second Crusade. He was apparently badly received at court and retreated in a huff to weather an illness in a cave (now covered over) near the Dean Bridge. There he was conducted to the healing waters of a spring by the local birds and before he left for France he publicly declared the outstanding virtues of this well.

This tale was probably invented to add romance to **St Bernard's Well**, which, according to tradition, was

TIP

Fishing for brown trout in the Water of Leith is allowed by permit (free) during the season of Apr–Sept (fly fishing only above Slateford, no spinning; available from fishing shops and water of Leith Visitor Centre or tel: 0131-529 7913).

BELOW: Dean Village in winter.

discovered by three boys fishing in the Water of Leith in 1760. The mineral spring immediately attracted attention when analysis showed that the water was very similar to the sulphur springs of Harrogate in Yorkshire. In 1788 the striking and atmospheric open-sided Roman temple which now contains it was designed by Alexander Nasmyth. At the centre of the pillared temple is a statue of Hygeia, the Greek goddess of health.

Stockbridge to Leith

The village of **Stockbridge** *(see pages 199–203)* grew up around an important fording point across the Water of Leith, and the present bridge – called simply Stockbridge – is a widened version of the stone one built *circa* 1785 to replace an earlier wooden one. An attractive section of walkway has been built between it and the smaller **Falshaw Bridge**, taking you close to the Royal Botanic Garden and the intriguingly named **Colonies**. These distinctive rows of workmen's houses (now much prized by young professionals who can't afford Georgiana) were built from 1861, and have trade symbols depicted in relief on their gable ends. There are groups of similar Colonies, built by the same company, elsewhere in Edinburgh.

The section of the walkway from Stockbridge through **Canonmills** ❺ (where the canons of Holyrood Abbey established a water mill and Robert Louis Stevenson was born, in Howard Place, in 1830) to **Bonnington** was one of the last to be completed. The final leg to Leith is not one of the more picturesque but it presents ample evidence of the river's industrial and commercial past. Here, growing in volume and prestige, Edinburgh's small but resourceful river also gives its first intimations of a modest maritime life. ❑

Map on page 186

ABOVE: the goddess of health presides over St Bernard's Well near Stockbridge. **BELOW:** Nasmyth's temple glorifies the riverside well.

(THE WEE SHOP)

BRUCE LINDSAY WALDIE LTD

APPROVED COAL & SMOKELESS
FUEL MERCHANTS ☞ Est.1889

PROPERTY OF THE CORSTORPHINE TRUST

VILLAGES

Some interesting and characterful old rural communities exist within Edinburgh, from Duddingston, in the shadow of Arthur's Seat, to Georgian Stockbridge and Cramond on the firth

Map on page 158

E very city other than those few which have been purpose-built from scratch has its villages; its mature rural pygmies which have been consumed by the expansive appetite of the urban giant. Some fare quite well in the digestive process, surviving more or less intact in substance and robust in identity; others are overwhelmed by the demands of new developments and new needs. Edinburgh's villages are particularly persistent, many giving their names to whole areas of the city and to countless streets. When people talk today of Corstorphine they don't mean the cluster of cottages tucked behind the busy artery which is one of Edinburgh's main exits to the west, but the large modern suburb whose most distinguished feature is Edinburgh Zoo on Corstorphine Hill.

Similarly, when they talk of **Newcraighall ❻**, they may mean the tiny mining community on the eastern boundary of Edinburgh, or they may mean the wider area now largely synonymous with recent massive retail and leisure development. For reasons of geography as much as through the deep-rooted traditions of miners and their families, the village had remained oddly isolated from the city, but now it threatens to be swamped by a sea of traffic, highstreet shops and leisure facilities.

PRECEDING PAGES: Cramond harbour. **LEFT:** old Corstorphine. **BELOW:** fishing on Duddingston Loch.

Glorious past

Agriculture, fishing and traditional industries are all represented by Edinburgh's villages, as well as associations with some of the city's past celebrities and, of course, with some of the major events in Scotland's disputatious history. There is, for example, a house in the cobbled Causeway of the village of **Duddingston ❼** which was occupied by Charles Edward Stuart on the eve of his most famous success, the Battle of Prestonpans. While his army camped on the flat ground east of the village, Bonnie Prince Charlie planned the strategy which was to defeat the Hanoverian troops of General John Cope and encourage the Jacobites to believe in the future of their doomed rebellion of 1745.

Today Duddingston is one of Edinburgh's best-preserved villages, given some protection from encroaching development by the bulk of Arthur's Seat and pretty little **Duddingston Loch**, which is now a nature reserve and a Christmas-card setting for ice skaters and curlers. And if there is any pub in Edinburgh which still has the weathered character of an old country pub it must be the **Sheep's Heid Inn** at Duddingston. It is said that this ancient hostelry was patronised by James VI, who presented it with an embellished ram's head in 1580, and for a long time a speciality of the house was the traditional, if grisly, Scots delicacy of boiled sheep's head.

The ancient Sheep's Heid Inn in Duddingston, named after the speciality of its kitchen.

Duddingston dates from the 12th century and owes its existence to the early church built on an elevation above the loch by the Abbot of Kelso, who had been gifted land by David I. **Duddingston Kirk**, the present church on that same pleasing site, is a characterful Norman building which is one of the oldest churches in Scotland still in use.

To the left of the main entrance is a little two-storey tower now called the **Session House**. But anyone familiar with Edinburgh's history will recognise it for a graveyard watchtower from which elders of the Kirk took turns to repel those body-snatchers whose trade in illegally acquired corpses made infamous the medical schools of 19th-century Edinburgh. To the right of the entrance is a "loupin-on-stane" (a mounting block for horse-riding parishioners) and the less charitable "joug's collar" – an iron collar and chain used to exhibit and humiliate 17th-century sinners, whose offences might have included blasphemy, adultery, drunkenness and failure to attend church regularly.

Rural thatched cottages

If Duddingston is the most "rural" village in central Edinburgh (it can be reached on foot by a pleasant stroll through Holyrood Park), then tiny **Swanston 8** is more truly in the country. On the southern boundary of the city, this charming cluster of farmsteads and whitewashed thatched cottages – the thatch alone makes them unusual in Scotland – has been spared the embrace of suburban developers for two reasons: at Swanston's back are the Pentland Hills, with lower slopes already colonised by two golf courses and an artificial ski slope; and at its front, separating farmland from city, is a more recent barrier – the land-gobbling Edinburgh bypass.

There was once a school in Swanston, serving rural children from the hinterland of Edinburgh, but not for 50 years; nor has the village a church, a pub, shops or a bus service. As Malcolm Cant has pointed out in his second volume of *Villages of Edinburgh*, Swanston lacks "many of the traditional essentials of village life" – possibly because the property-owning, car-driving classes who now occupy this prime retreat from the city don't need them.

Nor does Edinburgh much need Swanston, but there was a time when it did. In 1758, a thirsty and grimy Edinburgh Corporation obtained an Act of Parliament which allowed the city to use Swanston's fine spring water. The local landowner objected and a famous series of legal disputes followed; but in 1761 a water-house was built and Edinburgh began to drink Swanston water.

Home and inspiration

The piping of the water would lead indirectly to Robert Louis Stevenson's close association with Swanston. The building of the water-house was followed by a civic decision to build a more general meeting place, or as Stevenson put it: "It occurred to them that the place was suitable for junketing. Once entertained, with jovial magistrates and public funds, the idea led speedily to accomplishment; and Edinburgh could soon boast of a municipal Pleasure House. The dell was turned into a garden; and on the knoll that shelters it from the plain and the sea winds, they built a cottage looking to the hills."

Swanston Cottage, to which he referred, was enlarged around 1835, and in 1867 Thomas Stevenson, father of Robert Louis, became its tenant. The cottage was their "second home", used only in summer but for 13 years the romantic engine room, off and on, for many of Stevenson's novels and poems.

Map on page 158

"The hamlet is one of the least considerable... a few cottages on a green beside a burn. Some of them (a strange thing in Scotland) are models of internal neatness... the very kettle polished like silver..."

– R.L. STEVENSON ON SWANSTON

BELOW: eating fish and chips on the front at Portobello.

A BEAUTIFUL PORT

The seaside suburb of Portobello had its heyday in the 19th century as a popular resort with "an animation and gaiety superior to those of any other sea-bathing station in Scotland". When sea-bathing became popular the town was quick to exploit its extensive sandy strand and soon offered a promenade, pier, donkey rides and steamer trips across the Forth. It flourished into the 20th century, but after its pier was demolished in 1917 its appeal began to dwindle. Today, although its sands still attract local families, plans to regenerate the long promenade have been mooted and some new developments have gone ahead, Portobello is a ghost of its former self. The seedy amusement arcades and half-hearted funfair on the seafront have only a nostalgic appeal. Yet Portobello's dignified main street and handsome Georgian terraces testify to its prosperous past.

Portobello owes its fanciful name to a seafarer, George Hamilton, who fought the Spanish in Panama in 1739 and took part in the capture of Puerto Bello. He retired here and built the first house on this stretch of the estuary, calling it "Portobello". The community thereafter became established through its brick-making and ceramics industry. Its most famous son is Harry Lauder, the music-hall artist who caricatured the boozy, "pawky", sentimental Scot.

Sons of Colinton

Stevenson is also closely associated with the village of **Colinton** , which was first settled round the ancient church of Halis, or Hailes (a name which has lent itself to one of Edinburgh's newer peripheral housing estates, Wester Hailes) and which now occupies an interesting corner of the southern suburbs.

The village with its wooded dell flourished beside the Water of Leith, which was used to power a variety of mills in the 18th and 19th centuries. Stevenson's grandfather, Dr Lewis Balfour, was minister of the parish between 1823 and 1860, and his dignified manse beside the river was an important and much-loved fixture in the writer's boyhood. Balfour is buried in the graveyard of the 18th-century church, as is James Gillespie of Spylaw House *(see below)*. The church itself has some interesting historic features, too.

Like Swanston, Colinton was then very much in the country and, until his grandfather died, the sickly child Robert Louis Stevenson was often sent there to play with cousins and recuperate from his illnesses. "Out of my reminiscences of life in that dear place," he wrote in 1873, "all the morbid and painful elements have disappeared. I remember no more nights of storm; no more terror or sickness. I can recall nothing but sunshiny weather. That was my golden age."

Other distinguished sons of Edinburgh found Colinton an amiable alternative to city life. In the old village, tucked into a leafy shelf below the modern roadway, is **Henry Mackenzie's Cottage**, birthplace of the man of letters who is chiefly distinguished for one book, *The Man of Feeling*. Mackenzie, as a plaque informs you, was born in 1745 (the year of the Jacobite Rebellion) and died in 1831.

Under the arches of the viaduct of the station (opened in 1881, now disused) is a flight of steps leading to **Spylaw Park** and Spylaw House, which was built

BELOW:
Colinton Church.

in 1773 for Edinburgh's great benefactor James Gillespie. James and his brother John, bachelors both, were mill-owners and had a snuff factory and retail shop which made them very rich. Frugal and industrious to the last, James left his fortune for the endowment of a hospital for old people (geriatric patients, we would call them today) and a school for poor boys. His hospital was built in 1802 and his eponymous school, no longer for poor boys, is one of Edinburgh's top schools. A ruin in the grounds of another school – Merchiston Castle School – is all that remains of **Colinton Castle**, dating from the 16th century.

In the late 19th century, a branch line of the Caledonian Railway brought the village of Colinton within commuting distance of Edinburgh and many handsome villas, some from the drawing board of Sir Robert Lorimer, appeared.

The New Town village

Like most cities with an interesting history, Edinburgh inspires fierce territorial loyalties in its citizens. Like Glasgow, the city is broadly divided into two camps, North Side and South Side; but, where Glasgow's demarcation line is the Clyde, Edinburgh's is Princes Street. Once they have settled in central Edinburgh to the north or south of Princes Street, few householders would voluntarily change camps. And within these camps there are communities which are particularly binding. One of them is Stockbridge.

Stockbridge ⑩ begins where the steep downward slope of Edinburgh's Georgian New Town meets the Water of Leith, and is often called the New Town village. This gives it an immediate cachet, but until the last couple of decades of the 20th century it was essentially a working-class community, with much of its modest Georgian property run-down.

Map on page 158

In Redford Road, near Merchiston Castle School, the Covenanters' Monument remembers the 900 Covenanting rebels who camped in Colinton in 1666.

BELOW: an antique shop in Stockbridge.

Now, thanks to a conservation programme of restoration and stone-cleaning, its central position and its own intrinsic character, Stockbridge has become upwardly mobile, infiltrated by the wholefood and designer knitwear classes. But the social mix is still sufficiently rich to make it one of the least artificial yuppiedoms in the country. If many of its original shops have been replaced by retail outlets for herbal preparations, party accessories and (for some reason) charity clothes, it also supports some of the best food shops in Edinburgh and a scattering of small tradesmen and craftsmen.

Its history is not long by the capital's standards. Its neighbours to the west and east, Dean and Canonmills, are much older, and until 200 years ago Stockbridge was little more than the bridge which gives it its name and which crosses the Water of Leith at a point which was first a ford and then a wooden bridge for the movement of stock. A stone bridge was built around 1785, and widened about 1830. By then, Stockbridge was developing a strong identity.

Stockbridge residents display green fingers in the small front gardens of their Georgian terraces.

Raeburn's estate

That identity was given distinction by the portrait painter Sir Henry Raeburn, who was born humbly in Stockbridge in 1756 and who, after his talent had brought him fame, fortune and a knighthood, bought an estate and mansion house in his native village. St Bernard's House, now no more, was its principal residence and Raeburn took an interest in developing housing on his estate.

The exquisite **Ann Street**, with its cottage gardens and ornamental lamps (where houses now rank among the most expensive in Edinburgh) was named after his wife, Ann Leslie, and probably designed by the architect James Milne. (It is on the west bank of the river, reached via Leslie Place from Deanhaugh

BELOW:
Stockbridge keeps
up with the news.

Street; other fine residential streets in this corner of Stockbridge include St Bernard's Crescent, Danube Street, Carlton Street and Dean Terrace.) The main thoroughfare through the community, bustling **Raeburn Place**, is also a reminder of Scotland's greatest portrait painter.

Stockbridge has had a crop of other notable residents throughout its two centuries. The artist David Roberts was born in one of its oldest houses, the vernacular late 18th-century building **Duncan's Land**, which was constructed from stones from demolished houses in the Lawnmarket. (It's on Gloucester Street, just off the main road into Stockbridge from the New Town, and is now a Thai restaurant.) Professor Sir James Young Simpson, pioneer of anaesthetics, lived there for a time, as did the eccentric academic and journalist Christopher North, the publisher Robert Chambers (of the dynasty which still publishes dictionaries and reference books in Edinburgh) and George Meikle Kemp, architect of the Scott Monument.

In the 20th century Ann Street was the home, for a time, of an unrelated Kemp – the late Robert Kemp, journalist, playwright, man of letters and author of a modern version of the 16th-century Scots classic *The Thrie Estates*; while in **Comely Bank** – a pretty little Georgian terrace on the western edge of Stockbridge – No. 21 was the first married home of Thomas and Jane Carlyle.

Stockbridge institutions

In the past the area was particularly dense in churches, church schools and other institutions. Its oldest surviving church is **Stockbridge Parish Church** (on Saxe-Coburg Terrace), built in 1823 with a classical façade by James Milne. But the most distinctive is William Playfair's **St Stephen's** church on the street of

Map on page 158

BELOW: the glorious gardens of Ann Street.

that name, an imposing pile built between 1827 and 1828 for just under £19,000, which dominates the vista from the top of the New Town's Howe Street.

These days it is a useful landmark pointer to more secular affairs, namely for directing visitors to **St Stephen Street** – the narrow, atmospheric passage which, above all others, is quintessential Stockbridge today. Famous for its antique, junk and second-hand clothes shops, St Stephen Street is the mutually beneficial haunt of self-conscious individualists and alternative entrepreneurs.

Nearby, in parallel **Hamilton Place** and its continuation, **Henderson Row**, are two buildings which speak of very different styles of 19th-century philanthropy. The old Dean Bank Institution (now **Stockbridge Primary School**) was founded in 1832 for the "reformation of juvenile female delinquents", and was aimed specifically at those "who have no home, or worse than no home to go to, and who manifest a wish to return to better ways". Some of the crimes of these sad girls were pathetically paltry. Case histories tell of one who was "well educated but wholly ignorant of religion – had never received religious instruction – her fault was selling a book which had been stolen by her brother"; and another who was "seemingly friendless" and stole from her mistress.

For over 150 years an attractive building in its own arboreal grounds in Henderson Row was a school for deaf and dumb children. In 1977 Donaldson's School for the Deaf, reorganising its other premises in Edinburgh, sold the Henderson Row building to neighbouring **Edinburgh Academy**, which was also founded in the 1820s. But before that happened Donaldson's had a brief spell of glamour in another role: during the summer of 1968 it became the "Marcia Blaine School for Girls" in the film version of Muriel Spark's famous Edinburgh novella, *The Prime of Miss Jean Brodie*. Now it's a school for boys – and

The Stockbridge Colonies were built from 1861 by the Edinburgh Co-operative Building Company to provide quality housing for the working classes. They were the first of several Edinburgh developments along the same lines.

BELOW:
St Stephen's Church from the top of Howe Street.

traditionally the ethos of the highly conservative Edinburgh Academy has not been dissimilar to that of the fictional establishment of Marcia Blaine.

Houses by the river

On both sides of Stockbridge – the bridge itself – there are characterful sections of the **Water of Leith Walkway**, the recreational route which follows *the course of Edinburgh's modest little river from the southwest outskirts of the city to the port of Leith *(see The Water of Leith, page 185)*. The path to the east of the bridge gives a splendid view of the **Colonies**, built for working people in the late 19th century. One of the leading members of the far-sighted building company was Hugh Miller, a polymath from Cromarty, in the northeast of Scotland, who was a stonemason, writer, journalist and geologist and whose genius eventually became too much for him. He shot himself on Christmas Eve, 1856, not knowing that a Stockbridge street would soon be named after him.

By the river to the southwest of Stockbridge, in a leafy valley which is almost a gorge, is **Dean Village**, probably Edinburgh's best known and certainly its most quaint. It has existed for some 800 years, and many reminders of its ancient milling community survive in the vernacular architecture. In this book, the village is covered in detail in *The Water of Leith (pages 185–91)* rather than here, owing to its historically symbiotic relationship with the river.

Iron by the Forth

If the old economy of Dean Village can still be traced in many of its buildings, the industrial revolution mounted by the village of **Cramond ⓫** in the 18th century has all but vanished. It is common knowledge that Cramond's history

Map
on page
158

Lauriston Castle near Cramond contains Edwardian furnishings (open Apr–Oct daily except Fri; winter weekends pm; entrance fee).

BELOW: colourful Cramond.

Map on page 158

TIP

At low tide you can walk across to Cramond Island, uninhabited except by wildlife, but take care not to get stranded when the tide comes in.

BELOW: interesting old tombstones abound in the churchyard in Cramond.

is formidable; that its harbour was used by the Romans and that the excavated Roman fort was built in the 2nd century AD. But few now remember that this pretty, whitewashed village at the mouth of the **River Almond** was once a centre of the iron industry. It produced in the 1770s some 300 tons of rod iron a year and exported barrel hoops to the wine-growing areas of Spain, Portugal and Madeira and the rum and sugar producers of the West Indies.

There is now a calm riverside walk from the little marina where the Almond debouches into the Forth estuary, past the stone-lined cuttings which are all that remain of the quarry wharves, and past the shell of a forge which once contained two furnaces and the scanty residue of other iron and grain mills.

These days, people come to this picturesque enclave in the northwest suburbs of Edinburgh for other reasons: to visit its crow-stepped, whitewashed 17th-century inn overlooking the Forth; to take the little rowing-boat ferry across the River Almond in order to walk in the Dalmeny estate; or just to admire the views across to Fife and the postcard comeliness of the village.

Romans and Christians

The Romans came for other reasons, too. About AD 142 a garrison of almost 500 set about building a harbour and fort by order of Emperor Antoninus Pius, who established the frontier line across Scotland from the Forth to the Clyde. Eventually the Romans pulled back to the line of Hadrian's Wall between the Tyne and the Solway, but were back in Cramond under Septimius Severus, who launched a punitive assault on northeast Scotland a century later. The **Roman Fort** (in the car park behind the esplanade) was discovered in 1954.

Cramond Kirk, the 17th-century parish church (it has a 15th-century tower) nearby, is built on a site probably used by the early Christian communities who succeeded the Romans. The churchyard is fertile ground for those with an interest in old tombstones, while a few hundred yards to the north is **Cramond Tower**, a medieval defensive tower of obscure history which is now a private home.

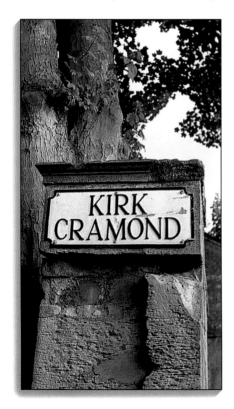

Between the tower and churchyard is **Cramond House** (*circa* 1680), which is now occupied by a clerk of the church, but was once the seat of the Inglis family. After inheriting in 1817, one of the Inglises, Lady Torphichen, completed Cramond's industrial decline by demolishing the oldest part of the village to extend the policies of Cramond House.

Edinburgh has many other villages, each with its claim to distinction. As well as the communities covered in other chapters – such as **Slateford** in the southwest (*The Water of Leith*), **Morningside** just south of the centre (*The Tenement Landscape*) and **Newhaven** in the north (*Leith and Newhaven*) – there is ancient **Restalrig** in the east, now surrounded by housing estates. It was once a place of pilgrimage for people afflicted with eye diseases, who came to bathe their eyes in an early 15th-century well, presided over by St Triduana. There is also **Davidson's Mains** just below Cramond, with ghost-ridden Craigcrook Castle, and **Liberton** in the southeast, whose name may be a corruption of Lepertown derived from a hospital for lepers which stood on a ridge outside Edinburgh.❏

The Outer Darkness

Edinburgh is one of Europe's most handsome cities and one of its most prosperous, yet neither the splendour nor the wealth is universal. The city has substantial pockets of some of the poorest amenities and rankest poverty in Britain.

As elsewhere in urban Scotland, its problems are "outer city" rather than the inner city deprivation found in England: it is ringed to the east, south and west with depressing, unhealthy and crime-ridden municipal housing estates. These "schemes", as they're known locally, have gained enduring notoriety, though some impressive recent attempts at self-help have demonstrated the fortitude of many residents. Now, at last, Craigmillar, The Inch, Niddrie, Oxgangs, Dumbiedykes, Pilton, Muirhouse and Wester Hailes can perhaps look forward to a better future.

A quarter of the city's population lives in municipal, or formerly municipal, housing. Some of the houses are of high quality, but many are not. Because 70 percent of them were thrown up in the great building boom of the 1950s and 1960s, they tend to suffer from bad design and poor workmanship and are now plagued with damp, condensation, sprawled concrete, faulty wiring, dire sound insulation, rotten security and eternally broken lifts. In some communities, a quarter of the properties are empty and boarded up.

Unemployment levels in large schemes like Craigmillar are up to three times the national rate; skills levels are low, crime levels high. But health standards provide perhaps the grimmest measure of inequality. Poor areas record significantly lower life expectancy than Edinburgh as a whole, and higher hospital admission rates for self-poisoning (including drug-related illness), self-harm and emergencies. Nor is deprivation confined to the estates. Around 5,000 people are registered homeless, and every night finds people sleeping rough in city-centre doorways.

In the last quarter of the 20th century, drug abuse reached awesome proportions on several of the schemes, creating both health problems, ranging from Hepatitis-B to Aids, and burgeoning crime, varying from house-breaking to violence between rival drug cartels. The schemes' lack of amenities for the young has also given rise to sporadic vogues for gang-fighting.

While bored middle-class kids, of which Edinburgh has plenty, can be as dangerous as their poorer counterparts, the magnitude of such problems has brought growing recognition that multi-disciplinary initiatives are needed to address social and economic exclusion. Local authorities have built ambitious partnerships with private capital and voluntary groups to attack urban deprivation, and have engaged the communities in determining their own futures. Housing is increasingly transferring out of local government ownership to tenant-based control; one such "New Housing Partnership" is regenerating Craigmillar by demolishing derelict properties and building more than 1,000 affordable new homes. Slowly, the sun may be starting to penetrate Edinburgh's darker corners. ❑

RIGHT: a typical drab municipal housing estate.

PARKS AND GARDENS

*In the very heart of Edinburgh is a large swathe of "countryside",
Holyrood Park, and dotted around the city a variety of parks and
an acclaimed botanic garden cater to every taste*

Map
on page
158

Edinburgh's dramatic cityscape, dominated by Holyrood Park's 823-ft (251-metre) Arthur's Seat and Salisbury Crags, is described in heart-stirring mode in Sir Walter Scott's novel, *The Heart of Midlothian* (set in 1736): "The prospect, in its general outline, commands a close-built, high-piled city, stretching itself out beneath in a form which, to a romantic imagination, may be supposed to represent that of a dragon; now, a noble arm of the sea, with its rocks, isles, distant shores, and boundary of mountains; and now, a fair and fertile champaign country, varied with hill, dale, and rock, and skirted by the picturesque ridge of the Pentland mountains."

Although there is rather less of the "fair and fertile champaign country" to be seen these days, modern Edinburgh contains some sizeable and appealing green spaces. Moreover, perhaps surprisingly, the essence of the city remains true to Scott's imagery. The spiky ridge of the Royal Mile still looks like a dragon's spine – presenting its best profile, perhaps, to the elevations in two of Edinburgh's major parks on the north side of the city, the Royal Botanic Garden and Inverleith Park. And the volcanic plug of Arthur's Seat and great, semicircular rampart of Salisbury Crags still form the city's centrepiece – and still bring a mood of wilderness to Edinburgh's largest park, whose northwestern edge is literally just behind the foot of the Royal Mile.

PRECEDING PAGES:
The Meadows.
LEFT: an encounter
in Princes Street
Gardens.
BELOW: the
palace in the park.

Spectacular Queen's Park

The royal estate of **Holyrood Park ⑫** (aways open; free), which (depending on the gender of the reigning monarch) is also known as the Queen's or King's Park, is a former hunting reserve. It is some 4 miles (6.5 km) in circumference, with two small lochs, a scattering of antiquities and a royal palace *(see The Old Town, page 117)* at its main entrance. The park never fails to startle visitors with its craggy style and spectacular scale, while annual events such as the New Year's Day triathlon and Fringe Sunday (when performers from the Edinburgh Festival Fringe hold a jamboree in the park) turn it into a huge, breezy, open-air theatre for locals.

The climb to the summit of **Arthur's Seat** is a popular hike, although idle mountaineers can reduce the effort by driving halfway up Queen's Drive (closed to vehicles Sun), the one-way road which circuits the park, leaving their cars at **Dunsapie Loch**. There is also parking at the foot of the hill at **St Margaret's Loch** (near the Palace) which, like Dunsapie, has a complement of swans, ducks and often greylag geese.

Nearby is **St Margaret's Well** and, a little farther up the hill, perched on a crag, the ruins of **St Anthony's Chapel**, both rather vaguely associated with people suffering from eye afflictions. The well is

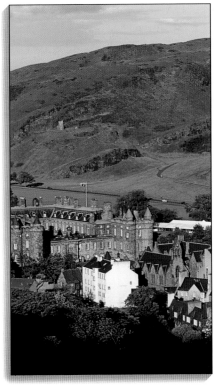

a late medieval conduit thought to have been established during the reign of James IV and moved to its present site from Restalrig in 1859; the chapel is believed to date from the 15th century and may be connected with a hospital founded by James I at Leith and committed to the care of victims of "St Anthony's Fire", the medieval name for erysipelas, a febrile disease.

Open-air murder

Holyrood Park is an uncomfortable place for wives by the evidence of two incidents, which took place two and a half centuries apart. One of Edinburgh's most notorious murders took place in the park on an October night in 1720, and those of morbid bent might take a passing interest in **Muschat's Cairn**, near the Willowbrae entrance, which marks the spot where the victim died.

The villain, Nicol Muschat, was a young surgeon and apothecary's assistant who married in 1719 and soon afterwards launched a bizarre series of attempts to kill his wife, Margaret Hall. First he tried to poison her with mercury; after spending weeks in agony, she recovered. Next he hired a gang of incompetent footpads who made several unsuccessful bids to waylay her. Then he decided to do the deed himself. He persuaded the ingenuous girl to accompany him into the park late at night on a jaunt to Duddingston village on the far side of Arthur's Seat. Then he cut her throat and left her body behind a wall, on the spot now marked by Muschat's Cairn. However, he was just as much a bungler as his predecessors and left so many clues behind that he was soon arrested, convicted and hanged in the Grassmarket.

In 1973, another young husband, a 21-year-old Dutch visitor called Ernst Dumoulin, celebrated his wedding day in Edinburgh by pushing his bride over

BELOW:
greylag geese
beside the loch
in Holyrood Park.

Salisbury Crags. There were no witnesses and he claimed her death was an accident. But the existence of a large insurance policy which he had taken out on her life a few days before aroused suspicions and Dumoulin was duly tried and convicted of murder in Edinburgh's High Court.

Despite this disagreeable association, the **Radical Road** where the bride's body was found is one of Edinburgh's favourite walks and viewpoints. In *The Heart of Midlothian* Sir Walter Scott advocates a notion that the best views of the city are to be had from the foot of Salisbury Crags, "marking the verge of the steep descent which slopes down into the glen on the southeastern side of Edinburgh". The path was built around the base of the Crags in 1820, two years after the novel was published, to give work to the unemployed.

Action-packed or mellow beauty

The Royal Botanic Garden and Inverleith Park sit side by side about a mile north of Princes Street. Both parks were once part of the Inverleith estate which gave the district its name, and their respective characters make them major crowd-pullers on fine Edinburgh days. Despite their proximity to each other, they not only represent two very different aspects of the recreational spectrum but two contrasting moods.

Inverleith Park ⓭ (always open; free) is breezy, energetic, expansive, action-packed. It has football, rugby and cricket pitches, a large model-boat pond and a well-stocked children's playground. Laid out by the city in 1890, it still contains at its east end the old Inverleith farmhouse which dates from the 18th century, but which was updated around 1900. Game-playing, as well as various other nuisances, is officially excluded from the quieter 70-acre (28-ha) **Royal**

Map on page 158

TIP

Inverleith Park's one oasis of tranquillity is a small formal rose garden, whose arboreal wall provides some shelter from hurtling dogs, gasping joggers and rogue cricket balls.

BELOW: strolling in the Royal Botanic Garden.

THE GLASSHOUSE EXPERIENCE

The interconnecting series of tropical and temperate glasshouses are the icing on the cake of the Royal Botanic Garden, presenting an exhilarating journey into another world (and an escape from the vagaries of Scottish weather) which encompasses several climatic zones.

You first enter into the warm Temperate House containing plants from Australasia and South Africa, its high roof and walls suspended by external pylons. At one end of a raised walkway above is the humid Tropical Aquatic House, memorable for its giant waterlilies (reared as annuals from seed) as well as economic crop plants including banana, coffee and rubber. The prescribed route then leads to the Orchid and Cycad House, containing 200-year-old cycad specimens, and the Fern House which recreates the conditions of a montane cloud forest.

From there, you come to the magnificent Victorian Palm Houses: the octagonal tropical house and the 70-ft (20-metre) high iron-roofed temperate house. Back along the central walkway is the South American Aquatic House featuring epiphytic bromeliads (pineapple family), followed by the Arid Land House containing succulents and cacti. Finally there are the newest additions, the Peat and Tropical Rock Houses. Now exit into the cold wind and lashing rain!

Map on page 158

Botanical browsing in the rockery.

BELOW:
Princes Street
Gardens in autumn.
RIGHT:
blooming youth.

Botanic Garden ⑭ (west gate on Arboretum Place, east gate on Inverleith Row; open daily 9.30am–dusk or 7pm in summer; free), which is a sumptuous, velvety, sheltered place. Even the hillock which supports Inverleith House, and which offers a spectacular panorama of the Edinburgh skyline, is well provided with mellow walls and opulent foliage to trap the sun.

The Botanic pre-dates Inverleith Park. The scientific interest in botany goes back a long way. Edinburgh's Royal Botanic Garden was founded in 1670 as a physic garden on a 40-ft sq. (4-metre sq.) site now obliterated by Waverley Station. It moved to Inverleith between 1822 and 1824, making it one of the oldest botanic gardens in Britain – and one of the best.

Enthusiasts identify as its star attractions the magnificent collection of rhododendrons, its heath and rock gardens (the former recreating Scottish landscapes, complete with Highland croft, and the latter crowned by a spectacular naturalistic waterfall) and the landscaping of exotic plants. Students of greenhouse architecture admire the contrast between the Victorian Tropical Palm House and the adventurous superstructures of the newer glass houses, designed in the 1960s and 1970s. (The **Glasshouse Experience** is open daily 10am–5pm or 3pm Nov–Feb; voluntary entrance fee.)

Local habituees of the gardens simply relish their heart-lifting beauty and voluptuous calm, and in summer those living nearby often just come in to sunbathe or read under a tree. For a few years they lamented the loss from **Inverleith House** of the National Gallery of Modern Art, which moved to new premises in 1984, but the building is now used for, occasionally very good, temporary art exhibitions (for details and current opening times, tel: 0131-248 2849; usually free).

Parks for everyone

Not all visitors find their way to these delightful parks, but few avoid being willingly swept into the great green abyss of **Princes Street Gardens** *(see The First New Town, page 140)*, that gorgeous gulf between bustling thoroughfare and Castle Rock which helps make Princes Street one of the most celebrated commercial arteries in Europe. Created in the valley of the drained Nor' Loch, these manicured formal gardens attract droves of shoppers and office workers during sunny lunchtimes, as well as tourists.

A popular public park with a rather different character – especially well used by students of the nearby university – is **The Meadows** ⑮, the common land of informal turf and leafy avenues to the south of the Old Town, behind the old Royal Infirmary. South of Melville Drive it runs into **Bruntsfield Links** which, in common with **Leith Links**, owes its survival as an open space to its former use as a golf course (Bruntsfield still has short-hole golf facilities). A "park" that is not visited casually, but which is well loved by families, is **Edinburgh Zoo** ⑯ (Costorphine Road; open daily; entrance fee) in the western suburb of Corstorphine. The zoo occupies a parkland setting on the side of Corstorphine Hill and has spacious animal enclosures. Its best-known residents are the penguins, a collection of several species which parade daily (weather permitting) outside their enclosure at 2.15pm. ❏

THE SEVEN HILLS OF EDINBURGH

 Map on page 158

A striking prospect from below, breathtaking views from the summit and an impressive geology and human history are all features of Edinburgh's principal, centrally sited hills

I t must have been a 20th-century marketing man who claimed for Edinburgh the topographical distinction of Rome, adding Scotland's capital to that mysteriously expanding list of European cities built on seven hills. (Prague is another which makes the same boast, as if some mystical urban virtue were endowed by such specific hilliness.)

Even by the late 19th century there was little of Edinburgh beyond the spreading verges of three hills, as Robert Louis Stevenson reported in 1878: "The ancient and famous metropolis of the North sits overlooking a windy estuary from the slope and summit of three hills. No situation could be more commanding for the head city of a kingdom; none better chosen for noble prospect. From her tall precipice and terraced gardens she looks far and wide on the sea and broad champaigns."

In those days, the three hills of Stevenson's "precipitous city" were the three which remain its most dramatic and alluring today: Arthur's Seat, Castle Hill and Calton Hill. But over the years, as the metropolis of the North found its metroland (despite the absence of underground railway), Edinburgh has acquired four more hills. Yet, for all the airy comeliness of the hills of Braid, West Craiglockhart, Blackford and Corstorphine, they seem bland, undistinguished suburban hummocks alongside the thrilling crags and aggressive profiles of the ancient three.

Sheer basalt rock

If, at 823 ft (251 metres), Arthur's Seat is the highest and the most oddly shaped – a "couchant rag-lion", Charlotte Brontë called it – then Calton Hill is the most eccentric and **Castle Hill** ⓱ the most formidable. The volcanic bastion supporting Edinburgh Castle is 435 ft (133 metres) above the sea (its sheer black rock makes it look even higher) and has been a stronghold from at least AD 600, when the Gododdin tribe occupied a fort on it. According to Sir William Brereton, Parliamentary Commander in the Civil War, when he visited Scotland in 1636 there were those who still called Edinburgh Castle "Castrum Puellarum", "because the kings of the Picts kept their virgins therein".

To stand at the base of Castle Hill and look upwards is to find your imagination falter before its forbidding basalt and the sanguinary adventures of history and prehistory which it has witnessed. Nothing can diminish it. Its stature keeps it secure from any lunatic scheme of architect or developer.

The history of Castle Hill is the history of **Edinburgh Castle** *(see pages 108–11)*, and legion

PRECEDING PAGES: Arthur's Seat from Castle Hill. **LEFT:** sledging on Arthur's Seat. **BELOW:** looking down at the city from the Castle.

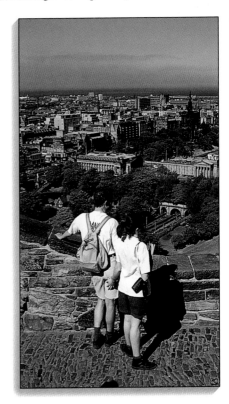

are its stories of siege, subterfuge, heroism, treachery, noble and ignoble acts. The cliffs themselves have played a part in Scotland's history. When the saintly Queen Margaret died in the castle in 1093, while it was under siege from Donald Bane, her body was secretly lowered down the rock and taken to her priory in Dunfermline. And in 1314, when the castle had been in English hands for 19 years during Scotland's Wars of Independence, it was retaken by the Earl of Moray and a handful of men who climbed stealthily up the cliffs.

The broad, battlemented **Esplanade** is the lofty stage above the city where the Festival-time Military Tattoo is held. Its history is less festive. Between 1479 and 1722 it was the favoured site for the burning of witches. Scotland's record in the persecution of old, eccentric women – and often young women who had made some local enemies – is a shameful one. More than 300 "witches" were burned on the Esplanade alone, on a spot marked by an Art Nouveau Witches' Well (on a wall to the right of the Esplanade's entrance).

Miniature Highland peak

Probably no one has misunderstood the nature of Edinburgh's hills more than the essayist William Hazlitt, who wrote in 1826: "Edinburgh alone is as splendid in its situation and buildings, and would have even a more imposing and delightful effect if Arthur's Seat were crowned with thick woods, and if the Pentland Hills could be converted into green pastures, if the Scotch people were French, and Leith Walk planted with vineyards."

The somewhat leaden satire of Hazlitt's observation doesn't diminish the crime of misrepresentation. Edinburgh's hills are, naturally and unalterably, the perfect emblems of Scotland's prevailing topography.

BELOW: the Castle in its lofty situation, framed by the fountain in Princes Street Gardens.

The **Pentlands** are a shapely outpost of the **Border hills** and **Arthur's Seat** ⑬, which crowns Holyrood Park *(see page 209)*, is a Highland peak in miniature. Dorothy Wordsworth recognised this: "We sate down on a stone not far from the chapel, overlooking a pastoral hollow as wild and solitary as any in the heart of the Highland mountains: there, instead of the roaring of the torrents, we listened to the noises of the city…" Nearly 200 years later, the noises of the city are very different, but now the thunder of traffic in the near distance sounds like the roaring of torrents, and it's just as possible, on winter mornings on Arthur's Seat, to believe yourself in the heart of the Highland mountains.

A long history

No one really knows which Arthur claimed the eminence for his seat. Some argue for the legendary king of the Round Table, and there is evidence that the Lothians lay in one of the British (Welsh) kingdoms before they were occupied by the Angles and Scots. But it may have been the 6th-century Prince Arthur of Strathclyde who gave the hill its name; then again – and more probably – the name may simply be a corruption of the Gaelic "Ard na Saigheid", meaning "height of the arrows".

Whatever its christening, Arthur's Seat was certainly defensively colonised in prehistory. The remains of four prehistoric forts can be traced with perseverance and difficulty on the hill and in the Dunsapie Loch and Salisbury Crags areas, suggesting that it was a major population centre in the first millennium AD and in the early centuries of the second one. More easily visible are the groups of cultivated terraces on the east flank of the hill, above and below Queen's Drive. They were once narrow ploughed fields, dating from the Dark Ages.

Map on page 158

It's a bit of a scramble to the top of Arthur's Seat but it is a popular climb.

BELOW: awaiting the solstice on Arthur's Seat.

The view from the top is simply magical. On clear days it embraces the narrow waist of Scotland, from the Firth of Forth to the Firth of Clyde, as well as the mountains of the **Trossachs**, those comely outriders of the great Highland massif, and, to the southeast, the romantic **Lammermuirs** and the Border hills.

It was not always thus. The name of "Auld Reekie" (Old Smoky) was acquired by Edinburgh in the 19th century when the peat and coal smoke from the multiplicity of chimneys in the Royal Mile produced a permanent pall over the city. The Clean Air Act has changed all that, but the grimy cloud that used to hang over Arthur's Seat is remembered in this piece of doggerel:

> *Arthur's Seat, ye're high and humpy*
> *But whit gars ye look sae grumpy?*
> *Perhaips the smeuch o' Auld Reekie*
> *Maks ye smairt, an' feel richt weerie?*

Strange fiction and fact

Naturally, this extraordinary urban mountain has not been ignored by writers and film-makers, but few have used it more dramatically than James Hogg in his classic allegory of the duality of human nature, *Private Memoirs and Confessions of a Justified Sinner* (1824). A key episode in the book is set on the summit of Arthur's Seat, where the tormented George Colwan is confronted by a giant apparition of his brother – "its dark eyes gleamed through the mist, while every furrow of its hideous brow frowned deep as the ravines on the brow of the hill" – and is later murdered by him and his satanic doppelgänger Gilmartin.

In the realm of fact, the hill was the scene of a macabre discovery in 1836, when five Edinburgh boys stumbled upon a cache of tiny coffins while out hunting rabbits. There were 17 of them, each 4 inches (10 cm) long with lids secured by brass pins and sides ornamented with designs in tin. Inside, fashioned in meticulous detail, were 17 diminutive figures. Their origin was never traced but, naturally, witchcraft was suspected – or that they represented the victims of Burke and Hare *(see page 167)*. Some of those miniature coffins are now displayed in the Museum of Scotland in Chambers Street.

Unfinished folly

> *Pompous the boast, and yet a truth it speaks*
> *A "modern Athens" – fit for modern Greeks*

This waspish comment on both Edinburgh and the Greeks was made by James Hannay in an edition of *The Edinburgh Courant* in 1860. By then, Edinburgh had lived for nearly 30 years with the "folly" which turned **Calton Hill ⑲**, which rises above the east end of Princes Street, into a hand-me-down Acropolis. The two hills can't really be compared, but echoes of the Athens rock are to be found in the steep crags and incomplete Parthenon of the **National Monument** on Edinburgh's Calton Hill – a monument more sheepishly known as "Scotland's Disgrace".

In 1822, when the city was still casting around for a suitable monument to commemorate the end of the Napoleonic Wars in 1815, various city luminaries, including Sir Walter Scott, Henry Cockburn and Lord

TIP

You can drive most of the way up Calton Hill and park near the northwest edge above the gully of Greenside, one of the sites in the city where witches were burnt.

BELOW: the Nelson Monument on Calton Hill.

Elgin, launched a public appeal. They wanted £42,000 "to erect a facsimile of the Parthenon" but barely half was subscribed. Nevertheless, the distinguished architect Sir William Playfair was appointed to the task along with C. R. Cockerell, whose job was to guarantee the accuracy of the reproduction, and great golden blocks of stone were hauled from Craigleith Quarry on the edge of the city to the top of Calton Hill. Work began in 1826 and came to a halt when funds dried up in 1829, with only part of the stylobate and 12 handsome columns and their architrave completed. Today, Edinburgh's heroic folly looks like a kind of flawless ruin of uncrumbled stone.

It is certainly the oddest building on the summit of Calton Hill but not the most preposterous; that honour must go to the **Nelson Monument** (open Apr–Sept: Mon pm and Tues–Sat; Oct–Mar: Mon–Sat till 3pm; entrance fee), built to honour the hero of Trafalgar in 1807. This circular tower is over 100 ft (30 metres) high with a flagstaff and a time-ball, which gives a visual signal to ships in the Forth at noon, on the top. The time-ball is in electric communication with the time-gun at the Castle and falls exactly when the gun is fired at 1pm. The battlemented base is composed of small rooms originally intended to give accommodation to disabled seamen but leased eventually, according to the records, to "a vendor of soups and sweetmeats". As James Grant wrote in the 1880s, it is "an edifice in such doubtful taste that its demolition has been more than once advocated". But he added, "with all its defects it makes a magnificent termination to the vista along Princes Street".

As indeed does the whole domed, towered and pillared mass of Calton Hill, which has a third major building on its summit. The cruciform-shaped **City Observatory**, with its characteristic green dome, was also designed by William

ABOVE: Burns Monument, on the side of Calton Hill, and, **BELOW**, the Stewart Monument above it, both copies of the Lysicrates.

Map on page 158

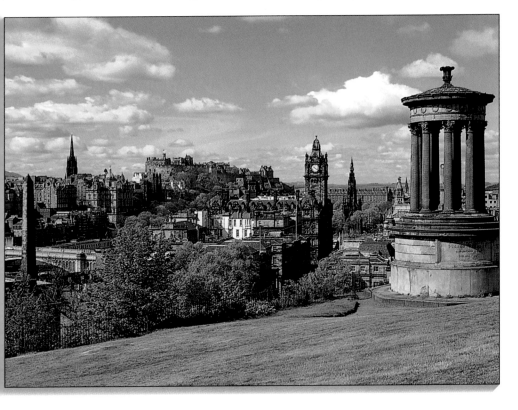

Playfair. It was built in 1818 for the recently formed Astronomical Institution, but the late 19th-century foretaste of pollution – smoke from the trains coming into Waverley Station – compelled the Astronomer Royal to relocate to Blackford Hill in the southern suburbs.

Panoramic views

For all its curiosities – and they also include a reproduction of the monument of Lysicrates in Athens, dedicated to an 18th-century Edinburgh University philosopher called Dugald Stewart, and a Portuguese cannon captured at Mandalay – the most satisfying spectacle of Calton Hill is the glorious view from its grassy plateau. The height and position of the hill make it a perfect standpoint for an all-round, close-up study of the city's central anatomy, as well as its relationship with Edinburgh's other hills and the waters of the Firth of Forth. "Leith camps on the seaside with her forest of masts" wrote Robert Louis Stevenson in 1879, evoking the mood and magic of Calton Hill in a series of stunning vignettes. The forest of ships' masts has dwindled to a copse, but the maritime life of Edinburgh's port can still be glimpsed in the superstructure of oil rig supply vessels, occasional cruise ships and British and foreign navy ships.

Much of Stevenson's intimacy with Calton Hill was acquired on assignations with prostitutes there, although today its sexual notoriety has been hijacked by gays looking for pick-ups (mainly after dark). Stevenson was too much of a poet, however, to neglect the view, with its opportunities for an exhilarating experience in urban voyeurism. "You turn to the city," he wrote, "and see children dwarfed by distance into pygmies, at play about suburban doorsteps; you have a glimpse upon a thoroughfare where people are densely moving;

BELOW: the incomplete National Monument, known as "Scotland's Disgrace".

Map on page 158

you note ridge after ridge of chimney stacks running downhill one behind another, and church spires rising bravely from the sea of roofs. At one of the innumerable windows, you watch a figure moving; on one of the multitude of roofs, you watch clambering chimney sweeps."

For anyone who loves Edinburgh with the clear-sightedness of Stevenson (who also loathed it), Calton is the paragon of hills. But, since his day, its 328 rocky feet (100 metres) have been almost overwhelmed, to the northwest, by the brutal bulk of the St James Centre – the shopping precinct which seems to have been built by people who hate Edinburgh.

Suburban hills

Pleasant walks above the city, but less intense experiences of it, are to be had on the four suburban hills. The most interesting are **Corstorphine Hill** ❷⓿ on the west side, home of Edinburgh Zoo since 1927, modelled on Stellingen Zoo near Hamburg and famous for its penguins, and **Blackford Hill** ❷❶, a steep shelf above the southern suburbs where the **Royal Observatory** stands (child-oriented multi-media Visitor Centre open Mon–Sat and Sun pm; entrance fee). It is now a joint research institution of the Science Research Council and the University of Edinburgh. At the foot of this hill is a public garden containing Blackford Pond, while to the west, topping Blackford's 539 ft (164 metres) by another 36 ft (11 metres), is wooded **West Craiglockhart Hill** ❷❷. The **Braid Hill** ❷❸ – or the Braids, as this boisterous plateau is locally known – is higher still at 675 ft (206 metres), and lies immediately to the south of Blackford. The last three all provide heart-stirring views of Edinburgh's place between the Firth of Forth and the Pentland Hills. ❑

Penguins on Corstorphine Hill.

BELOW: the Pentland Hills rim the city.

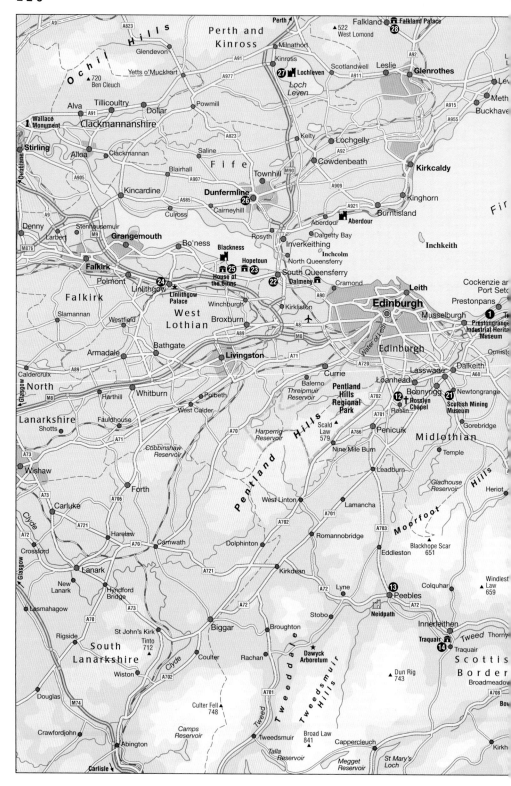

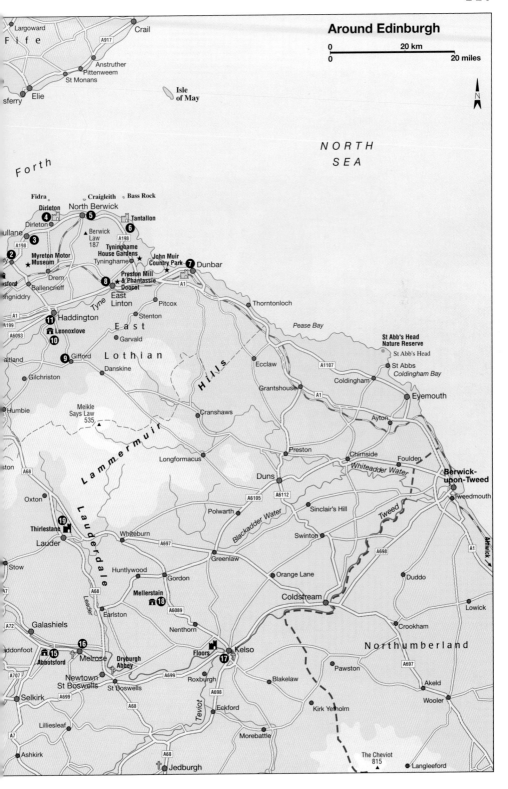

Around Edinburgh

0   20 km
0   20 miles

DAY TRIPS FROM EDINBURGH

This chapter suggests car tours taking in some of the top attractions in the Lothians, Borders and Fife – from abbey ruins to grand houses, and seaside resorts to rolling hills

Map on pages 226–27

T he scale of Scotland allows you to put Edinburgh comfortably in its context. An effortless day's outing from the capital brings you within reach of much of Scotland's past and present and the forces that have shaped the country: its critical topography, its rival clans, its dominant families and ecclesiastical powers and gifted individuals who have left their imprint on the land in castles, great houses, abbeys and museums.

There are plenty of playgrounds, too, within 50 miles (80 km) of the city: the beaches and golf courses of East Lothian, the elegant fishing river of the Tweed, the Lammermuirs, Pentlands and Border hills for riding and hillwalking and the Forth estuary for water sports. It shouldn't be forgotten, either, that Scotland's other great city, Glasgow, is less than an hour away by rail or road. There can be few countries in the world where it is possible to commute so swiftly between competing metropoli, and few neighbouring cities whose characters are so rewardingly different.

PRECEDING PAGES: Tantallon Castle. **LEFT:** pipe band at the Traquair Fair. **BELOW:** Seton Sands, just out of the city.

Pastoral home of golf

East of Edinburgh is the benign and affluent terrain (a county until 1975) of **East Lothian**, which many believe to be the most "English" of Scottish counties. Its rolling farmland is ornamented with pretty, prosperous villages and small towns, Scottish in their red pantiles and crow-step gables but English in their village greens. The reason why, for example, the village of Dirleton has its cottages and inns organised round a green instead of dispersed in the typical Scottish way is unclear; although it may have something to do with the expansion of the Anglian kingdom of Northumbria into southeast Scotland in the 7th century.

East Lothian's northern boundary is the **Firth of Forth**, characterised by a scattering of precipitous, bird-haunted islands and an attractive littoral of bays, beaches and machair – the sandy links which give it some of the best golf courses in the world. The most famous is Muirfield, near the village of Gullane, which takes its turn to host the Open Golf Championship (most recently in July 2002); the oldest is **Musselburgh**, where golf has been played since 1672. (The "Honest Toun" of Musselburgh, now cheek-by-jowl with Edinburgh's eastern suburbs, also has the oldest racecourse in Scotland).

The main route along the Forth coast is the A198, but it's worth making a detour on the B1348 through the industrial fringe of East Lothian (which has produced coal as well as crops) to the **Prestongrange**

The Myreton Motor Museum features old advertisements, signs and petrol pumps, as well as vehicles dating from 1896.

BELOW: the romantic ruin of Dirleton Castle, destroyed by Cromwell.

Industrial Heritage Museum ❶ (open Apr–Oct: daily; free; tel: 0131-653 2904). Sited on a former colliery with 800 years of mining behind it, the museum's relics of mining and other local industries include a Cornish beam engine which pumped water from the mine and a Hoffman kiln. Steam days, when you can travel on a steam train, are held on the first Sunday of the month from April to October. Nearby is **Prestonpans**, now one of a string of moribund mining communities but once (in 1745) the scene of Charles Edward Stuart's most famous victory. An small battle cairn just off the A198 commemorates the Prince's dawn raid on the government forces of General John Cope.

Coastal villages

Soon the drab residue of East Lothian's peripheral industry falls behind and the road continues through a series of picturesque coastal villages to pretty **Aberlady ❷**. On the approach to Aberlady from Longniddry is **Gosford House** (open late June–early Aug: Wed–Sun pm; entrance fee; tel: 01875-870201), home of the Earl of Wemyss. It isn't, perhaps, the most interesting of Scottish stately homes but admirers of the Adam dynasty of celebrated Scottish architects will enjoy the central part of the building, by Robert Adam. At the eastern edge of Aberlady is **Myreton Motor Museum** (open daily Feb–Nov; entrance fee; tel: 01875-870288), with a varied collection of vintage road transport.

Aberlady was once the port of the royal burgh of Haddington, 5 miles (8 km) inland, but there is virtually no trace of its maritime past. The bay where ships once anchored is now, at low tide, a vast mud flat. The next bay, with fine beaches and massive sand dunes, belongs to the village of **Gullane ❸**, which supports five golf courses. When you pass the road-end to Muirfield you will

also come close to bypassing **Dirleton ➍**, which you really should visit. The crowning glory of this exceptionally pretty village is 13th-century **Dirleton Castle** (open daily; Oct–Mar: closed Sun am; entrance fee; tel: 01620-850330), a romantic ruin on a grassy mound within beautiful walled gardens which contain a 17th-century bowling green. The castle was a stronghold of the Ruthven family, who were involved in the murder of Mary Stuart's favourite David Rizzio, and was also attacked by Edward I of England in 1298, during Scotland's Wars of Independence. It survived undiminished until 1650, when Cromwell destroyed it because it was a Royalist stronghold. The ruins are substantial, however, and from the battlements you can see south to the Lammermuirs, the hills that were the setting for Sir Walter Scott's novel *The Bride of Lammermuir*, and north to the hills of Fife. Prominent, too, are East Lothian's isolated volcanic plugs – conical Berwick Law and the whaleback of Traprain Law.

Biarritz of the North

Berwick Law dominates the handsome resort of **North Berwick ➎**, 2 miles (3 km) down the coast. The history of this old burgh, given royal status by Robert III, is not as benevolent as its appearance suggests today. On the rocky promontory which divides its two sandy bays is the ruin of the **Auld Kirk**, which has 12th-century foundations and a 16th-century porch. In 1591 the kirk was the scene of an infamous gathering of witches and wizards who were conspiring to encourage the Devil to cause the death of James VI.

In the 19th century North Berwick became known as the Biarritz of the North, when the coming of the railway gave it new status as a resort and inspired the building of the dignified hotels and guest houses which give the town so much of its charming, unspoiled character today. Although it has few artificial attractions, it nevertheless remains the perfect family resort, and an easy day out for the people of Edinburgh who swarm down the coast on summer weekends.

Its principal activities are the simple, innocent ones of childhood: picnics on the beach, putting and tennis, scrambles on the rocks (the East Bay has a boundary of exciting cliffs) or boat trips to the nature-rich islands of **Fidra**, **Craigleith** and the spectacular **Bass Rock**. Birdwatching has, however, taken on a more sophisticated dimension in North Berwick harbour with the opening in 2000 of the **Scottish Seabird Centre** (open daily; entrance fee; tel: 01620-890202) which, in addition to an exhibition and video on Scottish seabirds, shows live film of gannets and other birds (and seals) relayed from remote cameras set up on Fidra, the Isle of May and Bass Rock. This massive chunk of basalt lies about 1½ miles (2.5 km) out to sea and rises to a height of about 350 ft (105 metres). Although it is now uninhabited (except by seabirds: the gannets number 100,000), it bears traces of early fortifications, and it was put to its most famous use as a prison for Covenanters after 1671 and, later, for Jacobite prisoners who seized their jailers and held the fort for three years until they were pardoned.

There are vestiges of war, too, on the summit of **Berwick Law**, which is a steep but exhilarating climb

Map on pages 226–27

Puffins are among the seabirds that can be seen off the shore at North Berwick.

BELOW:
North Berwick harbour, a popular yachting base.

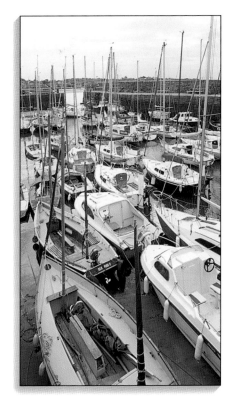

613 ft (187 metres) above the sea and where, on clear days, you can see north and westwards to the outriders of the Highlands. A ruined watchtower dates from Napoleonic times, when the Law was one of a chain of beacons prepared to warn of a French invasion, and an unseemly concrete bunker was put to similar use during World War II. The Law's most original endowment, however, is the arch made from the jaws of a whale, like a giant inverted wishbone, on its top. The venerable beeches on the east side of this attractive pyramid, incidentally, were planted in 1707 to commemorate the Act of Union, when the Scottish and English Parliaments became one.

Ruined castles

Three miles (5 km) east of North Berwick is one of Scotland's most dramatic castles: the clifftop **Tantallon Castle ❻** (open daily; Oct–Mar: closed Thur pm, Fri and Sun am; entrance fee; tel: 01620-892727), defended on three sides by vertiginous drops into the sea and on the fourth by a double moat. This gaunt, ruined sandstone fortress was a stronghold of the Douglases, the powerful Border family, and, although it dates from around 1375, it was never taken until 1651, when it fell to Cromwell's General Monk after 12 days of bombardment.

From Tantallon the A198 swings inland to join the A1 which soon afterwards reaches **Dunbar ❼**, a historic fortress port and royal burgh which is now a holiday resort. Today it promotes itself as the birthplace of the pioneer conservationist John Muir, who emigrated to America at the age of 11 and won himself the title of Father of the National Parks by, among other methods, taking Teddy Roosevelt on camping trips. A strip of coastal land, the **John Muir Country Park**, has been dedicated to his memory and the Muir family home in

The walled coastal town of Berwick-upon-Tweed, 3 miles (5 km) south of the Scotland-England border, has passed several times from one nation to the other and remains Scottish in character. The town's football team, Berwick Rangers, plays in the Scottish League.

BELOW: nesting gulls.

THE NATURE COAST

The siting of the Scottish Seabird Centre in North Berwick focuses the attention of tourists and day-trippers on an attraction of the East Lothian coast that keen birdwatchers have always appreciated. Camera technology and telescopes on the viewing platform of the 21st-century centre offer an easy introduction to observing – traditionally from the rocks or a boat – Scotland's largest colony of gannets on the sheer cliffs of Bass Rock, puffins on Craigleith, kittiwakes, guillemots, fulmars, cormorants, razorbills and several species of gull. Another rewarding location for observing seabirds, and the most important in southeast Scotland for cliff-nesting birds, is the more remote St Abb's Head near the English border.

Coastal nature reserves encompassing a variety of bird and animal habitats include Aberlady Bay, less than 10 miles (16 km) from Edinburgh, and the John Muir Country Park north of Dunbar, both of which are on the route outlined in the main text. At Aberlady a wooden footbridge leads across mud flats and a path continues through grassland and dunes to sandy Gullane beach, where nesting terns are protected. John Muir Park, where paths criss-cross 1,648 acres (667 hectares) along the varied shore and through woodland, is especially rich in overwintering waders.

Dunbar's 17th-century High Street is a small museum (John Muir Birthplace, 126–128 High Street; open Mon–Sun all year; free; closed for redevelopment until April 2003; tel: 01368 863353).

Only fragments remain of **Dunbar Castle**, which was defended by one of Scotland's most heart-stirring heroines, "Black Agnes", Countess of Dunbar. She held the stronghold by the harbour against the English for six weeks in 1339 (during Scotland's Wars of Independence) until it was relieved. The castle was also associated with Mary, Queen of Scots, who fled there with the duplicitous Darnley after the murder of Rizzio, and who later appointed her lover, the Earl of Bothwell, its governor. Her hostile half-brother, the Earl of Murray, razed it to the ground after Mary's defeat by her own nobles at Carberry Hill, and in 1650 Cromwell finished it off by using its stones to improve the harbour.

Inland attractions

Dunbar makes a good turning point for a journey back to Edinburgh via the A1 and its tributaries, giving you a chance to visit the quiet rural treasures of East Lothian's interior. For example, on the outskirts of the attractive village of **East Linton ❽** are picturesque **Preston Mill** on the River Tyne and, nearby, the **Phantassie Doocot** (B1407; both open Apr–Oct: Thur–Mon pm; entrance fee; tel: 01620-860426). The first is one of the oldest watermills still functional in Scotland, and the second is a beehive building which once gave house-room to 544 doves.

Of the county's inland villages, Stenton and Gifford (both on the B6370 south of the A1) are probably the most attractive and interesting. Like so many places of notoriety, **Stenton**'s appearance quite belies the sinister reputation it once had

Map on pages 226–27

TIP

A bit of action in East Lothian's quiet interior is provided by the Museum of Flight, at East Fortune airfield near East Linton (open daily; entrance fee; tel: 01620-880308), where aircraft chart the history of aviation and children go free.

BELOW: 18th-century Preston Mill in an idyllic rural spot.

The great Protestant reformer John Knox was from Haddington, where his name lives on in the Knox Academy.

for a particular enthusiasm for the burning of witches. Today it is a conservation area and the village green has a relic of more homely activities; its Wool Stone, or tron, was used for weighing wool at the wool fair. **Gifford** ❾ was the birthplace of the Reverend John Witherspoon, one of the signatories to the American Declaration of Independence and the first president of what is now Princeton University. It has two characterful inns and a pleasant walk beside a stream to the gates of **Yester House**, round which the village was neatly assembled in the 17th and 18th centuries.

The area's most distinguished grand home, situated on the road from Gifford to Haddington, is **Lennoxlove House** ❿ (guided tours Easter–Oct: Wed, Thur, Sun and some Sats, 2–4.30pm; entrance fee; tel: 01620-823720), the seat of the Duke and Duchess of Hamilton (since 1946). It was named after Frances Stewart, Duchess of Lennox, who in the 17th century was the model for the figure of Britannia used on Britain's coinage. Known as "La Belle Stewart", she was passionately but vainly pursued by Charles II. Lennoxlove House has a room devoted to Mary, Queen of Scots and contains her death mask and a French silver casket given to her by her first husband, Francis II of France.

Ancient market town

Lennoxlove is a stone's throw from **Haddington** ⓫, a fertile hunting ground for antiquarians. Its central streets still contain many of the buildings and still follow the design laid out between the 17th and 19th centuries. However, Haddington dates back to at least the 12th century when it was made a royal burgh by David I, and, although burned and occupied by the English several times since, it has long guarded its status as East Lothian's market town and administrative centre.

BELOW: the old rural way of life (inside Preston Mill).

Map on pages 226–27

Worth seeing is the 13th-century **St Mary's** church (on Sidegate), which contains the tomb of a famous daughter of Haddington – Jane Welsh, the wife of Thomas Carlyle, whose childhood home has been turned into a museum (2 Lodge Street; open Apr–Sept: Wed–Sat pm; entrance fee); and **St Mary's Pleasance**, the garden of Haddington House near the church (open daily; free), restored as a 17th-century garden. Haddington is closely bypassed by the A1, and its fast access to Edinburgh 17 miles (25 km) away has made it a favourite settlement of commuters. But the conservationists of East Lothian have preserved its essential character.

The Borders

The **Borders** region is a tourist centre in itself. It would be impossible to do justice to all its attractions in a day trip from Edinburgh, but it is easy enough to visit some of the principal ones: the great abbeys of Kelso, Jedburgh, Dryburgh and Melrose, Abbotsford (the home of Sir Walter Scott) and – for compulsive consumers – the woollen and tweed mills of the River Tweed, many of which have shops selling knitwear and cloth at bargain prices.

Rich sheep pasture and soft water from its famous fishing rivers give rise to conditions which once made the Borders prosper as a centre for producing quality textiles. However, today's economic conditions and overseas competition have not favoured the traditional practices of the mills in towns like Galashiels and Hawick. Tweed, peculiarly, takes its name only accidentally from the **River Tweed**. The Border weavers called their fabric "tweel", their dialect for twill, and a London merchant jumped to the wrong conclusion. Scenically, the Borders lack the drama of the Highlands, but have a distinctive beauty which is

The use of Border tweed by top dress designers such as Vivienne Westwood has made the woven fabric fashionable.

BELOW: ancient St Mary's Church in Haddington.

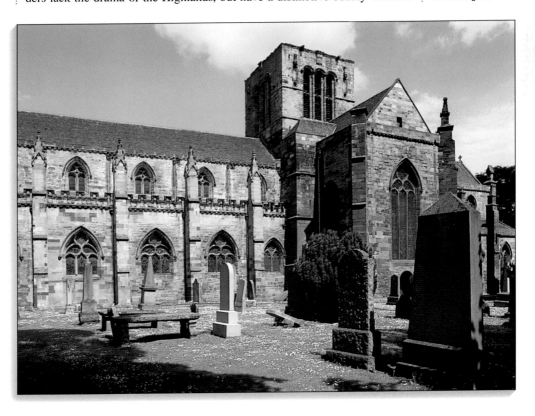

TIP

The Lochcarron of Scotland Cashmere and Wool Centre in Galashiels has a retail outlet and museum (open Mon–Sat all year and Sun pm June–Oct; free). Tours of the mill take place Mon–Fri at 10.30am, 11.30am, 1.30pm and 2.30pm).

BELOW: the Apprentice Pillar, Rosslyn Chapel.
RIGHT: bridge over the Tweed at Peebles.

more pastoral, less challenging. Border hills, some over 2,000 ft (610 metres), are shapely and rounded, rising from river valleys of natural woodland and increasingly planted with conifers. But there is still plenty of bare, lonely upland – moors and hills so desolate that it's difficult to appreciate those territorial imperatives which made this region so furiously contested. It is saturated – some might say stained – with the history of Scotland's old hostilities with England, and with the blood of its own feuding families. Its shattered castles, dismembered abbeys and spectacular local pageants – the Common Ridings which recall the days of *rievers* (freebooters) and moss-troopers – are today's testament to that savage past.

Touring the Borders

There are three main routes to the heartland of the Borders from Edinburgh: the A68 through Scott Country to Jedburgh, the A7 to Galashiels and Selkirk, and the A703 to the comely town of Peebles and the upper Tweed valley. There is always some argument as to whether Peebles is truly a Border town: it's only 23 miles (37 km) from Edinburgh and is certainly the region's most westerly outpost. But its substantial charm and striking setting on the Tweed make it a durable favourite with excursionists from Edinburgh.

For travellers with their own cars, it is possible to enjoy a comfortable and picturesque circular day trip down the A703 to Peebles and along the A72 through the broadening Tweed valley to Scott Country, that area which surrounds Abbotsford and the town of Melrose (by far the prettiest of Border towns), and return either via Lauder on the A68 or via Galashiels on the A7, taking in the lauded Scottish Mining Museum on the return through Midlothian. This, in the

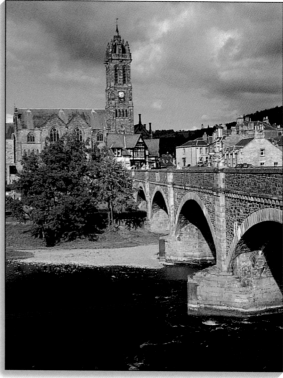

space of a full day, would give you the best possible introduction to the Borders and, although it's not suggested that you would have time to visit all the following places, they lie either on this route or within easy striking distance of it.

Map on pages 226–27

Pieces of antiquity

As you leave Edinburgh to travel south on the A703 (and A701) you should look for the signposts to **Rosslyn Chapel** ⑫ (open Mon–Sat and Sun pm; entrance fee; tel: 0131-440 2159), which lies to the east of the A701 beyond Roslin village, just a couple of miles (3 km) south of the city bypass. Within this small, 15th-century chapel (the burial place of the Sinclair family) is the most elaborate stone carving in Scotland, if not in Britain. The Seven Deadly Sins, the Seven Cardinal Virtues and a dance of death are extravagantly represented in bas-relief, but folk interest tends to focus on the Apprentice Pillar with its intricate and abundant flowers and foliage and on the numerous Green Men.

The story of the Apprentice Pillar has never been authenticated, but it's supposed to have been carved by an apprentice while his master was away. The work was so fine that when the master returned he flew into a jealous rage and killed the apprentice. Three carved heads at the end of the nave are alleged to depict the unfortunate youth, his grief-stricken mother and his master.

Entering the Borders from Midlothian, continue straight on at Leadburn, towards **Peebles** ⑬. A short riverside walk west from Peebles town centre takes you to **Neidpath Castle** (open Easter–Sept: Mon–Sat and Sun pm; entrance fee; tel: 01721-720333), a dour but well-preserved fortress on an eminence above the Tweed. It belonged first to the Frasers and then the Hays and was built between the 13th and 15th centuries. Like almost every other fortress in this re-

BELOW: inside Traquair House, one of the most interesting of the Border family seats.

gion, it was besieged by Cromwell. More can be seen at **Traquair House** (open Apr–Oct: daily pm, from 10.30am June–Aug; entrance fee; tel: 01896-830323), which claims to have been continuously inhabited since the 10th century. This mellow piece of antiquity lies across the river from **Innerleithen** (the village is on your A72 route from Peebles to Galashiels) and was a residence of William the Lion. Another 27 Scottish and English monarchs are said to have paid a visit, and when Bonnie Prince Charlie departed through its Bear Gates it was commanded that they remain closed until a Stuart regained the throne. They are, of course, still closed. Today, Traquair makes ale in its 18th-century brewhouse and welcomes visitors to its maze, craft workshops and summer fair, as well as the house itself.

Romantic museum

The mill town of **Galashiels** is the gateway to Scott Country and, being the least attractive of Border towns, a gateway that is best hurried through. You will find **Abbotsford House** (open late Mar–Oct: daily; Mar–May and Oct: closed Sun am; entrance fee; tel: 01896-752043) in parkland accessed from the B6360 off the A7, some 3 miles (5 km) out of the town, and find, too, that its mock baronial aspirations are everything you might expect from the romantic imagination of the man who invented the historical novel *(see page 69)*.

Abbotsford was very much Sir Walter Scott's own creation. He bought the farm in 1811 and in 1822 demolished the old farmhouse to build the main block which, today, is a museum to the Wizard of the North and his collection of curiosities. (He somehow acquired Napoleon's cloak-clasp, Rob Roy's purse, Burns's drinking glass and a lock of Bonnie Prince Charlie's hair.)

TIP

Adjoining the Traquair House Brewery, which produces three rich, dark ales, the Malt Loft contains an ale shop and a museum tracing the history of brewing on the premises.

BELOW:
the fanciful decor of Abbotsford House reflects the tastes of Sir Walter Scott.

Within sight of the house are the graceful triple peaks of the **Eildon Hills**, where Scott loved to walk, and where legend claims that King Arthur and his knights lie buried and Thomas the Rhymer was given his powers of prophecy by the Faerie Queen. Below the hills is the little town of **Melrose** ⓰, distinguished for the 12th-century Cistercian **Melrose Abbey** (open daily; Oct–Mar: closed Sun am; entrance fee; tel: 01896-822562), which was ruined by a combination of English invasion, religious reform and plundering of building materials. But much remains, including parts of the nave and choir which incorporate some of the best stone carving of their period.

From Melrose the ambitious collector of stones can strike out for all the Border abbeys, which lie within a few miles' drive of each other: **Dryburgh Abbey** (5 miles/8 km southeast of Melrose on the B6404; open daily; Oct–Mar: closed Sun am; entrance fee; tel: 01835-822381), with its remarkably complete cloister buildings; impressive **Jedburgh Abbey** (in the town 12 miles/20 km to the south on the A68; open daily; Oct–Mar: closed Sun am; entrance fee; tel: 01835-863925), founded by David I; and fragmentary remains of **Kelso Abbey** (near the town centre; open all year; free), one of the earliest completed by David I. Kelso was garrisoned as a fortress and, when the English Earl of Hertford entered the town in 1545, its garrison of 100 men (including 12 monks) was put to the sword and the abbey destroyed.

Adam masterpieces

Kelso ⓱, with its large and lovely Georgian square, is a market town and, like Melrose, the better for having no mills. It stands at the confluence of the Teviot and Tweed rivers about 12 miles (20 km) east of Melrose, and has long

Map on pages 226–27

Melrose Abbey is popularly believed to be the burial place of Robert the Bruce, who died in 1329.

BELOW: the ruins of Kelso Abbey.

THE BORDER ABBEYS

Scotland, especially the Borders, is full of abbeys that now lie ruined but were once powerful institutions with impressive buildings. During the reign of David I (1124–53), who revitalised and transformed the Scottish Church, more than 20 religious houses were founded. Outstanding among these is the quartet of Border abbeys: Dryburgh (Premonstatensian), Jedburgh (Augustinian), Kelso (Tironensian) and Melrose (Cistercian). All have evocative ruins, though perhaps it is Jedburgh, with tower and remarkable rose window still intact, which is Scotland's classic abbey.

It was not the Reformation of 1560 that caused damage to these abbeys but rather the selfishness of pre-Reformation clergy, raids in the 14th to 16th centuries by both English and Scots, the ravages of weather and activities of 19th-century restorers. The concern of the Reformation, spearheaded by firebrand John Knox, was to preserve, not to destroy, the churches the new religion needed. Monasteries continued to exist as landed corporations after the Reformation. Why upset a system that suited so many interests? After all, the Pope, at James V's request, had provided priories and abbeys for five of the King's bastard children to make their livings.

Floors Castle is the largest inhabited castle in Scotland, and was used as a location for the Hollywood film "Greystoke".

been associated with the Dukes of Roxburgh. Their family seat, **Floors Castle** (open Apr–Oct: daily; entrance fee; tel: 01573-223333) is just outside the town on the A6089. The castle was begun by William Adam around 1721 and given most of its present aspect by William Playfair in 1849. James II was killed in the grounds in 1460, when a cannon suddenly exploded.

The great architectural glory of the Borders, however, is **Mellerstain House ⓲** (open Easter and May–Sept: daily pm except Sat; Oct: Sat and Sun pm; entrance fee; tel: 01573-410225), which you can also reach by the A6089 from Kelso. Mellerstain is one of the finest achievements of Scotland's celebrated dynasty of architects, the Adam family. It was begun in 1725 by William Adam, who built both wings, and completed by his son Robert in 1778. Between them they created what many believe to be the loveliest 18th-century mansion in Scotland, and today it contains work by other distinguished names from the 18th and 19th centuries: furniture by Chippendale, Sheraton and Hepplewhite and paintings by Gainsborough, Constable and Veronese. From Mellerstain you can rejoin the A68 via minor roads for your return to Edinburgh or stop off at the home of the Maitland family, **Thirlestane Castle ⓳**, near Lauder (open Apr–Oct: daily except Sat; entrance fee; tel: 01578-722430) and view its sumptuous state rooms. The weary will enjoy, instead, the moment when the A68 breasts Soutra Hill on the western slopes of the Lammermuirs to open up a panorama of Edinburgh and the Firth of Forth.

Paintings and coal

The winding A7, parallel to the A68, offers alternative points of interest, though it's less thick with stately homes. Three miles (5 km) west of the Border town of

Selkirk, south of Galashiels, is the home of the Scotts of Buccleuch, **Bowhill House** ⓴ (open in July only: daily pm; entrance fee; tel: 01750-22204). Art lovers who are visiting the region during its short opening season will be interested to know that it is one of the Borders' finest "art galleries" – along with Mellerstain – with paintings by Van Dyck, Reynolds, Gainsborough, Canaletto and Raeburn. (The country park in which it stands, with woodland walks, is open as the house plus late Apr–Aug, daily except Fri, for a reduced entrance fee.)

On the last stretch of the A7 before it reaches the Edinburgh bypass is a rather less genteel but fascinating museum, well worth visiting either on a day out of Edinburgh or as the main focus of a shorter trip. The **Scottish Mining Museum** ㉑ (open daily; entrance fee; tel: 0131-663 7519), in the preserved small mining town of **Newtongrange**, offers lively tours of the Lady Victoria Colliery (which closed as a working mine in 1981) led by former miners. Five million pounds were pumped into the museum in the late 1990s to introduce interactive attractions including remote-controlled "magic helmets" and a "virtual" coalface, but it's still an authentic experience.

On the Forth

For citizens of Edinburgh there is some peculiar, psychological imperative to go east or south, rather than west or north, on days out from the city. Perhaps they feel the hinterland to the east and south is more truly theirs; whereas to the west, another city (Glasgow) begins to impose its identity on the land, and to the north there is the barrier of the Forth estuary. Crossing the Forth Road Bridge, on which tolls are payable (for those heading north only), tends to represent a necessary journey rather than a carefree jaunt. Yet among the most

Map on pages 226–27

Every June Selkirk hosts the oldest and largest of the Common Ridings festivals traditional in the Borders. During this time horse riders ritually check the boundaries of the town's land, as in medieval times.

LEFT: Sir Walter Scott towers over Selkirk, where he was Sheriff.
BELOW: sheep jam in the Borders.

Hawes Inn in South Queensferry was the scene of David Balfour's abduction in Robert Louis Stevenson's classic novel "Kidnapped".

BELOW: Hopetoun House, completed by William Adam.

popular coach tours from Edinburgh are day trips along the M9 to Stirling and beyond – the Trossachs and Loch Lomond – to give people a taste of the Highlands; or across the Forth to the Fife coast, following it as far as St Andrews. We shall not be so ambitious.

There is plenty of interest and appeal in the lower Forth valley and enough to preoccupy the visitor to Fife without driving more than an hour from Edinburgh city centre (there are also good train services to some of these places). Begin with the bridges themselves, and the ancient ferry crossing of **South Queensferry** ㉒ which now huddles beneath them. The two giant bridges provide spectacular contrast in engineering design: the massive humped girders of the **Forth Rail Bridge**, opened in 1890, and the delicate arch of the suspension bridge (**Forth Road Bridge**), opened in 1964.

During the season there are boat trips from the village to the island of **Inchcolm** with its ruin of St Colm's Abbey, which gets a mention in Shakespeare's *Macbeth*. (The *Maid of the Forth* departs from Hawes Pier under the rail bridge up to three times daily in summer and at weekends mid-Apr–June and early Oct; tel: 0131-331 4857.) The abbey was first a priory founded for Augustinians in 1123 by a grateful Alexander I, who was shipwrecked on the island and helped by the resident hermit.

Fine homes

On the south shores of the Forth, on either side of the bridges, are the homes of two of Scotland's noble families. To the east is **Dalmeny House** (open July and Aug: Sun–Tues pm; entrance fee; tel: 0131-331 1888), built in 1815 and home to the Earls of Rosebery. The fifth earl married the richest heiress in Eng-

land, became prime minister in 1894 and saddled three Derby winners. He was an expert on Napoleon, and memorabilia of the dictator fills the Napoleon Room. Also of note are tapestries from Goya cartoons, portraits by Reynolds, Gainsborough and Raeburn, and 18th-century furniture.

To the west is **Hopetoun House** ❷ (open Apr–Sept: daily; entrance fee; tel: 0131-331 2451), home to the earls of that name. This glorious Adam building was begun by William Bruce in 1699 and completed by William Adam and his sons, and contains paintings by Gainsborough, Canaletto and Raeburn. Magnificent views of the Forth bridges can be enjoyed from the rooftop. The large, delightful grounds are full of rare specimen trees. Other pockets of prettiness in **West Lothian** exist but require perseverance. Unlike its counterpart in the east this Lothian becomes more industrial the farther you travel from Edinburgh, and only a few miles upriver from the Dalmeny and Hopetoun estates is the oil terminal and petro-chemical plant of **Grangemouth**. The plant's flare stacks punctuate views across the flat basin of the Forth like fiery exclamation marks.

Royal burgh and palace

However, between Edinburgh and Grangemouth, speedily reached by the M9, is one of Scotland's oldest towns, home to the well-preserved ruins of its most magnificent palace. **Linlithgow** ❷ received its charter from David I and the town was probably a significant royal residence from then on. **Linlithgow Palace** (open daily; Oct–Mar: closed Sun am; entrance fee; tel: 01506-842896), set beside a loch, was built by James I in the 15th century and was the scene of some key events in Scottish history. In 1513 Queen Margaret, unknowingly a widow, waited here for the return of her husband James IV from the disastrous

Map on pages 226–27

TIP

As well as making trips to Inchcolm Island, the *Maid of the Forth* operates summer sealife cruises around the islands of the Forth, looking for seals, dolphins, minke whales and seabirds; also evening jazz cruises (Fri and Sat).

BELOW: inside Hopetoun House.

Battle of Flodden, in which the king and most of the Scottish nobility were killed by the English. Mary, Queen of Scots was born here in 1542, while her father, James V, lay dying across the Forth in Falkland Palace, and a few years later Linlithgow was host to Edinburgh University, whose scholars had fled the city for fear of the plague. Charles I was the last monarch to sleep in the palace while he contemplated making Linlithgow his Scottish capital, and between 1651 and 1659 the town was garrisoned by Cromwell.

Neglect and fire – the building was gutted when it was occupied by soldiers of the Duke of Cumberland in the aftermath of the 1745 Jacobite rebellion – have destroyed the roof and interiors, but the shell of the palace is intact. Together with its large inner courtyard, containing an elaborate fountain, it gives an impressive idea of the scale and elegance of this fortified palace and the considerable style in which Scotland's monarchs lived. (The fountain was a wedding present from James V to Mary of Guise and was said to have overflowed with wine on the day of their marriage.)

Alongside the palace, and topped with a controversial "crown of thorns" spire which was lowered by helicopter in 1964, is the ancient, mainly 15th-century **St Michael's** church (open daily in summer; Oct–Mar: closed weekends), the largest pre-Reformation church in Scotland. Spare a thought for James IV, who saw an apparition in the south transept which warned of his doom at Flodden. The church and the palace can be glimpsed by motorists on the M9.

Dark histories

From the M9 above Linlithgow you can also thread your way down to the Forth River again and the promontory which supports **Blackness Castle** (open

BELOW:
Linlithgow Palace, where Mary, Queen of Scots was born.

Map
on pages
226–27

Apr–Sept: daily; Oct–Mar: closed Thur pm, Fri and Sun am; entrance fee; tel: 01506-834807) – a 15th-century fortress which juts out into the Forth like the bow of a great stone ship and which, for a while, was one of Scotland's most dramatic youth hostels. Blackness was one of the four important Scottish castles which, under the terms of the Act of Union in 1707, was permitted to maintain its fortifications. It was used as a state prison in Covenanting times and as a powder magazine in the 1870s, and today is just a public relic.

The nearby **House of the Binns** ㉕ (open May–Sept: daily pm except Fri; entrance fee; tel: 01506-834255), however – which contains portraits, period furniture and porcelain – is still occupied by the Dalyell family, whose most famous ancestor was "General Tam" Dalyell. (The name is pronounced *Dee-ell*, and the present Tam Dalyell is a Labour Member of Parliament.) During the Civil War General Tam was a staunch Royalist who was captured at Worcester but escaped from the Tower of London to serve the Tsar in Russia until summoned home by Charles II. He then became a scourge of the Covenanters, who were doubtless responsible for the story that, on his death, his body was carried off by the Devil.

The Kingdom of Fife

To venture across one of the great bridges into **Fife** is indeed to enter a new kingdom. (The stubborn, prickly Fifers fought a successful action to hang on to their region's ancient title when Scotland's old shires were reorganised into new administrative units.) A whole chapter could be written on Fife: its meandering coast and pastoral interior, clasped between the estuaries of Forth and Tay, its attractive fishing villages and old mining communities. The elegant and

BELOW: guarding the fortress, Blackness Castle.

Tour guides at Falkland Palace will explain the rules of "royal" (or real) tennis, the game of kings played on the court here since 1539.

BELOW: the old fishing village of Crail in Fife.

venerable university town of St Andrews, with its famous golf courses, is in Fife, and so – by way of contrast – is Kirkcaldy, which to Scots will always be associated with making linoleum. Two or three destinations in Fife are readily reached from Edinburgh by the M90, which cuts through the region on its way to Perth. Each gives some idea of the versatility of this highly individual region and its significance in Scotland's history.

The town of **Dunfermline** ㉖ has been a royal burgh since at least the 11th century, and, although Fife's more recent industrial history has put its imprint on it, Dunfermline's **Abbey**, **Monastery** and **Palace** ruins (complex open Apr–Sept: daily; Oct–Mar: closed Thur pm, Fri and Sun am; entrance fee; tel: 01383-739026) have close links with the nation's monarchs. Robert the Bruce is buried below the pulpit of the Abbey Church (closed in winter). The choir of this 12th-century church was rebuilt in 1818, when Bruce's body was found wrapped in a shroud of embroidered gold and encased in lead. Little is left of the Palace of Dunfermline, but it was occupied by Mary, Queen of Scots in 1561 and was the birthplace of a succession of monarchs, including Alexander I, David I and David II, James I and the children of James VI of Scotland and I of England, including the future Queen of Bohemia and Charles I.

Dunfermline is also celebrated as the birthplace of Andrew Carnegie, the industrial tycoon who made his fortune in the steel and iron mills of Pennsylvania and then gave much of it away in philanthropic gifts. Dunfermline wasn't forgotten (it owes its swimming pool, library and public park to Carnegie, as well as an annual festival of music and drama) and Dunfermline has not forgotten the boy who spent his youth there before his family emigrated to America. Their modest house has been transformed into the

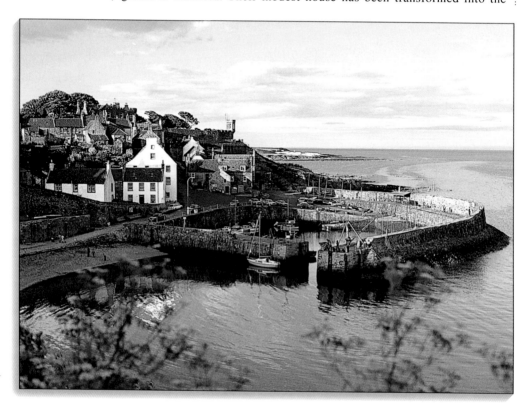

Map on pages 226–27

Andrew Carnegie Birthplace Museum (open Apr–Oct: Mon–Sat and Sun pm; entrance fee; tel: 01383-724302).

Stuart prison and home

Two places in Fife are irrevocably associated with the Stuart dynasty: **Lochleven Castle ㉗** (open Apr–Sept: daily; entrance fee; tel: 07778-040483), on an island on the loch reached by ferry from Kinross, from which Mary, Queen of Scots made a romantic escape, only to be defeated at the Battle of Langside and forced to seek the inhospitable protection of her English cousin Elizabeth I; and the favourite royal residence of **Falkland Palace ㉘** (open Mar–Oct: Mon–Sat and Sun pm; entrance fee; tel: 01337-857397), built by James IV and embellished by James V, Mary's father, who died there as his daughter was born with the resigned words: "God's will be done. It cam' wi' a lass and it'll gang (go) wi' a lass."

The dying king feared for the Stuart line, which was established through marriage to the daughter of Robert the Bruce. In fact Mary's son, James VI of Scotland and I of England, would become the first king to rule over both countries. The Renaissance palace complex contains the beautiful Chapel Royal and is surrounded by lovely gardens.

Loch Leven, by the town of **Kinross**, and Falkland, in the shadow of the **Lomond Hills**, lie within a few miles of each other (take the A91 east from just north of Kinross, then the A912 to reach the palace). The grim little island fortress where Mary suffered and the pretty Renaissance palace which she loved as much as her father did represent extremes of fortune for the Stuarts. They make a fitting "double" for pilgrims fascinated by their story. ❑

BELOW: the gardens of Falkland Palace, a favourite retreat of the Stuarts.

INSIGHT GUIDES

TRAVEL TIPS

Insight FlexiMaps

Maps in Insight Guides are tailored to complement the text. But when you're on the road you sometimes need the big picture that only a large-scale map can provide. This new range of durable Insight Fleximaps has been designed to meet just that need.

Detailed, clear cartography
makes the comprehensive route and city maps easy to follow, highlights all the major tourist sites and provides valuable motoring information plus a full index.

Informative and easy to use
with additional text and photographs covering a destination's top 10 essential sites, plus useful addresses, facts about the destination and handy tips on getting around.

Laminated finish
allows you to mark your route on the map using a non-permanent marker pen, and wipe it off. It makes the maps more durable and easier to fold than traditional maps.

The world's most popular destinations
are covered by the 125 titles in the series – and new destinations are being added all the time. They include Alaska, Amsterdam, Bangkok, Barbados, Beijing, Brussels, Dallas/Fort Worth, Florence, Hong Kong, Ireland, Madrid, New York, Orlando, Peru, Prague, Rio, Rome, San Francisco, Sydney, Thailand, Turkey, Venice, and Vienna.

INSIGHT GUIDES
The world's largest collection of visual travel guides

CONTENTS

Getting Acquainted

The Place

Edinburgh is the capital of Scotland, a country of 30,405 sq. miles (78,772 sq. metres), which is constitutionally part of the United Kingdom but self-governing in domestic affairs.

Location: Situated between the Pentland Hills, which rise to 1,898 ft (578 metres), and the south coast of the Firth of Forth, Edinburgh is at 55°57N 3°13W.

Geography: Notable for its hills and bridges, the city can count five extinct volcanoes within its limits. The most commanding is Arthur's Seat (823 ft/251 metres) which, surrounded by Holyrood Park, creates an unexpected sense of open country within the city.

Population: Approximately 450,000.

Religion: Christian (Presbyterian, other Protestant denominations, Roman Catholic). The majority adheres to the Presbyterian Church of Scotland which has a Calvinistic ethos valuing hard work and independent thinking.

Time zone: Greenwich Mean Time (GMT) and British Summer Time.

Currency: Scotland has the same currency, the pound sterling (£), as the rest of the UK.

Weights and measures: Britain is only half way to accepting the metric system: foods and packaged goods are sold in grammes (a change that has only recently been fully implemented and that older people find difficult); beer comes in pints and half pints; road signs give distances in miles, but petrol is sold in litres.

Electricity: 240 volts is standard. Hotels will usually have dual 110/240 volts sockets for razors.

International dialling code: To call Edinburgh from overseas, dial the local number for an international line, followed by 44 for the UK, 131 for Edinburgh, then the seven digit telephone number. From Edinburgh, dial 00 for an international line.

Government

Scotland was governed as a region of the United Kingdom from the 1707 Act of Union with England until 1999, when it gained home rule. In a referendum in 1997 the Scots voted for the restoration of their own parliament, which convened for the first time on 12 May 1999 in the Assembly Hall, The Mound, Edinburgh. The Parliament is due to move to purpose-built premises at Holyrood in mid-2003. The system of proportional representation used in the election resulted in a coalition government between Labour and the Liberal Democrats plus a slight revival in the fortunes of the Conservatives. The next elections to the Parliament should take place in mid-2003.

While Scotland continues to be governed from Westminster, London, in matters such as defence, and has representatives in the UK Parliament, debate over the viability of Scottish MPs (Members of the UK Parliament) having a say in English affairs while English MPs have no influence over the Scottish Parliament (the so-called West Lothian Question). One potential outcome could be the Scottish National Party's goal of full independence for Scotland.

The **Scottish Parliament Visitor Centre** (corner of the High Street/ George IV Bridge; tel: 0131-348 5000; www.scottish.parliament.uk) gives some insight into the workings of the Parliament. Open 9am–5pm Mon–Fri (sometimes at weekends during the Festival). To book to visit the Parliament in session, tel: 348 5411.

Local government of Edinburgh is by two elected councils: Lothian Regional Council and Edinburgh City Council. Local elections are held every four years. Both the City Chambers and the Regional Chambers are on the Royal Mile. The Region is responsible for education, planning, transport, the police and fire services throughout Lothian Region; the City for housing, recreational facilities and sanitation within the city.

Economy

Traditionally, Edinburgh's economy was based on beer, biscuits and books. Brewing on a large scale continues, but takeovers have brought closures and redundancies. Printing and publishing still exist, but the biscuit manufacturers have moved out of town. As in the rest of Scotland, traditional heavy industry has seriously declined, recent casualties being the closure of the last deep mine (at Longannet on

Climate

Who dares generalise about Edinburgh weather?

In late May and June there may be a spell of glorious sunshine so that everyone forecasts a marvellous summer. In July it rains, especially at weekends. In August God tosses a coin to decide whether to drown the Festival. In September and October blue skies and biting winds confuse everyone. The rest of the year it is cold.

For those who trust figures, the coldest months are January and February with average daily temperatures ranging from 1°C (34°F) to 6°C (42°F). August is the warmest month, reaching an average high of 18°C (64°F).

Keen winds and rain make warm clothing and sturdy umbrellas a must at any time of year. Formal dress is seldom de rigueur, even in swanky hotels or the dress circle of the theatre.

the Forth) and of the last engineering works at Leith Docks. The new big employers are finance and tourism.

Within Europe, Edinburgh's financial centre now ranks fourth in importance after London, Paris and Frankfurt. The financial institutions deal mainly in investment and unit trusts.

Tourism in Edinburgh is growing and is evident year-round, from the summer Festival to the ever-growing New Year (Hogmanay) celebrations. The establishment of the Scottish Parliament in Edinburgh has further contributed to a property and business boom in the city.

As the Scottish centre of medicine, law and banking, Edinburgh boasts a prominent professional class, its most picturesque manifestation being the robed and wigged advocates who emerge at lunchtime from the courts on the High Street.

Business Hours

Most offices are open Monday–Friday 9am–5 or 5.30pm, and may well be closed between 1 and 2pm. Banks stay open at lunchtimes but tend to close slightly earlier in the evening. Building societies, but not normally banks, also open on Saturday mornings. See also *Shopping Hours* in the *Shopping* section.

Public Holidays

In addition to the major British public holidays, which are 1 and 2 January, Good Friday, Easter Monday, and 25 and 26 December, **Scottish national holidays** are: May Day (first Monday in May); Spring Holiday (Monday in late May); and Summer Holiday (first Monday in August).

In Edinburgh, there are additional **local holidays** (not universally taken): Edinburgh Spring Holiday (third Monday in April), Victoria Day (third Monday in May) and Edinburgh Autumn Holiday (third Monday in September).

Planning the Trip

When to Go

Summer is the generally preferred time to visit to coincide with milder weather. See also the *Festivals* section in these Tips. During Festival time in August the city centre gets very crowded.

Entry Regulations

Enquiries about passports and visas should be made to the relevant embassy – see *Practical Tips*. Visitors to the UK may only bring in the Customs Allowances of alcoholic drinks, tobacco and perfume. The limits for duty-paid good for travellers within the EU are 800 cigarettes or 1kg tobacco, 10 litres of spirits, 20 litres of fortified wine, 90 litres of wine and 110 litres of beer. Visitors from non-EU countries can import 200 cigarettes or 250g tobacco, 2 litres of wine and either 2 litres of fortified wine or 1 litre of spirits.

For further information contact the Customs and Excise National Advice Service on 0845-010 9000 (0208-929 0152 if calling from outside the UK), www.hmce.gov.uk.

Animal Quarantine

Birds and mammals will normally be quarantined for six months. Details of the regulations about bringing animals into and out of the UK and a full list of quarantine kennels are available from www.defra.gov.uk/animalh/quarantine. The average cost of keeping a dog in kennels is £200 a month. In Europe, the Pet Travel Scheme (PETS) allows pet dogs and cats from certain countries to enter the UK without quarantine as long as they meet certain criteria. See the 'defra' website for details.

Health

Ezra Pound is reported to have said of Edinburgh: "Most of the denizens wheeze, sniffle, and exude a sort of snozzling whnoff whnoff, apparently through a hydrophile sponge." Apart from the common cold, the only unpleasant contagious disease prevalent in Edinburgh is Aids. European Union countries have a reciprocal agreement for free medical care, but medical insurance is advisable. Everyone will receive free emergency treatment at a hospital casualty department.

Tourist Information

Edinburgh and Scotland Information Centre, 3 Princes Street (on top of Princes Mall shopping centre), tel: 0131-473 3800, esic@eltb.org, www.edinburgh.org. Extensive information on Edinburgh. Also provides accommodation services, transport and events ticket sales, and an exchange bureau. A useful shop sells maps and guidebooks. Open May–Sep: Mon–Sat 9am–7pm, Sun 10am–7pm (closes 8pm July/Aug), Oct–Apr: Mon–Wed 9am–5pm, Thur–Sat, 9am–6pm, Sun 10am–5pm.
VisitScotland, 23 Ravelston Terrace, EH4 3TP, tel: 0131-332 2433, info@visitscotland.com, www.visitscotland.com. The former Scottish Tourist Board, provides information on all areas of Scotland.

Money Matters

The British pound is divided into 100 pence. The coins used are 1p, 2p, 5p, 10p, 20p, 50p, and £1. However, although the £1 coin is widely used, £1 notes issued by the

Special Needs

Children

An excellent publication, *Edinburgh for the Under-Fives* (£5.95), published by the National Childbirth Trust, provides a lot of ideas for desperate parents. Available at most bookshops. (ISBN 0951239775).

Lesbian, Gay and Bisexual

- Lothian Gay and Lesbian Switchboard, tel: 0131-556 4049 (7.30–10pm daily)
- Edinburgh Lesbian Line, tel: 0131-557 0751 (7.30–10pm Monday and Thursday)
- Edinburgh Lesbian, Gay and Bisexual Centre, 58a–60 Broughton Street, tel: 0131-478 7069
- Edinburgh Bisexual Group, www.egroups.com/group/edinburghbisexuals

Disabled

- UPDATE, 27 Beaverhall Road, tel: 0131-558 5200, Scotland's national disability information service
- Grapevine, tel: 0131-475 2370, for venue and transport accessibility enquiries

Scottish banks still circulate along with notes of £5, £10, £20, £50 and £100. (Technically, Scottish notes are legal tender in England and Wales, but some shops will not accept them. English banks will readily change them for you.)

Traveller's cheques can be cashed at banks, *bureaux de change* and many hotels, though the best rates are normally available at banks.

Access (or MasterCard) and Visa are the most commonly acceptable credit cards, followed by American Express and Diners Club. Small guest houses and bed-and-breakfast places may not take credit cards.

Getting There

BY AIR

Edinburgh Airport lies 8 miles (13 km) west of the city centre. Scheduled flights run to and from various English and Irish airports and the Highlands and Islands, and several European cities including Amsterdam, Brussels and Paris. British Airways and British Midland both run comprehensive services to and from London Heathrow. EasyJet and Go operate low-cost flights from London (Luton/Gatwick and Stansted respectively) to Edinburgh. Scot Airways and British European both fly to Edinburgh from London City. Aer Lingus flies from Dublin. During the summer there are also various charter flights from Europe and North America. Coach and taxi connections into the city centre take about 20 minutes.

Scheduled transatlantic flights arrive in Glasgow and Prestwick, from where Scottish Citylink (08705 50 50 50) and Stagecoach (0141-552 4961) run regular bus services into Edinburgh. The bus journey takes about two hours.

There are plenty of porters at Edinburgh Airport. If you have difficulty finding one, ask at the Information Desk. Payment is at your discretion, but £1 is a reasonable tip.

Edinburgh Airport: general flight enquiries: 0131-333 1000
KLM UK: (0870) 5 074 074
British Airways: (0870) 55 111 55, www.british-airways.com
British Midland: 0131-344 5600, www.britishmidland.com
Easyjet: (0870) 6 000 000
Go: (0845) 607 6543, www.go-fly.com
Servisair (for other airlines flying to Edinburgh): 0131-344 3111

BY RAIL

The main line to Edinburgh runs up the east coast from London Kings Cross. Journey times from London are between four and a half and five hours (but up to seven hours on a Sunday) and north of Berwick the line passes along the impressive coastline. The journey on the west coast line from Euston takes over six hours. The overnight trains also travel this line. Edinburgh has two railway stations, Waverley and Haymarket at, respectively, the east and west ends of the city centre. Waverley is the main station, but Haymarket is nearer the airport. For all rail passenger enquiries, tel: (0845) 748 4950.

There are porters at Waverley and Haymarket stations. To make sure of help for disabled or infirm travellers contact the appropriate rail operator: Scotrail (0845 605 7021), GNER (08445 7225 444), Virgin (0845 744 3366).

BY ROAD

From London take the M1 and then link up to the M6. This motorway runs along England's west coast, and is the best road for the main part of the journey. After Carlisle, the motorist can choose between: the A7, a rather slow tourist route through the Borders; the A701 from Moffat, which is a high, winding, remote road, but probably the fastest; or the A702 through Biggar, the main trunk road, skirting the Pentland Hills. Motorway addicts can follow the A74 to the outskirts of Glasgow and join the M8 into Edinburgh. The 400-mile (650-km) journey from London takes about eight hours.

The east coast road from London to Edinburgh is the scenic but slow A1. Stretches of the A1 have been converted to motorway A1(M).

BY BUS

National Express (08705 80 80 80, www.nationalexpress.co.uk) runs daily coaches between London's Victoria Coach Station and Edinburgh. The journey takes 8½ to 9½ hours. Traditionally very inexpensive, the coach companies now offer a "deluxe" option.

Practical Tips

Media

NEWSPAPERS

The Scotsman, published in Edinburgh since 1817, is the city's – and ostensibly the nation's – quality daily paper. It is rivalled on the national level by the more dynamic Glasgow paper *The Herald*. *The Scotsman* gives sound coverage of national and international news, and is strong on the arts. The *Evening News*, its sister paper, covers local Edinburgh news and interest. The *Daily Record* is the most widely-read Scottish tabloid.

Scotsman Publications ventured into the quality Sunday paper market in 1988 with *Scotland On Sunday*. The English Sunday papers responded with a rash of Scottish sections, covering Scottish concerns with varying degrees of accuracy, and the *Sunday Herald* was launched in 1999.

The celebrated *Sunday Post*, last bastion of small-town conservatism, is still a source of amused national pride. Edinburgh also has a number of small, council-supported "community newspapers" serving semi-autonomous areas of the city and providing a platform for local wrangling.

The free daily newspaper *Metro* (Mon–Fri), available at Waverley and Haymarket Stations and on LRT and First Bus buses, has useful listings of events.

MAGAZINES

Scottish magazines are thin on the ground. There is nothing to compare with London's *Spectator*

or (hope springs eternal) the *New Yorker*. The *Edinburgh Review* is a wide-ranging, heavyweight cultural journal. Sundry literary magazines (*Lines Review, Cencrastus, Chapman*) publish poetry, prose and criticism. More recent additions on the scene are the Scottish Arts Council funded *Product* and monthly upmarket lifestyle magazine *Caledonia*. *The List* (fortnightly) provides watertight coverage of the arts in Edinburgh and Glasgow and invaluable listings of events.

RADIO AND TV

BBC Radio Scotland (FM 92.4-94.7 MW 810kHz/370m) is a national network with news, music and talk programmes. Radio Forth (FM 97.3 MW 1548kHz) is the local commercial station. BBC Scotland and Scottish Television (STV) are the Glasgow-based television stations which add Scottish news, features and drama to the national network.

Post and Telecoms

POST

The Central Post Office is in the St James Centre (Kings Mall), at the east end of Princes Street, tel: (0845) 722 3344 (Monday 9am–5.30pm, Tuesday–Friday 8.30am–5.30pm, Saturday 8.30am–6pm). Other city centre post offices are at 40 Frederick

Banking

Banks with branches throughout Edinburgh are the Bank of Scotland, Royal Bank of Scotland, Clydesdale and Lloyds-TSB. City centre branches of most banks (and building societies) can be found in George Street, Hanover Street or Shandwick Place. The English banks Barclays and HSBC have one branch each in the city, at 1 St Andrew Square and 76 Hanover Street respectively.

Street and 7 Hope Street (west end of Princes Street), tel (both): 0845 722 3344; and 33 Forrest Road (near the university), tel: 225 3957. They are open Monday–Friday 9am–5.30pm and Saturday 9am–12.30pm (Frederick Street branch closed Saturday).

Some post offices are housed within newsagents and are open slightly different hours. Some close for lunch and most take a half day on Wednesday. For advice on mail services phone (08457) 740 740; counter services (0845) 722 3344.

TELEPHONE

The area code 0131 should be dialled before an Edinburgh telephone number when calling from anywhere else in the UK.

The traditional red telephone box has been replaced by modern glass booths. Some of these are operated by coins (£1, 50p, 20p, 10p), others by credit card or phonecards which can be purchased from newsagents and post offices. Phone boxes are scattered throughout the city, and there is a bank of them at the central post office.

To make enquiries about British Telecom services call 0800 309409. To call the Operator, dial 100; International Operator, dial 155; Directory Enquiries, dial 192; International Directory Enquiries, dial 153; the Talking Clock, dial 123; telemessage/telegrams, dial 0800 190190.

Most banks open Monday–Friday; hours vary but some branches close as early as 4pm. Most building societies also open on Saturday morning, as do the Clydesdale and Lloyds-TSB (Hanover Street branches), and the Royal Bank of Scotland (142/144 Princes Street).

Cashpoint machines are sited outside most banks and are usually open at all times. See also *Planning the Trip: Money Matters*.

FAX

The St James Centre Post Office shop (tel: 0845-722 3344) has a fax machine for inland faxes. It costs 50p per sheet. There are several other fax bureaux in the city centre.

Tipping

Most restaurants do not add a service charge to the bill. In this case, it is normal (but not compulsory) to give a 10–15 percent tip. Check the bill carefully; if a charge for service is included, there is no need to pay extra unless you wish to reward exceptional service. If the service has been very poor, the service charge can be subtracted from the bill.

A similar percentage tip should be paid to hairdressers and taxi drivers. A tip of about £1 minimum is appropriate for porters at transport terminals or in your hotel. It is not necessary to tip in self-service establishments or pubs.

Religious Services

The main Sunday services are usually at 11am. Many churches also hold a Sunday evening service.
Albany Church for the Deaf, Greenside Parish Church, Royal Terrace, tel: 319 1841.
Associated Presbyterian Church, Viewforth Parish Church Gilmore Place, tel: 445 3673.
The Central Mosque, 50 Potterrow, tel: 667 0140.
Charlotte (Baptist) Chapel, 13 South Charlotte Street, tel: 225 4812.
Church of Jesus Christ of Latter Day Saints, Dalkeith Chapel, Newbattle Road, Dalkeith, tel: 654 0630.
Greyfriars Kirk, Greyfriars Place, tel: 225 1900 (Gaelic service every Sunday at 12.30pm.)
Methodist Church, Central Hall, 2 West Tollcross, tel: 221 9029.
St Andrew's Orthodox (Greek Russian) Church, 23a George Square, tel: 667 0372.

St Columba (Free Church of Scotland), Lawnmarket, tel: 225 5996.
St Giles' Cathedral (Church of Scotland), High Street, tel: 225 4363.
St Mary's (Catholic) Cathedral, Broughton Street, tel: 556 1798.
St Mary's (Episcopalian) Cathedral, Palmerston Place, tel: 225 6293.
Sikh Temple (Guru Nanak Gurdwara) 1 Mill Lane, Leith, tel: 553 7207.
Synagogue Chambers, Edinburgh Hebrew Congregation, 4 Salisbury Road, tel: 667 3144.
Ukranian Catholic Church of St Andrews, 6 Mansionhouse Road, tel: 667 5811.

Embassies and Consulates

American Consulate General, 3 Regent Terrace, tel: 556 8315.
Australian Consulate, Melrose House, 69 George Street, tel: 624 3333.
Canadian Consulate, Standard Life House, 30 Lothian Road, tel: 220 4333.
Consulate General of The

People's Republic of China, Romano House, 43 Station Road, tel: 316 4789.
The Royal Danish Consulate, 215 Balgreen Road, tel: 337 6352.
French Consulate General, 11 Randolph Crescent, tel: 225 7954.
German Consulate, 16 Eglinton Crescent, tel: 337 2323.
Icelandic Consulate, 45 Queen Street, tel: 220 5775.
Consulate General of Ireland, 16 Randolph Crescent, tel: 226 7711.
Italian Consulate General, 32 Melville Street, tel: 226 3631.
Japanese Consulate General, 2 Melville Crescent, tel: 225 4777.
Netherlands Consulate, 1 Thistle Street, tel: 220 3226.
Royal Norwegian Consulate General, 86 George Street, tel: 226 5701.
Polish Consulate, 2 Kinnear Road, tel: 552 0301.
Consulate General of the Russian Federation, 58 Melville Street, tel: 225 7098.
Spanish Consulate General, 63 North Castle Street, tel: 220 1843.
Swedish Consulate General 22 Hanover Street, tel: 220 6050
Swiss Consular Agency, 66 Hanover Street, tel: 226 5660.

Emergencies

In emergencies, phone 999. No money is needed to make a 999 call from a public call-box: just dial, and ask for the Fire, Police or Ambulance service.

For non-urgent enquiries contact a local police station or the **Police Information Centre**, 188 High Street, (next to Parliament Square) tel: 226 6966, open 10am–10pm summer, 10am–6pm winter. All these stations are continuously staffed:
Gayfield Square Police Station, Gayfield Square (off Leith Walk), tel: 556 9270.
West End Police Station, Torphichen Place, Haymarket, tel: 229 2323.
Leith Police Station, Queen Charlotte Street, tel: 554 9350.
St. Leonard's Police Station, 14 St. Leonard's Street, tel: 662 5000

Lost Property & Left Luggage
Lost Property Department, Police Headquarters, Fettes Avenue, tel: 311 3141. There are Left Luggage lockers at Waverley Station and the Bus Station.

Medical Services
There is a 24-hour Accident and Emergency department at the Royal Infirmary, 1 Lauriston Place, tel: 536 1000 (in mid-2003 the Infirmary moves to new premises at Little France, Old Dalkeith Road). There is a minor injuries unit at the Western General, Crewe Road, tel: 537 1000, (9am–9pm, Mon–Sun).

There is an emergency dental clinic at the Dental Hospital, 39 Lauriston Place, tel: 536 4900. It is open Mon–Fri 9am–3pm.

Getting Around

On Arrival

If you arrive in Edinburgh by air, taxis will be on hand to take you into the city centre. The journey takes about 20 minutes and should cost £12–15. Alternatively, a bus service runs every 10–20 minutes; it takes slightly longer but costs just £3.30 or £5 for an open return ticket (children £2/£3). There are also a number of car hire firms based at the airport should you wish to travel independently. If you arrive by train, simply walk up the Waverley Steps and out into the Princes Street throng. The Tourist Information Centre is at the top of the steps.

On Foot

There are many ways to get around the city centre, but under your own steam is by far the best option. Edinburgh has a compact city centre, and you can see almost all of the major sites on foot. Maps of both the New and Old Town are readily available, and delving into the many nooks and crannies the city has to offer is a day out in itself. The Royal Mile in the Old Town has numerous closes to explore, whilst across Princes Street the New Town has an architectural charm all of its own.

On a sunny day, the views from the top of Arthur's Seat, the Scott Monument or the Royal Botanic Garden will take your breath away. Beware though: the many hills and steps that make up the city's contours can leave you equally short of puff. Guided walking tours may also be undertaken, mainly in summer (see *Culture* section).

By Bus

If you wish to explore beyond the city centre (or are just feeling too tired to walk the length of Princes Street), then travelling by bus is the easiest method. The bus station at St Andrew Square is currently closed for reconstruction (due to reopen in late 2002), so in the meantime most buses start their journey on St Andrew Square, North St David Street or Waterloo Place.

Lothian Region Transport (LRT) and First Edinburgh are the main bus companies operating in the city and Lothians. They run services on popular routes every 10–20 minutes. Fares start at 50p, but Daysavers at £2.20 (adults) and

By Bicycle

Cycling is a good way of getting around as central Edinburgh is quite small, but watch out for cobbled streets. Edinburgh is probably the most cycle-friendly Scottish city, but it still has some way to go. Some of the main roads in Edinburgh have cycle lanes and there are cycle routes in and around the city. The excellent local cycling organisation, Spokes, publishes a useful Edinburgh cycle map, tel: 313 2114, www.spokes.org.uk, available at the Tourist Information Centre, bike shops and bookshops. The 6,000 km (3,728 mile) North Sea Cycle Route which links seven countries passes through Edinburgh, www.northsea-cycle.com. Edinburgh Bicycle Co-operative at 8 Avlanley Terrace, tel: 228 1368 has a good range of clothing and spares as well as bikes.

Edinburgh Cycle Hire, 29 Blackfriars Street, tel: 556 5560. Daily 9am–7pm. Deposit required.
Bike Trax, 11 Lochrin Place, tel: 228 6633. Monday–Friday 9.30am–6pm, Saturday 9.30am–5.30pm, Sunday noon–5pm. Deposit required.

£1.50 (children) are great value. Under 5s travel free. Weekly and monthly saver tickets are also available. On city buses the correct change is required. If you're venturing further afield, Scottish Citylink and Stagecoach, among others, travel to Glasgow, Fife, the Borders and many other destinations.

For information on all bus companies, their routes and timetables, phone Traveline on 0800 23 23 23 (free from within Edinburgh and Lothians) or 0131-225 3858 (from outside the region). For information on LRT services only, tel: 0131-555 6363; First Edinburgh tel: 0131-454 9997. The Traveline office is at 2 Cockburn Street, open 8.30am–5.30pm Monday–Friday.

There is a free bus running between the four National Galleries of Scotland, hourly service Monday to Saturday from 11am, Sunday from 12 noon, tel: 624 6200.

Taxis

Black taxis are readily available throughout the city centre, with numerous companies operating 24 hours (although you will struggle to get one late on Friday and Saturday nights). You can either phone for a taxi (this will cost slightly more) or simply hail one in the street. To improve your chances of catching one, go to one of the recognised taxi ranks: on Hanover Street, North St Andrew Street, Rutland Street (outside Caledonian Hotel), Lothian Road (outside Sheraton Hotel), Hope Street (outside Frasers), Waverley Bridge and at Haymarket and Waverley stations. The fare is displayed inside the cab, and prices go up at peak times (evenings and public holidays).
City Cabs: 228 1211
Central Radio Taxis: 229 2468
Capital Castle Taxis: 228 2555
Radiocabs: 225 9000

By Car

Driving around the outskirts of Edinburgh is relatively easy, but the city centre is often choked with traffic and the many one-way systems can be problematic. Cars can only travel westbound up Princes Street, and once you've got to your destination parking is a whole new challenge. Many spaces are pre-allocated to "permit holders only" (sold to city residents), so look out for the "pay and display" zones or parking meters. Edinburgh traffic wardens are infamous for their diligence, and parking fines are £30 a time. If you're planning to journey out into the rest of Scotland, however, there are a number of reasonably priced car hire firms.

At the Airport
Avis, tel: 344 3900
Europcar, tel: 333 2573
Hertz, tel: 333 1019

City Rentals
Arnold Clark, 1/13 Lochrin Place, Tollcross, tel: 228 4747
Avis, 100 Dalry Road, tel: 337 6363
Europcar, 24 East London Street, tel: 557 3456
Hertz, 10 Picardy Place, tel: 556 8311
Lo-Cost Hire, 1a Wardlaw Terrace, tel: 313 2220
Thrifty Car Rental, 42 Haymarket Terrace, tel: 337 1319

Where to Stay

Choosing a Place

Tourism in Edinburgh is becoming a year-round trade with more and more hotels opening to cope with extra demand. There is a wide choice of accommodation in Edinburgh, whether you're looking for a family-run guest house, a backpackers' hostel or a deluxe hotel.

A large number of centrally located bed and breakfast and guest houses offer value for money, traditional Scottish cuisine and a friendly welcome. Hotel accommodation is wide ranging, with a mix of chain hotels, family-run, stylish or deluxe establishments. University campus accommodation is good value but is often on the outskirts of the city and is only usually available during the Easter and summer holidays. Edinburgh is fast becoming a backpackers' paradise, with a steady rise in the number of hostels, the majority of them located in the city centre.

How do you select a place to stay? VisitScotland has changed its system of grading accommodation so that quality only is now assessed. The Quality Assurance Scheme lets you know that trained and impartial inspectors have visited the property. Star gradings range from one star (fair and acceptable) to five stars (exceptional/world class).

You are strongly advised to book in advance. During Festival time (August) and Hogmanay (December and early January) accommodation is at a premium.

Hotels

Albany Hotel, 39 Albany Street, tel: 556 0397, fax: 557 6633, email: info@albanyhoteledinburgh.co.uk, www.albanyhoteledinburgh.co.uk Refurbished listed Georgian building on quiet New Town street just north of Princes Street. Variety of rooms, some small. 21 rooms. **£££**
Ailsa Craig Hotel, 24 Royal Terrace, tel: 556 1022/6055, fax: 556 6055, email: ailsacraighotel@ednet.co.uk, www.townhousehotels.co.uk. Elegant, reasonably priced hotel with stunning views over the Forth and Calton Hill. This hotel won the Golden Pillow Award in 1999. 18 rooms. **£**
Apex International Hotel, 31–35 Grassmarket, tel: 300 3456, fax: 220 5345, email: international@apexhotels.co.uk, www.apexhotels.co.uk Five-storey hotel in the lively Grassmarket, with fantastic views of the Castle. New bar and restaurant offers world cuisine, with the capacity to seat over 150. 175 rooms. **££–£££**

Search and Booking Services

The best way to go about booking your accommodation is to get in touch with the **Central Reservations Office** of Edinburgh and Lothians Tourist Board, tel: 0131-473 3800 or email esic@eltb.org. They can find and book accommodation according to your requirements for a £3 booking fee (£1 per person for five or more people). Check out their website www.edinburgh.org. For hostels and caravan/camping parks, book direct with the establishment.

Accommodation can also be booked from any of the following branches of the travel agent **First Option:** UK Arrivals at Edinburgh Airport, tel: 333 5119; Waverley Steps (entrance to Princes Mall), tel: 557 0905, and Waverley Station, tel: 557 0034. There is a £5 maximum booking fee for UK residents or £7.50 for overseas reservations.

Apartments

Canon Court Apartments,
20 Canonmills, tel: 474 7000,
fax: 474 7001, e-mail:
info@canoncourt.co.uk
www.canoncourt.co.uk
43 luxury serviced apartments in
city centre location, close to the
Royal Botanic Garden. Available
on a daily or weekly basis. **£££**

Balmoral Hotel, Princes Street,
tel: 556 2414, fax: 557 3747, email:
reservations@thebalmoral.com,
www.roccofortehotels.com
Edinburgh's premier hotel. Many
rooms with Castle view. Health club
with swimming pool. 188 rooms.
£££–££££

Bank Hotel, 1 South Bridge, tel:
622 6800, fax: 622 6822, e-mail:
bank@festival-inns.co.uk. Former
bank half way along the Royal Mile,
converted into a café-bar with
bedrooms above. 9 rooms. **£–££**

Bruntsfield Hotel, 69 Bruntsfield
Place, tel: 229 1393, fax: 229 5634,
email: bruntsfield@queensferry-
hotels.co.uk,
www.thebruntsfield.co.uk
A friendly, Victorian townhouse with
superb views, an excellent location
and an award-winning restaurant,
The Potting Shed. 74 rooms. **££–£££**

Caledonian Hilton Hotel, Princes
Street, tel: 222 8888, fax: 222
8889, email: ednchhirm@hilton.com,
www.hilton.com
This vast, turn-of-the-century red
sandstone building, the "Grande
Dame" of Edinburgh hotels, is
constantly being upgraded. Many
rooms with view of Castle. 249
rooms. **££££**

Carlton Hotel, 19 North Bridge, tel:
472 3000, fax: 556 2691, email:
carlton@-paramount-hotels.co.uk,
www.paramount-hotels.co.uk
Splendidly situated in the heart of
the city, this imposing Victorian mass
has long been a favourite Edinburgh
hotel. 197 rooms. **££–£££**

Channings, 15 South Learmont
Gardens, tel: 315 2226, fax: 332
9631, email:
reserve@channings.co.uk,
www.townhousecompany.co.uk
A series of five adjoining
Edwardian houses facing a
cobbled, quiet street a few minutes
away from the city centre. Country
house public rooms; individually
furnished bedrooms, a tad on the
small side. Pleasant patio. 46
rooms. **£££**

Dunstane House Hotel, 4 West
Coates, Haymarket, tel: 337 6169,
fax: 337 6060, email:
reservations@dunstanehousehotel.
co.uk,
www.dunstanehousehotel.co.uk
Privately run, listed 1850s Victorian
mansion house in the west end of
the city, with original features,
cornices and stained glass
windows. 16 rooms. **£–££**

Edinburgh City Travel Inn Metro,
1 Morrison Link, tel: 0870 238
3319, fax: 228 9836,
www.travelinn.co.uk
This property in the city centre is
part of an unpretentious, functional
modern chain. 281 rooms of
which 137 are family rooms.
£–££

George Inter-Continental Hotel,
19–21 George Street, tel: 225
1251, fax: 226 5644, email:
edinburgh@interconti.com,
www.intercontinental.com
A distinguished, well-established
property in the heart of the city.
Rooms at rear of top two floors
have superb views of Fife. 195
rooms. **££–££££**

Hilton Edinburgh Airport Hotel,
Edinburgh International Airport,
tel: 519 4400, fax: 519 4466, email:
res.manager@edinairport.stakis.co.
uk, www.hilton.com. Built in 1995,
20–30 minutes from city centre.
150 rooms. **£–£££**

Menzies Belford Hotel, 69 Belford
Road, tel: 332 2545, fax: 332 3805,
email: belford@menzies.co.uk,
www.menzies@hotels.co.uk
Located on the leafy banks of the
Water of Leith yet within minutes of
the city centre on the bus route.
144 rooms. **££–£££**

Hilton Edinburgh Grosvenor Hotel,
Grosvenor Street, tel: 226 6001,
fax: 220 2387, email: reservations
@edinburgh.stakis.co.uk,
www.hilton.com Situated at the
west end of town across from
Haymarket railway station. 189
rooms. **£–£££**

Holiday Inn Crowne Plaza,
80 High Street, tel: 557 9797,
fax: 557 9789, email:
rescpedinburgh@allianceuk.com,
www.crowneplazaed.co.uk
This modern, vernacular hotel sits
comfortably on the Royal Mile.
Leisure centre; on-site parking. 238
rooms. **££–£££**

Holiday Inn Express Leith,
Britannia View, Ocean Drive, Leith,
tel: 555 4422, fax: 555 4646,
email: reservations@hiex-
edinburgh.com, www.hiexpress.com
A new hotel in the heart of Leith,
overlooking the Royal Yacht
Britannia. Children stay free. 102
rooms. **£**

Holiday Inn North,
107 Queensferry Road, tel: 332
2442, fax: 332 3408, email:
reservations@hiedinburghnorth.fsn
et.co.uk, www.edinburgh-
north.holiday-inn.com
A typical Holiday Inn property with
grand panoramic views. Two miles
(3 km) north of town but on main
bus route. 119 rooms. **£–££**

Hotel Prices

Prices are per person in a double
room.
- **£** = £30–50
- **££** = £50–75
- **£££** = £75–110
- **££££** = over £110

Hotel Ibis, 6 Hunter Square,
tel: 240 7000, fax: 240 7007,
email: h2039@accor-hotels.com,
www.ibis-hotels.com.
Brand new modern hotel situated
just off the Royal Mile. 99 rooms. **££**

Howard Hotel, 34 Great King Street,
tel: 557 3500, fax: 557 6515,
email: reserve@thehoward.com,
www.thehoward.com
Three interconnected 18th-century
town houses in the New Town result
in a magnificent classical hotel. All
bedrooms different and all made
the more comfortable by
contemporary bathrooms.
Splendid breakfast. 18 rooms.
££££

Hotel Prices

Prices are per person in a double room.
- **£** = £30–50
- **££** = £50–75
- **£££** = £75–110
- **££££** = over £110

Inverleith Hotel, 5 Inverleith Terrace, tel: 556 2745, fax: 557 0433, email: info@inverleithhotel.co.uk, www.inverleithhotel.co.uk
Family-run Georgian house hotel overlooking the Royal Botanic Garden. 8 rooms. **£**

Ramada Jarvis Edinburgh Murrayfield Hotel, Ellersly Road, tel: 337 6888, fax: 313 2543, email: sales.edinburgh@ramadajarvis.co.uk, www.jarvis.co.uk
Edwardian country house retaining its original charm and tranquillity; recently refurbished. Two miles (3 km) from city centre. 57 rooms. **££**

Learmouth Ramada Jarvis Hotel, 18–20 Learmonth Terrace, tel: 343 2671, fax: 315 2232, email: rs.learmouth@ramadajarvis.co.uk, www.jarvis.co.uk
Terraced houses converted into a quiet, elegant hotel, a short distance from Princes Street. 62 rooms. **£–££**

Ramada Jarvis Mount Royal Hotel, 53 Princes Street, tel: 225 7161, fax: 220 4671, email: sales@ramadajarvis.co.uk, www.jarvis.co.uk
Superbly located in Princes Street with splendid views of the Castle. 158 rooms. **££**

Jurys Edinburgh Inn, 43 Jeffrey Street, tel: 200 3300, fax: 200 0400, email: bookings@jurysdoyle.com, www.jurysdoyle.com
Prime city centre location within walking distance of Edinburgh's major tourist attractions. 186 rooms. **£–££**

Malmaison, 1 Tower Place, Leith, tel: 468 5000, fax: 468 5002, email: edinburgh@malmaison.com, www.malamaison.com
A former seamen's mission, the Malmaison is an award-winning contemporary hotel situated on the waterfront of Leith. Excellent restaurant. 60 rooms. **££–£££**

Marriott Dalmahoy Hotel & Country Club, Long Dalmahoy, Kirknewton, tel: 333 1845, fax: 333 1433, email: reservations. dalmahoy@marriotthotels.co.uk, www.marriott.com\marriott\edigs
A grand mansion to the west of the city and 3 miles (5 km) from the airport. Leisure facilities include two championship golf courses. 215 rooms. **£££**

Point Hotel, 34 Bread Street, tel: 221 5555, fax: 221 9929, email: sales@point-hotel.co.uk; www.point-hotel.co.uk
Minimalist, stylish hotel, centrally located with Castle views and within walking distance of Edinburgh's major theatres. 140 rooms. **££**

Prestonfield House Hotel, Priestfield Road, tel: 668 3346, fax: 668 3976, email: info@prestonfieldhouse.com, www.prestonfieldhouse.com
Surrounded by formal gardens and a golf course, yet a mere 5 minutes drive from city centre. Stay here and you are following in the footsteps of Bonnie Prince Charlie, Benjamin Franklin and Dr Johnson. 31 rooms of which 26 are in a modern extension which in no way interferes with the ambience of the distinguished 16th-century baronial mansion. **£££**

Roxburghe Hotel, 38 Charlotte Square, tel: 240 5500, fax: 240 5555, email: info@roxburghe.macdonald-hotels.co.uk, www.macdonaldhotels.co.uk
Situated on Edinburgh's grandest square, just off Princes Street, this refurbished "county" hotel has some grand bedrooms as well as smaller rooms. 197 rooms. **££–£££**

Royal British Hotel, 20 Princes Street, tel: 556 4901, fax: 557 6510, email: royalbritish@cairn-hotels.co.uk, www.cairnhotelgroup.com
A comfortable landmark property immediately opposite the main railway station. 72 rooms. **£££**

Royal Terrace Hotel, 18 Royal Terrace, tel: 557 3222, fax: 557 5334, email: reservations.royalterrace@principal hotels.co.uk, www.lemeridien.com.
Georgian terrace buildings on a cobbled street, minutes from the east end of Princes Street, constitute this handsome chintzy hotel. Complete leisure club and large private garden. 108 rooms. **££–££££**

Sheraton Grand Hotel, 1 Festival Square, tel: 229 9131, fax: 229 6254, email: grandedinburgh.sheraton@sheraton .com, www.sheraton.com
Refurbished hotel within a stone's throw of the exhibition centre and several major theatres. Many rooms with superb views of Castle. Spa; on-site parking. 261 rooms. **£££–££££**

Guest House Prices

Prices are per person in a double room.
- **£** = less than £20
- **££** = £20–30
- **£££** = over £30

Thrums Private Hotel, 14–15 Minto Street, Newington, tel: 667 5545, fax: 667 8707 email:thrumshotel@lineone.net, www.thrumshoteledinburgh.com.
Detached Georgian house with garden, 3 miles (5 km) south of city centre. 14 rooms. **£**

Guest Houses

Abcorn Guest House, 4 Mayfield Gardens, tel: 667 6548, fax: 667 9969, email: abcorn@btinternet.com, www.abcorn.co.uk
A detached Victorian villa with private parking on the main bus route, 2 miles (3 km) to southeast of city centre. 7 en-suite rooms. **££–£££**

Airlie Guest House, 29 Minto Street, 667 3562, fax: 662 1399, email: airlieguesthouse@btinternet.com, www.airlieguesthouse.co.uk/

Non-smoking guest house near the the city centre. 8 rooms (5 en suite). **£–£££**

Amaryllis Guest House, 21 Upper Gilmore Place, tel/fax: 229 3293, email: ghamaryllis@aol.com, www.airlieguesthouse.co.uk Centrally located guest house in quiet residential area. 5 rooms (4 en suite). **£–££**

Ashlyn Guest House, 42 Inverleith Row, tel/fax: 552 2954, email: reservations@ashlyn-edinburgh.com. Listed Georgian house close to Botanic Garden and 2 miles (3 km) from city centre. Non-smoking; dinner served. 8 rooms (5 en suite). **££–£££**

Ballarat Guest House, 14 Gilmore Place, tel: 229 7024, fax: 622 1265, email: ballarat.house@virgin.net Cosy and friendly guest house in close proximity to city centre and theatres. 5 rooms (1 en suite). **£–££**

Balquhidder Guest House, 94 Pilrig Street, tel: 554 3377, email: reservations@balquhidderedinscot.com, www.olstravel.com/guest/balquhid. A former church manse, built in 1857, this centrally located Victorian detached house offers a warm family welcome. 6 rooms (5 en suite). **££**

Bonnington Guest House, 202 Ferry Road, tel/fax: 554 7610, email: bonningtongh@btinternet.com. Townhouse built in 1840, situated in Leith, 20 minutes from city centre and on main bus route. Private parking. Bedrooms non-smoking. 6 rooms (3 en suite). **££–£££**

Cameron Toll Guest House, 299 Dalkeith Road, tel: 667 2950, fax: 662 1987, email: camerontoll@msn.com, www.edinbed.com Be entertained with bagpipe music while you enjoy your evening meal (table licence) in an imposing guest house about 2 miles (3 km) southeast of city centre. Parking. 11 rooms (10 en suite). **££–£££**

University Accommodation

Note: Prices brackets are as guest house ranges.

Heriot-Watt University, Riccarton, tel: 451 3669, fax: 451 3199 email: info@eccscotland.com, www.ecc.scotland.com. At extreme western fringe of city but open all year round. **££**

Napier University, 219 Colinton Road, tel: 445 4427, email: vacation-lets@napier.ac.uk. About 3 miles (5 km) south of city centre. Single and twin rooms. Summer holidays only. **££**

Queen Margaret University College, 36 Clerwood Terrace, tel: 317 3310. Residential area, 4 miles (6 km) west of city centre on main bus route. Excellent sports facilities. Car parking available. Single and twin rooms. May–August only. **£–££**

University of Edinburgh:
Edinburgh First, 18 Holyrood Park Road, tel: 651 2007, fax: 667 7271, email: edinburgh.first@ed.ac.uk, www.edinburghfirst.com Conveniently situated close to the Commonwealth Pool and Holyrood Park. Easter and summer holidays only. **££–£££**

Classic Guest House, 50 Mayfield Road, tel: 667 5847, fax: 662 1016, email: info@classichouse.demon.co.uk, www.classichouse.demon.co.uk Elegant Victorian guest house, on main bus routes about 2 miles (3 km) southeast of city centre. 4 rooms (3 en suite). **£–££**

Dukes of Windsor Street, 17 Windsor Street, tel/fax: 556 6046, email: info@dukeofwindsor.com. Centrally situated restored Georgian townhouse. Continental, rather than customary hearty Scottish, breakfast. On-street parking. 10 en-suite rooms. **££–£££**

Galloway Guest House, 22 Dean Park Crescent, tel/fax: 332 3672, email: galloway-theclarks@hotmail.com. In lively Stockbridge district, popular with bright young things, 1 mile (2 km) north of Princes Street. 10 rooms (6 en suite). **££**

Georgian House, 29 Gayfield Square, tel: 557 2063, fax: 530 0146, email: georgianhouse@hotmail.com, www.leisurenet.co.uk.georgianhouse. Exclusive Georgian townhouse in quiet tree-lined cul-de-sac. Non-smoking. 4 en-suite rooms. **£££**

International Guest House, 37 Mayfield Gardens, tel: 667 2511, fax: 667 1112, email: intergh@easynet.co.uk Victorian guest house on main bus route, about 2 miles (3 km)

southeast of city centre. Private parking. 9 en-suite rooms, 4 of which are singles. **££–£££**

Joppa Turrets, 1 Lower Joppa, tel/fax: 669 5806, email: stanley@joppaturrets.demon.co.uk, www.joppaturrets.demon.co.uk. For those who must be by the seaside. On the beach at Joppa but close to bus routes and 5 miles (8 km) from city centre. Parking no problem. 5 rooms (3 en suite). **££–£££**

Kirklands Guest House, 128 Old Dalkeith Road, tel/fax: 664 2755, www.firstcity.force9.co.uk. Near Holyrood Palace and on main bus route. Large car park. 9 rooms (7 en suite). **£–££**

Leamington Guest House, 57 Leamington Terrace, tel: 228 3879, fax: 221 1022, email: lemgh@globalnet.co.uk Family run guest house in quiet residential area. Close to city centre, theatres and shops. 8 rooms (4 en suite). **££–£££**

Salisbury Guest House, 45 Salisbury Road, tel/fax: 667 1264, email: Brenda.Wright@btinternet.com, www.members.edinburgh.org/salisbury. Georgian listed building near Holyrood Palace and Royal Mile. 12 rooms (9 en suite). **££–£££**

Six Mary's Place Guest House, 6 Mary's Place, off Raeburn Place, tel: 322 8965, fax: 624 7060, email: info@sixmarysplace.co.uk.

Georgian town house near city centre. Dining conservatory and gardens. Home cooked vegetarian cuisine. Non-smoking. 8 rooms (2 en suite). **££–£££**

Stuart House, 12 East Claremont Street, tel: 557 9030, fax: 557 0563, email: june@stuartguesthouse.co.uk, www.stuartguesthouse.co.uk. Refurbished Georgian house 3 miles (5 km) north of city centre. Non-smoking. Dinner served. 6 rooms (5 en suite). **£££**

The Thirty-Nine Steps, 62 South Trinity Road, tel: 552 1349, email: thirtyninesteps@eh53nx.freeserve.co.uk, www.thirtyninesteps.com. Victorian house situated close to Botanic Garden and the city centre. Parking available. 7 rooms (6 en suite). **££–£££**

Hostels

The Scottish Youth Hostel Association (SYHA)

Tel: (01786) 891400 (information), (08701) 553255 (reservations), email: reservations@syha.org.uk, www.syha.org.uk (website gives details of all SYHA hostels in Scotland). Prices at the Edinburgh hostels range from around £12–18 You must be a member but you can join at any hostel. Current annual membership costs £6. There are two SYHA hostels in Edinburgh, both of them open all year round:

Eglinton Youth Hostel, 18 Eglinton Crescent, tel: 337 1120. Facilities include a self-catering kitchen, laundry room and internet access.

Bruntsfield Youth Hostel, 7 Bruntsfield Place, tel: 447 2994. TV, pool table and a self-catering kitchen are among the facilities. Advance booking is advisable during the summer months. Reduced prices for under 18s.

INDEPENDENT HOSTELS

Prices range from around £10–15 for dormitory beds and £15–25 per person for a shared room, and vary seasonally at some hostels. Most

Camp Sites

All-inclusive prices range from around £9–14 per person.

Drummohr Caravan Park, Levenhall, Musselburgh, tel: 665 6867; fax: 653 6859, email: bookings@drummohr.org, www.drummohr.org. Open March–October. Caravans and tents. Sheltered park with excellent facilities on the eastern edge of the city, close to East Lothian countryside.

Edinburgh Caravan Club, Marine Drive, tel: 312 6874. All year round. Caravans and 2-man tents. All facilities including disabled units and children's play area.

Mortonhall Caravan Park, Frogston Road East, tel: 664 1533, fax: 664 5387, email: enquiries@mortonhallcp.demon.co.uk. Open March–October. Tents of any size and caravans. Facilities include licensed shop, bar and restaurant. Disabled toilets and shower.

hostels offer the 7th night free, have self-catering kitchen facilities and 24-hour access for residents. Advance booking is advisable during the summer months.

Belford Hostel, Belford Church, 6–8 Douglas Gardens, tel: 225 6209, 220 2200 (reservations), email:info@hoppo.com, www.hoppo.com Open all year round. Hostel within historic church offers dormitory accommodation and double/twin rooms. Internet access. 127 beds.

Brodie's Backpacker Hostel, 12 High Street, tel: 556 6770, email: reception@brodieshostels.co.uk. Open all year round with female only and mixed dorms on the Royal Mile. Internet access, no curfew and friendly staff. 54 beds.

Castle Rock Hostel, 15 Johnston Terrace, tel: 225 9666, email: castle-rock@scotlands-top-hostels.com. Close to Edinburgh Castle. Dormitory accommodation with an additional charge for breakfast.

Internet access, laundry service and films shown every night. 250 beds.

Edinburgh Backpackers Hostel, 65 Cockburn Street, tel: 220 1717, (reservations) 220 2200, email: info@hopp.com. Very central. Dormitories plus double and twin. Common rooms and licensed café/122 beds.

High Street Hostel, 8 Blackfriars Street, tel: 557 3984, email: highstreet@scotlands-top-hostels.com, www.scotlands-top-hostels.com

Just off the Royal Mile, this popular hostel has separate male/female dorms. Free walking tour of Royal Mile at 10am every day. Also run MacBackpackers Tours, reasonably priced hostel-based bus tours around Scotland. 140 beds.

Royal Mile Backpackers, 105 High Street, tel: 557 6120, email: royalmile/@scotlands-top-hostels.com, www.scotlands-top-hostels.com

City centre dormitory accommodation (separate female dorms). Free walking tour and MacBackpackers Tours – see High Street Hostel. 38 beds.

Where to Eat

Eating Out

Edinburgh has one of the largest numbers of restaurants and cafés per capita in the world, with eateries to suit every taste and budget. From small delis and sandwich shops to plush restaurants and trendy diners, no dietary requirement is left uncatered for.

Stroll around the city centre perusing menus and checking out interiors or, if you're short of time and require more information than the following listings give, let the experts guide you. There are a number of excellent food guides available, including *The List Eating & Drinking Guide*, which features over 700 restaurants, bars and cafés in Edinburgh and Glasgow, and the *Edinburgh Food Guide*, both of which you'll find on sale in book shops and newsagents. *The List* also has an Eating and Drinking website, www.list.co.uk.

A firm favourite in Edinburgh and the choice of many of the more upmarket establishments is "Scottish" cuisine. Blending some of the country's finest produce – seafood, beef and game as well as fresh fruits and vegetables – with a French approach to cooking, there are many good Scottish restaurants to choose from.

If you're looking for a more continental feel, then there is also a large number of Italian restaurants dotted around the city centre, plus a fair amount of Chinese, Indian and Thai establishments. Edinburgh is also home to some of the best vegetarian restaurants in Britain. For a light meal, try one of the many cafés, bistros and bars

Restaurant Prices

Prices are per person for a two-course evening meal excluding wine.
- **£** = under £10
- **££** = £10–20
- **£££** = over £20

serving food into the early hours of the morning.

Restaurants

SCOTTISH

The Atrium, 10 Cambridge Street, tel: 228 8882. Located in the foyer of the Traverse Theatre, this is one of the most stylish places in town. Sophisticated, imaginative menu served in mellow, contemporary ambience with excellent service. **£££**
The Dial, 44–46 George IV Bridge, tel: 225 7179. Bold, innovative, sophisticated interior. Relaxed

Top Ten Cafés

Café Florentin, 8 St Giles Street, tel: 225 6267. French café on two floors, serving great coffee, croissants, soups, salads and some irresistible cakes and pastries.
Café Hub, Castlehill, Royal Mile, tel: 473 2067. Housed in the International Festival building, this new café is brightly furnished, with an impressive food and wine menu. Outdoor terrace in the summer.
Caffeine, 154 Dundas Street, tel: 07855 777071. Excellent range of coffees, served with sandwiches and ciabattas with tasty and interesting fillings. Closed Sat/Sun.
Elephant House, 21 George IV Bridge, tel: 220 5355. Popular coffee house serving a huge range of exotic teas and coffees, plus great cakes and pastries.
Favorit, 30 Leven Street, tel: 221 1800 and 19 Teviot Place, tel: 220 6880. New York deli meets Italian café. Two stylish eateries serving filling wraps and some

eating with a Mediterranean bias. When all other eateries have closed their kitchens The Dial still functions. Good value lunch. **££**
fitz(Henry), 19 Shore Place, Leith, tel: 555 6625. Be assured of a very fine dining experience indeed at this award-winning restaurant. Exciting ingredients cooked and presented in innovative ways. **£££**
Howies, 75 St Leonard's Street, tel: 668 2917; 208 Bruntsfield Place, tel: 221 1777; 63 Dalry Road, tel: 313 3334; 4–6 Glanville Place, Stockbridge, tel: 225 5553. This 10-year-old family-run chain is a firm favourite with Edinburgh locals, and for good reason. Affordable, flavoursome and each branch is slightly different. **££**
Jackson's, 209–213 High Street, tel: 225 1793. Atmospheric basement restaurant serving imaginative Scottish cooking in somewhat cramped space. Very popular with tourists. Set lunch an excellent bargain. **£££**

luscious fruit drinks. Open early morning until late.
Fruitmarket Cafeteria, Fruitmarket Gallery, 45 Market Street, tel: 226 1843. Soak up some contemporary art, then relax with a coffee and some tasty soup, Macsween's haggis or *nachos*.
Glass & Thompson, 2 Dundas Street, tel: 557 0909. Cosy deli serving first rate home baking and soups. Some outdoor seating in the summer.
Helios Fountain, 7 Grassmarket, tel: 229 7884. Self-service non-smoking vegetarian café in a craft shop. Delicious organic muffins, sweet and savoury bakes.
Laigh Bake House, 117a Hanover Street, tel: 225 1552. Now 100 percent organic. Popular with young and old, and deservedly so.
Valvona & Crolla, 19 Elm Row, Lieth Walk. tel: 556 6066. An Edinburgh legend, this popular Italian deli serves extravagant food at high prices, but it's usually worth every penny.

Martin's, 70 Rose St North Lane, tel: 225 3106. Difficult to find this small, well established restaurant but well worth the trouble. Limited but confident menu with best cheeseboard in town. Excellent discreet service. **£££**

Oloroso, 33 Castle Street, tel: 226 7614. Stunning setting in a penthouse space with glass walls and a penthouse space with glass walls and a roof terrace. Excellent food cooked to precision. Reasonable bar snacks also available. **£££**

Restaurant Martin Wishart, 54 The Shore, Leith, tel: 553 3557. One of the best restaurants in the city (the only one with a Michelin star), opened in 1999. Imaginative and dynamic cooking. Menu changes daily. **£££**

Rogue, Scottish Widows Building, 67 Morrison Street, tel: 228 2700. New in 2001, this trendy restaurant and bar allows you to eat as little or as much as you want, from a sandwich to the full works. **££**

Stac Polly, 29 Dublin Street, tel: 556 2231 and 8 Grindlay Street, tel: 229 5405. Unashamedly Scottish in every respect, each branch has its own individual style, with the food almost always of a high standard. Friendly service. **£££**

The Tower, Museum of Scotland, Chambers Street, tel: 225 3003. Situated at the top of Edinburgh's magnificent new museum, a good table at this excellent restaurant affords you not just a great meal, but a wonderful view too. Good value pre-theatre menu. **£££**

The Witchery, 352 Castlehill, Royal Mile, tel: 225 5613. New-wave cooking served in two restaurants, each with unusual atmosphere. Upstairs is dark and atmospheric – beams and oil lamps – while downstairs is bright with lots of greenery and small outdoor terrace. Choice of 900 wines. Fast turnover. **£££**

CHINESE

Chinese Home Cooking, 34 West Preston Street, tel: 668 4946.

Straightforward Cantonese cooking. Bring your own bottle. **£**

Dragon Way, 74 South Clerk Street, tel: 668 1328. A sensory overload of dragons and Chinese paraphernalia, with an impressive menu to match. **££**

Kweilin, 19 Dundas Street, tel: 557 1875. Large, sumptuous space serving authentic Cantonese dishes, especially strong on seafood. Many swear this is the best Chinese in town. **££**

Restaurant Prices

Prices are per person for a two-course evening meal excluding wine.
- **£** = under £10
- **££** = £10–20
- **£££** = over £20

FRENCH

Duck's at Le Marché Noir, 2–4 Eyre Place, tel: 558 1608. An elegant restaurant offering informal yet sophisticated dining. The cuisine combines Scottish and French elements. Extensive, interesting wine list. **£££**

Jacques, 8 Gillespie Place, tel: 229 6080. Uncomplicated, quality food in authentic surroundings, with the feel of a French rural town. Close to the Theatre Royal. **££**

Le Café Saint-Honoré, 34 N.W. Thistle Street Lane, tel: 226 2211. Step into this pleasant bistro down a cobbled lane in the New Town, leave Scotland behind and enter France. Good value lunch and "Apres Cinq" (5–7pm) menu. Imaginative dishes and a decent wine list. **£££**

La Cuisine l'Odile, 13 Randolph Crescent, tel: 225 5685. Tuesday–Saturday noon–2pm. Simple bistro in the basement of L'Institut Français d'Écosse. Limited menu of delightful, inexpensive dishes. Booking advised. **£**

Pompadour, Caledonian Hilton Hotel, Princes Street, tel: 222 8888. Possibly Edinburgh's most elegant and formal dining room.

Secluded tables offer wonderful views of the Castle. Classic wines and impeccable service. **£££**

Le Sept, 7 Old Fishmarket Close, tel: 225 5428. Down a cobbled close off the Royal Mile, this long-established restaurant specialises in fish and crêpes. Simple, pub-style tables (a few outdoors). **££**

INDIAN

Indian Cavalry Club, 3 Atholl Place, tel: 228 3282. The paramilitary uniforms of the staff should not be off-putting. This upmarket Indian restaurant with an emphasis on steaming attempts, with a fair amount of success, to blend brasserie and Indian restaurant. Better than average wine list at reasonable prices. **££**

Kalpna, 2 St Patrick Square, tel: 667 9890. Gujerati and southern Indian vegetarian food in a non-smoking restaurant. Decent, moderately priced wine list. **£–££**

Lancers, 5 Hamilton Place, tel: 332 3444. Elegant space with three rooms serving Bengali and north Indian cuisine. Modest wine list. **££**

Shamiana, 14 Brougham Street, tel: 228 2265. Kashmir dishes served in this rather elegant Indian restaurant. Excellent Tandoori and curry. Booking essential, open evenings only. **££**

ITALIAN

Ferri's Restaurant, 1 Antigua Street, Leith Walk, tel: 556 5592. Good food in a cheerful environment, open evenings only. **££**

Librizzi's, 69 North Castle Street, tel: 226 1155. Specialising in fish dishes, this Sicilian restaurant is bright and stylish and the home-made pasta is a treat. **£££**

Pizza Express, 23 North Bridge, tel: 557 6411; 32 Queensferry Street, tel: 225 8863; 1 Deanhaugh Street, tel: 332 7229; 36-37 The Shore, Leith. Reliable standby with reasonable prices. The Deanhaugh Street branch is in an old clock tower by the Water of Leith. **£**

Ristorante Tinelli, 139 Easter Road, tel: 652 1932. Small, unpretentious restaurant with a limited menu of superb North Italian food. Splendid cheese selection. **££**

JAPANESE

Yumi of Edinburgh, 2 West Coates, tel: 337 2173. Formal Japanese dining in a large sandstone house, with a variety of set menus. Contains a Tatami room where you kneel down to eat. **£££**

MEXICAN

Blue Parrot Cantina, 49 St Stephen Street, tel: 225 2941. This basement restaurant in Stockbridge is small and dimly lit but perfectly formed. The menu's not bad either and the food is authentically spicy. Good range of Tequilas and cocktails. **££**

Viva Mexico, 41 Cockburn Street, tel: 226 5145. Cosy restaurant that transfers the diner back to the atmosphere of old Mexico. Food (for some) on the spicy side. Good selection for vegetarians. Great margaritas. **££**

SEAFOOD

Café Royal Oyster Bar, 17a West Register Street, tel: 556 4124. An Edinburgh institution where the ambience is everything. Victorian stained glass and polished wood. Always bustling. **£££**

Creelers, 3 Hunter Square, tel: 220 4447. Seafood restaurant just off the Royal Mile from which you can watch buskers on the square. Great langoustines. Carnivores are not denied their pleasures. **££–£££**

Skippers Bistro, 1a Dock Place, Leith, tel: 554 1018. Intimate, cosy restaurant with wood-panelled booths. Friendly service and some of the best seafood in town. **£££**

The Shore Bar and Restaurant, 3/4 The Shore, Leith, tel: 553 5080. Charming fish restaurant, with dark wooden panelling and a real fire. Eat in the restaurant or the bar. **££**

The Waterfront, 1c Dock Place, Leith, tel: 554 7427. An old custom's office on the water's edge with a brand new conservatory, offering imaginative, Mediterranean flavours and an impressive wine list. Outdoor tables in summer. **££**

SPANISH

Igg's, 15 Jeffrey Street, tel: 557 8184. Small, family-run restaurant with an excellent reputation for wonderful food, including game, seafood and a full *tapas* menu. **£££**

THAI

Siam Erawan, 48 Howe Street, tel: 226 3675. The city's top Thai restaurant with authentic Thai food and laid-back waiters. Good wine list. Booking essential. **££**

Sukhothai, 23 Brougham Place, tel: 229 1537. Good range of Thai dishes and obliging service. Good choice of seafood dishes. **££**

TURKISH

Nargile, 73 Hanover Street, tel: 225 5755. Light and airy, comprehensive menu with signature dish of the meza, a tapas-style selection of Middle Eastern starters. **££**

VEGETARIAN

Bann UK, 5 Hunter Square, tel: 226 1112. Just off the Royal Mile. A stylish interior design and exciting menu make this not just one of the best vegetarian restaurants in Scotland, but all of Britain. Serves main meals throughout the day, and *tapas*-style snacks up to 11pm. **££**

Black Bo's, 57 Blackfriars Street, tel: 557 6136. Food bursting with flavour and a relaxed, informal atmosphere courtesy of the very creative chef and owner. **££**

Henderson's Salad Table, 94 Hanover Street, tel: 225 2131. Self-service basement diner with menu changing through the day. Low-key live music most evenings. **££**

Bistros

The Apartment, 7–13 Barclay Place, tel: 228 6456. Mediterranean and Asian influences. Great food, large portions, trendy yet welcoming atmosphere. **££**

blue, 10 Cambridge Street, tel: 221 1222. Impossibly stylish and perennially popular place to eat and/or drink. Housed in the Traverse Theatre complex. **££**

Daniel's Bistro, 88 Commercial Street, Leith, tel: 553 5933. A lively eatery in converted whisky warehouses near Leith Docks. Fine Scottish produce and traditional French regional dishes. **££**

The Dome Bar & Grill, 14 George Street, tel: 624 8624. Housed in a former bank, this large, airy venue is good for either a main meal or a day-time drink while shopping on George Street. **££**

Maxies Wine Bar and Bistro, 5b Johnston Terrace, tel: 226 7770. Varied international cuisine served by helpful and friendly staff. Good for seafood. **££**

Peckhams Underground, 155 Bruntsfield Place, tel: 228 2888. Beneath the Peckhams shop. Flop into a plush red sofa and enjoy an eclectic range of food and wine. **££**

Culture

WALKING TOURS

Auld Reekie Tours, 45 Niddry Street, tel: 557 4700. Underground city horror tours daily every hour from 12.30–3.30pm and 7–10pm. Start at Tron Kirk.

City of the Dead Haunted Graveyard Tour, Candlemaker Row, tel: 225 9044 or 0771 5422 750. Haunted tour starting by St Giles' Cathedral at 8.30pm and 10pm daily.

The Edinburgh Literary Pub Tour, 97B West Bow, tel: 226 6665. Daily in July and August at 6pm and 8.30pm; Thursday–Sunday at other times (Friday only November to March) at 7.30pm. Starts at Beehive Inn, Grassmarket.

Geowalks, 23 Summerfield Place, tel: 555 5488. Guided walks up Arthur's Seat along Water of Leith and in East Lothian, March to November.

Mercat Walking Tours, Mercat House, Niddry Street South, tel: 557 6464. Day-time historical walks and haunting evening walks, with an optional pub visit in evening. Royal Mile Walk daily all year at 10.30am/Mary King's Close Tour, daily 11.30am–9.30pm; Underground Vaults Tour every hour from 11am–4pm (noon and 4pm only October to April); Ghosts and Ghouls Tour all year at 7pm and 8pm. Start at Mercat Cross outside St Giles', Royal Mile.

Witchery Tours, 537 Castlehill, Royal Mile, tel: 225 6745. Costumed walking tours start at The Witchery restaurant (352 Castlehill). Book in advance for the Murder and Mystery Tour (nightly, after dark, all year) or Ghosts and Gore Tour (daily in daylight, May to August).

BUS TOURS

Guide Friday Tours, 133–135 Canongate, tel: 556 2244 email: edinburgh@guidefriday.com, www.guidefriday.com. Guided open-top bus tours where you can jump on and off around the city, departing throughout the day from Waverley Bridge.

Edinburgh Tour, Lothian Region Transport, 27 Hanover Street, tel: 555 6363, email: info@edinburghtour.com, www.edinburghtour.co.uk. Tours of Edinburgh. Open-top and enclosed buses, seven languages. Book at the tourist information office or the Hanover Street or Waverley Bridge ticket centres.

MacBackpacker, 105 High Street, tel: 558 9900, email: enquiries@macbackers.com. Informal, hostel-based tours of the Highlands, for budget travellers.

MacTours, 11a James Court, tel: 220 0770, email: enquiries@mactours.com, www.mactours.com. Vintage open-top bus tours of the city daily from Waverley Bridge.

Scotline Tours, 87 High Street, tel: 557 0162, email: info@scotlinetours.com, www.scotlinetours.com. Tours of the city and surrounding areas, the Borders, St Andrews, Loch Lomond etc. Can be booked at the tourist information office.

Details of individual museums, castles, historic houses and other cultural attractions are given in the main body of text. The following bodies administer many of them, and in some cases offer special multi-attraction passes and/or free admission for members. Many attractions have extended opening hours during the Festival.

City of Edinburgh Museums and Galleries

City Art Centre, 2 Market Street, tel: 529 3993, email: enquiries@city-art-

Edinburgh offers rich opportunities to the ancestor hunter. In **New Register House** at the east end of Princes Street are records of every birth, marriage and death in Scotland since 1855, the national censuses since 1841, and parish records from even earlier. For a fee of about £17 a day you can inspect the records and should be able to trace several generations. Information may be found in New Register House, tel: 314 4433, and in the **Central Library** on George IV Bridge, tel: 242 8000.

The serious ancestor hunter should read *Scottish Roots* by Alwyn James, which explains the various records in great detail, or *Tracing your Scottish Ancestors* by Catherine Cory. The **Scottish Roots Ancestral Research Service**, 16 Forth Street, tel: 477 8214 provides an expert service in genealogy, but is also restricted to Scottish records.

Those keen to belong to a clan even though your name is Hui Bing, Watanabe or Berkovitch should visit the **Clan Tartan Centre**, 70–74 Bangor Road, Leith, tel: 553 5161; **Edinburgh Old Town Weaving Company**, tel: 555 Castlehill, tel: 226 1555 provides an expert service in genealogy, but is also restricted to Scottish records. There, with the assistance of computers, you may find that you are really a Stuart, Macduff or McGregor.

centre.demon.co.uk, www.cac.org.uk
City of Edinburgh museums are the Museum of Childhood, The People's Story, Museum of Edinburgh, The Writers' Museum, Brass Rubbing Centre, Lauriston Castle, Queensferry Museum, Newhaven Heritage Museum, Nelson Monument and the Scott Monument; galleries are the City Art Centre and the Travelling Gallery.
Opening hours: Core hours are

Out and About with Children

The following attractions in and near Edinburgh are recommended for the whole family. All of them charge an entrance fee with reductions for children, except for the Royal Museum, the Museum of Scotland, and the Museum of Childhood, which are free for everyone.

Deep Sea World, North Queensferry, tel: (01383) 411880, www.deepseaworld.com. Open Monday–Sunday, 10am–6pm. Travel across the Forth Bridge to this excellent marine centre, featuring the longest underwater walkway in the world, touch pools, sharks and lots of amazing fish and other sea creatures. Dive with sharks (over 16's only), behind-the-scenes tours, special feeding times.

Our Dynamic Earth, Holyrood Road, tel: 550 7800, www.dynamicearth.co.uk. Open April to October daily 10am–6pm; November to March, Wednesday–Sunday 10am–5pm. One of Edinburgh's newest attractions takes you back 4,500 million years to the Big Bang and then works forward to present day. A great, interactive event.

Edinburgh Butterfly and Insect World, Dobbies Garden World, Lasswade, tel: 663 4932, www.edinburgh-butterfly-world.co.uk. Open daily: March to October 9.30am–5.30pm; November to February 10am–5pm. Tropical environment featuring free-flying butterflies plus insect displays. In the Bugs and Beasties room visitors are invited to handle tarantulas and minibeasts.

Edinburgh Zoo, Corstorphine Road, tel: 334 9171, www.edinburghzoo.org.uk. Open daily: April to September 9am–6pm; October to March 9am–4.30pm. The world's largest penguin enclosure and Europe's largest colony of penguins. The 2.15pm penguin parades (weather permitting), when the birds mingle with visitors, are great fun; also sealion feeding times at 11.15am and 3.45pm. Other events on a less regular basis – check with the zoo.

Museum of Childhood, 42 High Street, tel: 529 4142, www.cac.org.uk. Open Monday–Saturday 10am–5pm, Sunday in July and August noon–5pm.

In some ways, parents get more out of this than children, with plenty of nostalgia. Younger children can have fun dressing up, playing tea parties and seeing what mummy and daddy used to play with when they were little.

Royal Museum and Museum of Scotland, Chambers Street, tel: 247 4219/247 4422. www.info@nms.ac.uk. Open Monday–Saturday 10am–5pm, Sunday noon–5pm (Tuesday 8pm). Separate but inter-linked museums in two very different buildings. The Royal Museum is a traditional museum in a Victorian building with a fantastic, soaring entrance hall (kids love the huge clock and the fishponds here) and contains a huge number of artefacts. Children will be most interested in the exhibits on the natural world and on scientific and technological development.

Adjacent and connected to it on various levels is the new **Museum of Scotland**, tracing the history of Scotland on six floors. Great views from the Roof Terrace. No entrance fee.

Monday–Saturday 10am–5pm, with Sunday opening during the summer. Admission to the majority of City of Edinburgh museums is free, but during Festival time some places charge a small entry fee. The City Art Centre charges for special exhibitions.

Historic Scotland

Longmore House, Salisbury Place, tel: 668 8800, www.historic-scotland.gov.uk. Historic Scotland properties in or near Edinburgh include Edinburgh Castle and Blackness, Craigmillar, Crichton, Dirleton and Tantallon castles. Entrance fees vary.

Opening hours vary, but the core hours in summer are: April to September daily 9.30am–6.30pm (except Edinburgh Castle: daily 9.30am–6pm). Standard hours from

October to March are: Monday–Saturday 9.30am–4.30pm, Sunday 2–4.30pm (Edinburgh Castle: daily 9.30am–5pm).

Special deals: Scottish Explorer Ticket offering unlimited access to all Historic Scotland properties. A three-day pass costs £15 (concessions £11, family £30); for a seven-day pass £15 (£11) and for a 14-day pass £20 (£15). Or you can become a Friend of Historic Scotland for a year at a cost of £30 (£23/£53). Friends get free entry to all Historic Scotland properties and discounted entry to English Heritage, Welsh Cadw and Manx National Heritage properties, plus a quarterly magazine, 20 percent discount in Historic Scotland shops and invitations to membership events and holidays.

National Museums of Scotland

Chambers Street, tel: 247 4219, www.nms.ac.uk

National museums include the Royal Museum and Museum of Scotland in central Edinburgh, the National War Museum in Edinburgh Castle, Granton Research Centre in the suburbs, and the Museum of Flight in East Lothian.

Opening hours for the Royal Museum and Museum of Scotland are: Monday–Saturday 10am–5pm (Tuesday until 8pm), Sunday noon–5pm. Admission free.

Special deals: A National Museums Pass entitles you to free entry for one year to 15 museums in Scotland, costing £8 for adults, concessions £5, family ticket £15.

The National Trust for Scotland
28 Charlotte Square, tel: 243 9300, www.nts.org.uk
Centrally located properties are Gladstone's Land and the Georgian House. Outside the city are the House of the Binns, Inveresk Lodge Garden, Newhailes (opened 2002) Malleny Garden and Preston Mill. Entrance fees and opening times vary.
    Special deals: Annual membership of the National Trust for Scotland (NTS) currently costs £30 for an individual or £50 for a family. Reduced rates for under 25's and senior citizens. Life membership also available. Members gain free admission to NTS properties in Scotland, England, Wales and Northern Ireland and receive a colour magazine.

Art Galleries

Edinburgh has a large number of diverse galleries, with something to suit every taste, and a thriving contemporary art scene which is gaining an international reputation. Entry is free to all public and commercial galleries, but for special exhibitions and during Festival time (August), many galleries introduce an admission charge. Opening hours are also extended during the Festival.

PUBLIC GALLERIES

The national galleries and other principal galleries are further discussed in the *The Visual Arts* chapter. Details of the National Gallery of Scotland, Scottish National Portrait Gallery and Royal Scottish Academy are also given in *The First New Town*, while *The Water of Leith* chapter includes the Scottish National Gallery of Modern Art and Dean Gallery.

National Galleries of Scotland
tel: 624 6200, email; nginfo@nationalgalleries.org, www.nationalgalleries.org
Dean Gallery, 73 Belford Road. Open Monday–Saturday 10am–5pm, Sunday noon–5pm. The newest of

the national galleries, situated near the Scottish National Gallery of Modern Art and complementing it with a modern collection including the sculpture of Eduardo Paolozzi, Dada and Surrealism. Also temporary exhibitions.
National Gallery of Scotland, The Mound. Open Monday–Saturday 10am–5pm, Sunday noon–5pm. The most senior of the national galleries. Scotland's finest collection of European paintings from the Renaissance to Post-Impressionism. Temporary exhibitions include the annual airing of Turner's watercolours in January.
Scottish National Gallery of Modern Art, 75 Belford Road. Open Monday–Saturday 10am–5pm, Sunday noon–5pm. Beyond bijou Dean Village, set in wonderful grounds. An impressive collection of 20th/21st-century art. Temporary exhibitions throughout the year.
Scottish National Portrait Gallery, 1 Queen Street. Open Monday–Saturday 10am–5pm, Sunday noon–5pm. Famous Scots from the 16th century to the present day. Notable programme of temporary exhibitions.
City Art Centre, 2 Market Street, tel: 529 3993. Open Monday to Saturday 10am–5pm; Sunday only, 2–5pm. Council-run gallery on five floors, the home of the City of Edinburgh's impressive collection of Scottish art. Also hosts a varied programme of temporary, contemporary exhibitions.
Collective Gallery, 22–28 Cockburn Street, tel: 220 1260. Open Wednesday–Saturday noon–5pm, Sunday 3–5pm. After an extensive, Lottery-funded refurbishment, this gallery is now bigger and brighter. Regular temporary exhibition programme showcasing the work of up-and-coming contemporary artists.
Fruitmarket Gallery, 45 Market Street, tel: 225 2383. Open Monday–Saturday 11am–6pm, Sunday noon–5pm. Situated opposite the City Art Centre, this stylish gallery is one of Edinburgh's finest contemporary art spaces, attracting home-grown talent and high-profile international artists.

Inverleith House, Royal Botanic Garden, Inverleith Row, tel: 248 2849. Open daily (except Tuesday), 10.30am–5.30pm. An exciting exhibition programme of art and sculpture, complemented by stunning views of Edinburgh's dramatic skyline. Callum Innes, Andy Goldsworthy and Carl Andre are among the artists who have exhibited here.
Royal Scottish Academy, The Mound, tel: 225 6671. Exhibitions gallery in front of the National Gallery. Closed until summer 2003.
Stills Gallery, 23 Cockburn Street, tel: 622 6200. Open Tuesday–Saturday 10am–5pm. Across the road from the Collective Gallery; one of Edinburgh's most dynamic art spaces featuring work by photographic artists from around the globe. Also houses a café and photographic and digital labs.
Talbot Rice Gallery, Old College, University of Edinburgh, South Bridge, tel: 650 2211. Open Tuesday–Saturday 10am–5pm. This gallery houses a small permanent collection of work, with the main focus on temporary exhibitions featuring international and Scottish artists.

COMMERCIAL GALLERIES

The following list represents the best of the city's many gallery salerooms.
Bourne Fine Art, 6 Dundas Street, tel: 557 4050, www.bournefineart.co.uk. Open Monday–Friday 10am–6pm, Saturday 11am–2pm.
Calton Gallery, 10 Royal Terrace, tel: 556 1010, www.caltongallery.co.uk. Open Monday–Friday 10am–6pm, Saturday by appointment. Specialist dealers in 19th- and 20th-century Scottish and marine paintings and watercolours.
Edinburgh Printmakers, 23 Union Street, tel: 557 2479. Open Tuesday–Saturday 10am–6pm. The place to purchase limited edition prints or take part in workshops

Film: Multiplexes and Arthouse Cinemas

Cameo, 38 Home Street, tel: 228 4141. Stylish, independent cinema showing a mix of arthouse, cult and classic movies and new releases. Weekly late-night screenings and Sunday double bills. Licensed bar – drinks can be taken into auditorium.

Dominion, 18 Newbattle Terrace, tel: 447 2660 (recorded information), 447 4771 (bookings and enquiries). Cosy, four-screen cinema in Morningside showing new releases. Licensed bar also serves food.

Filmhouse, 88 Lothian Road, tel: 228 2688, www.filmhouse.demon.co.uk. An arthouse cinema, although not only film fanatics will find something of interest. Three screens show well-constructed special seasons and a basic diet of interesting international movies. This is the main venue for the Edinburgh International Film Festival in August. Licensed café-bar.

Odeon, 7 Clerk Street, tel: 0870 5050007. Commercial new releases on five screens. This is Edinburgh's main venue for film premieres, so the licensed, tartan bar has seen a few international stars on its stools.

Odeon Wester Hailes, Westside Plaza, 120 Wester Hailes Road, tel: 0870 5050007. A fair hike out of the well-served city centre, this cinema excels in its eight screens and comfortable seating. Licensed bar.

Star Century, Ocean Terminal, Leith, tel: 553 0700. Wall to wall screens and deep, comfy seats in this new 12 screen complex within Ocean Terminal. Commercial new releases.

UCI, Kinnaird Park, Newcraighall Road, tel: 0870 010 2030. In the suburbs, but this cinema has 12 screens and shows just about every film opening in a given week. Licensed bar, restaurant and bowling alley in the complex.

UGC Cinemas, Fountain Park, Dundee Street, tel: 0870 902 0417. Part of a leisure complex in the city's Fountainbridge area, the UGC has 13 screens, including a luxurious (and expensive for punters) premiere screen. The complex includes a licensed bar, restaurant and nightclub.

Warner Villages, Omni, Leith Walk. New 12-screen cinema.

and courses; the gallery also has a strong exhibition programme featuring work by local and international artists.

Ingleby Gallery, 6 Carlton Terrace, tel: 556 4441. www.inglebygallery.com. Open Tuesday–Saturday 10am-5pm. This gallery space on the ground floor of a Georgian townhouse attracts big names, past shows having included the work of Howard Hodgkin, Callum Innes, Sean Scully and Patrick Heron.

Open Eye Gallery, 75–79 Cumberland Street, tel: 557 1020, www.openeyegallery.co.uk. Open Monday–Friday 10am-6pm, Saturday 10am-4pm. New Town gallery featuring the work of Scottish artists and beyond, with regular shows of paintings and applied arts. See also *The Visual Arts*.

The Scottish Gallery, 16 Dundas Street, tel: 558 1200, www.scottish-gallery.co.uk. Open Monday–Friday 10am-6pm, Saturday 10am-4pm. New Town gallery featuring both traditional and modern art by a range of well-known and not so well-known artists. Frequent shows of jewellery, ceramics and other applied arts.

Torrance Gallery, 36 Dundas Street, tel: 556 6366, www.torrancegallery.co.uk. Changing exhibitions of contemporary art. Open Monday–Friday, 11am-6pm, Saturday 10.30-4pm.

Scottish Entertainment

At several locations an evening of Scottish entertainment with lots of bagpipe music and tartan may be enjoyed. Dinner is usually included in the admission price. These entertainments are mounted for the visitor rather than for the locals.

Jamie's Scottish Evening, King James Thistle Hotel, Leith Street, tel: 556 0111. April to October, nightly at 6.45pm.

Scottish Evening, George Inter-Continental Hotel, 19-21 George Street, tel: 225 1251. May to September, Sunday, Tuesday, Thursday and Friday at 7.30pm.

A Taste of Scotland, Round Stables, Prestonfield House, Priestfield Road, tel: 668 3346. April to October, Sunday–Friday at 7pm. Superb historical setting.

CEILIDH DANCES

Those seeking something more authentic may want to sample a ceilidh dance – the word "ceilidh" is Gaelic and means a gathering. These days expect energetic traditional dancing to live folk music, and do not let inexperience put you off as most events feature official callers to demonstrate the steps.

Assembly Rooms, 54 George Street, tel: 220 4349. Occasional events throughout the year. This is an excellent venue so it's well worth attending a ceilidh here if you have the opportunity.

Caledonian Brewery, 42 Slateford Road, tel: 623 8066, www.claedonian–brewery.co.uk Ceilidhs are irregular, although there are usually at least two a month on Saturday nights. Doors open 7pm.

St Bride's Centre, 10 Orwell Terrace, tel: 346 1405. Again, events are irregular, but in the winter months, especially, there is often a ceilidh every weekend.

Theatre

Bedlam Theatre,
11b Bristo Place, tel: 225 9873,
www.bedlamtheatre.co.uk. Beautiful,
Gothic former church, now home to
the Edinburgh University Theatre
Company whose productions, while
occasionally dire, have also won
prestigious awards. The Fonts
festival in February of new Scottish
theatre writing is the highlight of the
calendar.

Brunton Theatre, Ladywell Way,
Musselburgh, tel: 665 2240. Well
worth the trip out of the city centre,
this is a well-appointed venue,
although the concrete exterior
leaves a little to be desired. The
Brunton is frequently host to
touring companies, comedians
and musicians.

Edinburgh Festival Theatre,
13–29 Nicholson Street, tel: 529
6000, www.eft.co.uk
As Edinburgh's newest theatre
venue (1994), the Festival Theatre
is the Edinburgh base of Scottish
Ballet and Scottish Opera, as well
as the venue of choice for the
bigger touring theatre and dance
productions. A recent merger with
the King's Theatre, however, means
that not everything that graces the
stage is highbrow.

Edinburgh Playhouse, 18–22
Greenside Place, tel: 0870 606
3424, www.edinburgh-
playhouse.co.uk. The Playhouse is
Edinburgh's biggest venue, making
it a popular option for touring
comedians and musicians, although
its mainstay, except during the
International Festival, is visiting
productions from London's
West End.

King's Theatre, 2 Leven Street,
tel: 529 6000, www.eft.co.uk
An Edwardian theatre in the plush,
traditional mould, the King's has
now merged with the Festival
Theatre (see above). Both share
booking and programming facilities,
although the King's tends to attract
the more mainstream touring
events and popular amateur
productions.

Netherbow Arts Centre, 43–45
High Street, tel: 556 9579/2647,
www.storytellingcentre.org.uk
Converted from part of the historic
John Knox House, the Netherbow
specialises in small-scale touring
and community events, in particular
children's theatre and traditional
storytelling events. It hosts the
International Storytelling Festival
in November.

Royal Lyceum Theatre,
Grindlay Street, tel: 248 4848,
www.lyceum.org.uk
As Edinburgh's repertory theatre,
the Lyceum is not cutting edge. It
mainly airs the classics but also
stages the occasional new play
(often very successfully). All house
productions are previewed with a
free Friday night performance –
joining the queue before 7pm
should guarantee a ticket.

St Bride's Centre, 10 Orwell
Terrace, tel: 346 1405. A
community-led programming policy
means the fare here is a mixed, if
interesting, bag. Of most interest to
the visitor are the Ceilidh nights
(see *Scottish Entertainment*) and
the varied touring productions.

Theatre Workshop, 34 Hamilton
Place, tel: 226 5425. Although it's
a small, unassuming theatre, the
Theatre Workshop's contribution to
the city's theatrical diversity should
not be underestimated. As well as
staging innovative community
projects, the venue hosts a diverse
range of unusual touring productions.

Traverse Theatre,
10 Cambridge Street, tel: 228
1404, www.traverse.co.uk
Edinburgh's most exciting
contemporary theatre. With a
programme tailored to promote
new writing, it has become a
centre of excellence in the genre.
The Monday Lizard events (last
Monday of each month) feature
short scripts performed by
professional actors in the bar. The
venue is also a popular stopping
place for new touring productions,
including dance-based shows. (see
*Triumph of the Traverse Theatre
page 123*).

Comedy

During the Edinburgh Festival
Fringe, Edinburgh is awash with
comedians, but things are a bit
quieter during the rest of the year.
Pub-based comedy shows come
and go, so it's worth keeping an
eye out for posters to find out
what's going on. However,
Edinburgh has a few established,
year-round venues:

Edinburgh Playhouse, 18–22
Greenside Place, tel: 0870 606
3424, www.edinburgh-
playhouse.co.uk Generally hosts
any big-name comedians in town.

Fin MacCool's, 161 Lothian Road,
tel: 622 7109. three to four acts
on a Saturday night. Also raw
comedians on a Thursday.

The Gilded Balloon, 233 Cowgate,
tel: 226 6550,
www.gildedballoon.co.uk

The Gilded Balloon's main
business is organising Scottish
tours for middle-ranking
comedians, who'll usually perform
here when they come to
Edinburgh. Also hosts occasional
local stand-up events.

Snatch Club, The Liquid Room,
9c Victoria Street, tel: 225 2564.
Resident cabaret act with Harry
Ainsworth (aka Garth Brooks).

The Stand, 5 York Place, tel: 558
7272, www.thestand.co.uk
Edinburgh's only purpose-built
comedy venue, with some sort of
laughathon every day. Weekday
events include a comedy quiz and
a stand-up beginners' night, with
standard five-act shows taking
place Thursday–Saturday. Gay
comedy 2nd Tuesday of the month
(OOT: Out on Tuesday).

Music and Dance

See also *Pubs with Live Music*
under *Nightlife*.

The Corn Exchange, New Market
Road, Gorgie, tel: 443 2437,
www.ece.uk.com
A recent addition to Edinburgh's
rock scene, The Corn Exchange is
the right size to attract the biggest

contemporary bands (Blur played the inaugural concert). Outside the city centre, but gigs regularly sell out.
Edinburgh Festival Theatre, 13–29 Nicolson Street, tel: 529 6000, www.eft.co.uk
The Edinburgh base for Scottish Opera and Scottish Ballet. Their productions are held in high esteem and often involve new takes on the classics. The bigger touring shows also stop here.
Edinburgh Playhouse, 18–22 Greenside Place, tel: 0870 606 3424, www.edinburgh-playhouse.co.uk
Edinburgh's biggest all-seater which hosts visiting big-name musicals, rock, jazz and folk artists, although – because it's primarily a theatre – it lacks the atmosphere of some other venues.
Henry's Jazz Cellar, 8 Morrison Street, tel: 467 5200. A pub during the day, this is Edinburgh's dedicated jazz venue at night. Something on every night, although the Monday and Tuesday shows are often DJ-only affairs. The programme ranges from traditional and bop to cutting-edge jazz fusion.
The Liquid Room, 9c Victoria Street, tel: 225 2564, www.liquidroom.com
A regular programme of well-known rock/pop acts competes with this venue's other identity as a nightclub.
The Pleasance Cabaret Bar, 60 The Pleasance, tel: 650 2349. This student union bar is also the home of Edinburgh Folk Club. Regulars on the scene often drop in and there are some lively open-mic sessions.
The Queen's Hall, Clerk Street, tel: 668 2019. The mainstay here is classical music, with regular visits from touring outfits as well as a winter programme from ensemble-in-residence, the Scottish Chamber Orchestra. As a cosy, medium-sized venue, it is also host to middle-ranking jazz and folk artists.
Reid Concert Hall, Teviot Row, Bristo Square, tel: 650 2423. The property of Edinburgh University, this is the main venue for performances of the faculty of music – which are generally classical but include the occasional night of experimental and electronic music – although local and

touring ensembles also play here. Also houses an important collection of historic instruments (see website: www.music.ed.ac.uk/euchmi/).
St Cecilia's Hall, Niddry Street (off Cowgate), tel: 650 2805. Another university venue, St Cecilia's is the city's oldest concert hall (1762). Again the programme is mainly classical, including student performances and visiting outfits. Houses the university's collection of early keyboard instruments (see *The Old Town*, page 128).
Usher Hall, Lothian Road, tel: 228 1155, www.usherhall.co.uk. Full-scale concert hall (capacity 2,200), built by the brewer Andrew Usher at the turn of the 20th century. Reopened at the end of 2000 after refurbishment, it is the Edinburgh base of the Royal Scottish National Orchestra and its music programme includes some of the world's biggest classical names.
The Venue, 17–21 Calton Road (behind Waverley Station), tel: 557 3073, www.edinburghvenue.co
Long-established rock and pop venue which hosts both touring acts and local band events.

Nightlife

Pubs

Most pubs in Edinburgh now sell "real ale" – cask-conditioned beer in various strengths (60°, 70° and 80°) made by Scottish brewers, large and small. Ask for, for example, 80/- ("eighty shilling"). Connoisseurs should look out for Caledonian 70/- and 80/-, which are made using traditional methods in a Victorian brewery in the city. Most pubs have a reasonable selection of malt whiskies.

Licensing hours in Edinburgh are liberal. If you try hard enough, so they say, you can drink for 22 out of 24 hours. Certainly, there is no shortage of pubs which are "open all day", which usually means from about 11am until midnight or 1am. Licenses are often extended until 3am during the August festival season; for year-round late-night drinking try the Cowgate and Bristo Square areas of the city.

Most bars are bearable, and some of the traditional drinking haunts shouldn't be missed. The following selection is a bit special:
The Barony Bar, 81–85 Broughton Street, tel: 557 0546. Situated in trendy Broughton Street, the Barony is a refreshingly old-fashioned bar with a real coal fire and hearty pub grub.
Bennets, 8 Leven Street, tel: 229 5143. A bar in the traditional mould in the city's Tollcross area, Bennets also boasts a choice of at least 100 malt whiskies.
Café Royal Circle Bar, 19 West Register Street, tel: 556 1884. Tucked away at the east end of Princes Street, this is a classy joint, with tiled walls and leather upholstery as well as a fine range of beers and a gourmet menu.

The Canny Man's, 237 Morningside Road, tel: 447 1484. Sometimes intimidating and with undeniably cantankerous staff, The Canny Man's is still an Edinburgh institution (see *The Tenement Landscape* chapter, *page 172*). Every ornament is steeped in history, and the huge range of whiskies, wines and cigars is the best in the city.

Clarkes Bar, 142 Dundas Street, tel: 556 1067. Traditional, unpretentious real ale pub for the discerning drinker.

Diggers (The Athletic Arms), 1 Angle Park Terrace, tel: 337 3822. Nicknamed for its proximity to a graveyard, this bar is an excellent choice for a pint of 80/- and is a perennial favourite among sports fans (with televised matches).

Greyfriars Bobby, 34a Candlemaker Row, tel: 225 8328. Named after the famously faithful dog (whose grave can be visited in the churchyard behind the pub), Greyfriars Bobby is an ideally placed stopping-off point on the sightseeing trail.

King's Wark, 36 The Shore, Leith, tel: 554 9260. The Shore area of Leith has been the subject of a very successful redevelopment, yet the King's Wark still has a traditional port pub feel to it. It is cosy, relaxed and offers an excellent seafood menu.

Milne's, 35 Hanover Street, tel: 225 6738. A cavernous traditional bar in the city centre, Milne's offers a changing array of speciality ales.

PUBS WITH LIVE MUSIC

Drinking is a popular pastime in Scotland, but that doesn't mean you can't experience some culture at the same time. Several of Edinburgh's hostelries have built their reputation on their live music slots, and in many others you'll find regular music residencies and even the occasional spontaneous jam.

The Antiquary, 77–78 St Stephen Street, tel: 225 2858. Cosy cellar bar with a lively open folk session every Thursday from 9pm.

Casinos

If you want to gamble at a casino, the law requires that you become a member of the club 24 hours before you play, although restrictions maybe changed in the near future. Membership is free. Dress code varies between venues.

Cascades Casino, 2 Ocean Drive, Leith, tel: 553 7505.

Ladbroke Maybury Casino, 5 South Maybury, tel: 338 4444.

Stanley Berkeley Casino Club, 2 Rutland Place, tel: 228 4446.

Stanley Edinburgh Casino Club, 5b York Place, tel: 624 2121.

The Beat Jazz Basement, 1 Chambers Street, tel: 220 4298. Cosy, subterranean venue, with jazz every night from 10pm. Weekdays more traditional, weekends more modern.

Bridge Jazz Bar, 82 South Bridge, tel: 478 2510. Eight gigs a week, usually free entry. 9pm–1am.

Ensign Ewart, 521 Lawnmarket, tel: 225 7440. A great spot near the Castle for Scottish folk music at weekends.

Finnegan's Wake, 9b Victoria Street, tel: 226 3816. Irish theme bar which offers Celtic rock and folk on a nightly basis.

Hebrides, 17 Market Street, tel: 220 4213. This small pub is a great venue for folk music on Thursday, Friday and Saturday night.

Malt Shovel, 11–15 Cockburn Street, tel: 225 6843. Swing jazz on Tuesday night – the longest running pub residency in Edinburgh.

Sandy Bell's, 25 Forrest Road, tel: 225 1156. Long renowned for live folk music.

Trafalgar Suite, Waterloo Buffet, 3 Waterloo Place, tel: 556 7597. Resident jazz band on a Sunday evening – mainstream progressive and experimental.

Whistle Binkies, 6 Niddry Street, tel: 557 5114. Late-opening pub with nightly music. Folk-rock, covers bands and blues are the mainstays.

Nightclubs

Edinburgh has a bustling club scene, with every taste catered for, whether it's charty tunes you crave or the underground sounds of drum and bass and hip hop. Nightclubs are generally licensed until 3am (extended to 5am during the Edinburgh Festival in August). Apart from a few specialist "glam" nights, the dress code is fairly casual.

La Belle Angele, Hastie's Close (off The Cowgate), tel: 225 7536, www.la-belle-angele.co.uk Stylish venue, large enough to host big-name DJs but not too big to lose its intimacy. Club nights showcase cutting-edge dance music across the genres.

The Bongo Club, 14 New Street, tel: 558 7604, www.thebongoclub.co.uk. Always under threat of closure, The Bongo Club relies heavily on arts subsidies to put on a genre-defying array of live music and DJ events. An arts venue during the day and for the duration of the Edinburgh Festival, this club always comes up with something a little different.

The Citrus Club, 40–42 Grindlay Street, tel: 622 7086, www.citrus-club.co.uk Popular with students, this club specialises in indie, rock, chart and party sounds Thursdays–Saturday.

The Establishment, 3 Semple Street, tel: 229 7733, Relaxed club lounge, from 4pm. R&B night on Saturdays.

Club Mercado, 36 Market Street, tel: 226 4224. Trendy spot with wrought-iron decor, well suited to glam events. Also the venue for infamous after-work drinking sessions on a Friday.

Eros & Elite, Fountainpark, Dundee Street, tel: 228 1661, www.nightclub.co.uk A custom-built venue within a leisure complex, Eros & Elite is in fact two clubs. Both specialise in chart, party and commercial dance music, but Elite has a strict over 25's policy.

Ego, 14 Picardy Place, tel: 478 7434. A converted casino hosting club nights on Fridays and

Saturdays, from house and dance to "kitsch retro" and party events. Also has gay club nights, (see under *Gay Nightlife*).

Gaia, 28 King's Stables Road, tel: 229 7986, www.edin-out.com Mainstream dance, disco and party tunes are the speciality of this two-floored venue, which pulls capacity crowds at weekends. Studenty.

La Belle Angele, 11 Hasties Close, tel: 225 7536. Variety of club nights on Fridays and Saturdays. Week nights it's a music venue hosting a range of local and touring bands.

The Liquid Room, 9c Victoria Street, tel: 225 2564, www.liquidroom.com

Gay Nightlife

The Broughton Street/Picardy Place area (known as the Gay Triangle) is the main focus of the city's gay nightlife, although most dance club nights in the city centre have a gay-friendly atmosphere. Useful contacts are the Lothian Gay And Lesbian Switchboard (tel: 556 4049), which operates 7.30–10pm daily, and Gay Men's Health (10a Union Street, tel: 558 9444), a drop-in centre which offers counselling and support services. *Scotsgay* magazine lists what's on, available from C.C. Blooms.

Angel Delight, The Venue, 17–21 Calton Road, tel: 557 0751. Monthly, women-only superclub on the top floor every fourth Friday. There's also a regular residency for DJ Michelle of Manchester's famous Poptastic night, who brings her "ShagTag" system with her.

Blue Moon Café, 1 Barony Street, tel: 556 2788. A trendy, relaxed café-bar with a straight-friendly atmosphere. The menu is extensive and reasonably priced. As a hub of gay activity, this is an excellent place to find out what's on around town.

Out of the Blue downstairs (tel: 478 7048) is less straight-friendly and sells gay merchandise and tickets for gay-oriented events.

C.C. Blooms, 23–24 Greenside Place, tel: 556 9331. The city's only dedicated gay nightclub, C.C.'s has a bar upstairs and a small but always packed club downstairs. The music policy ranges from camp disco classics and retro tunes to high energy dance. Open nightly.

Joy, Ego, 14 Picardy Place,

tel: 478 7435. Upfront gay club, every second Saturday. Joy Infoline: 467 2551. The same venue also hosts Vibe on a Tuesday, and Lush on a Friday.

Laughing Duck, 24 Howe Street, tel: 220 2376. Very popular, non-cruisy atmosphere in this tastefully refurbished bar.

Nexus, 60 Broughton Street, tel: 478 7069. Café-bar and restaurant, great food at reasonable prices.

New Town Bar, 26b Dublin Street, tel: 538 7775. Male-oriented, Cruisy bar, popular with male professionals. **Kaleidoscope** a mixed disco, runs 10pm–2am Friday and Saturday, 9am–1am Thursday and Sunday.

Planet Out, 6 Baxter's Place (Leith Walk), tel: 524 0061. Brightly-coloured gay-oriented bar, which attracts a crowd intent on partying or building up to a night out clubbing. Note: Planet Out doesn't open until 4pm weekdays.

Queer Sunday, Ego, 14 Picardy Place, tel: 478 7434. Weekly gay club night, with offshoots on Thursday and Friday as well. The atmosphere is glam with party tunes and regular PAs from popular pop acts.

Solas Café, Solas HIV and Aidscentre, 2/4 Abbeymount, tel: 661 0982. Good home cooking. Tuesday and Thursday 11am–7.30pm, Wednesday and Friday 11am–4pm.

The Stag and Turret, 1 Montrose Terrace, tel: 661 6443. Busy bar, set over two floors, which attracts a slightly older crowd. Entertainment includes pool, karaoke and women-only events.

Open Tuesday–Sunday, with underground dance tunes at the weekends and more student-oriented party nights during the week. Also a regular live music programme.

Negociants, 45–47 Lothian Street, tel: 225 6313. Best known as a popular café-bar, but the basement operates as a nightclub of sorts called "Medina". The music ranges from funk to dance to hip hop. Free admission on Wednesday nights.

Opal Lounge, 51 George Street, tel: 226 2275. Contemporary dance/acid/funk at a popular venue.

Peppermint Lounge, Blair Street, tel: 622 6811. Relaxed atmosphere, popular with young professionals. Two rooms, one funk, one mainstream.

The Potterrow, Bristo Square, tel: 650 2656. An Edinburgh University Students' Association venue, where student ID is required. If you are not a student, or accompanied by one, contact the venue in advance to find out about temporary membership. One of the best sound systems in Edinburgh and regular residencies for dance superclubs like Cream.

Po Na Na, 43b Frederick Street, tel: 226 2224, www.ponana.com A Moroccan-style bar-cum-club, keeping its good-time vibe going with DJs every night. Often reaches capacity at weekends, so arriving early is advised.

Studio 24, Calton Road, tel: 558 3758. With a long history as a music venue and cinema, the somewhat drab Studio 24 is now home to underground clubs, including goth and rock nights as well as techno events.

The Venue, 17–21 Calton Road, tel: 557 3073, www.edinburghvenue.com In addition to its live music programme, The Venue operates as a nightclub Thursday–Saturday, with occasional mid-week events. With three floors, it is adaptable for big-name guest DJs or smaller events.

Why Not? 14 George Street, tel: 624 8311. Upmarket haunt of the "it people".

Festivals

The Festival City

Edinburgh is very much a festival city, with an international reputation for its summer arts gatherings. The month of August is when things reach fever pitch as the city plays host to no less than six major events – collectively often referred to simply as "the Festival". At other times of the year, too, there is plenty going on, the biggest event outside the summer season being Hogmanay (New Year) which has grown hugely in recent years.

Summer Arts Festivals

See also the chapter on *The Edinburgh Festival*.

Edinburgh International Festival
Office at: The Hub, Castlehill
Information tel: 473 2001,
bookings tel: 473 2000,
email: boxoffice@eif.co.uk
www.eif.co.uk
Three weeks over August and early September. This is the granddaddy of them all, featuring invited international companies from the realms of music, opera, theatre and dance. Venues throughout the city.

Edinburgh Festival Fringe
Festival Fringe Society office at: 180 High Street
Information tel: 226 0026,
bookings tel: 226 0000,
email: admin@edfringe.com
www.edfringe.com
Officially three weeks in August, but some performances take place throughout the month. The offshoot of the International Festival, although the Fringe has grown into the biggest arts festival in the world, featuring everything from internationally renowned theatre companies to small student productions, and taking in drama, comedy, dance, music and every conceivable mixing of the genres. Performances take place at numerous venues, with street entertainment along the Royal Mile and on The Mound during the daytime.

Edinburgh International Book Festival
Office at: The Scottish Book Centre, 137 Dundee Street
Information tel: 228 5444,
bookings tel: 624 5050,
email: admin@edbookfest.co.uk,
www.edbookfest.co.uk
Last three weeks in August. Gathers together the great and the good from the literary world for readings and discussions, including a much-praised children's programme. Over 600 events with more than 500 authors. Takes place in marquees in Charlotte Square.

Edinburgh International Film Festival
Office at: Filmhouse, 88 Lothian Road
Information tel 229 2550, bookings tel: 623 8030, email: info@edfilmfest.org.uk
www.edfilmfest.org.uk
Last two weeks in August. Another established event in the world calendar: a series of premieres, cult films and lectures by prominent faces in the film industry. The main venue is the Filmhouse, but screenings also take place at other cinemas in the city.

Edinburgh International Jazz and Blues Festival
Office at: c/o Assembly Direct, 89 Giles Street.
Information/bookings, tel: 467 5200, www.jazzmusic.co.uk
Late July and the first week in August. The best of national talent and visiting jazz players of world-class calibre. See also *Pubs and Performers*. Various venues.

Edinburgh Military Tattoo
Office at: 32 Market Street
Information and bookings tel: 225 1188, email:
edintattoo@edintattoo.co.uk
www.edintattoo.co.uk
Three weeks in August. A spectacular Scottish musical pageant, performed nightly (except Sunday) outdoors on the Castle Esplanade and televised across the world.

Other Festivals

Hogmanay
Details from the Edinburgh and Lothians Tourist Board or website:
www.edinburghshogmanay.org
Four days over the New Year. Features a range of arts and cultural events in the lead-up to and aftermath of a mammoth New Year's Eve street party. The party is one of the biggest in Britain, with music, street entertainment, fireworks and plenty of seasonal cheer; however, access to the city centre is restricted to pass holders. Passes (free) are limited and are quickly snapped up, so you will need to apply well in advance of your visit.

Edinburgh International Science Festival
Information tel: 220 1882,
bookings tel: 473 2070,
www.sciencefestival.co.uk.
Two weeks in April. Caters for all levels of knowledge, from pre-school children to university professors. There are plenty of hands-on experiments to get involved with, as well as exhibitions, outdoor events and lectures.

Children's International Theatre Festival
Information, tel: 225 8050,
bookings, tel: 248 1404
www.imaginate.org.uk.
Approximately five days at the end of May/beginning of June. Attracts children's theatre experts from around the world for a brief but colourful fling.

- **Programmes** can be obtained from the festival offices, the tourist information office or city bookshops.
- **For on-line information** about all of Edinburgh's festivals visit www.edinburghfestivals.co.uk.
- **Advance bookings** are taken for International Festival performances from April and for Military Tattoo performances from December the previous year. Demand for seats at the latter, particularly, is very high and early booking is recommended. For Fringe events, it is often only necessary to book in advance for big-name or short duration shows. Bookings are taken from around mid-June.
- **The Hub** on Castlehill is open year-round. You can book here for all the main festivals.
- *The Guide* magazine is published every day during the summer festivals, with full up-to-date listings; look also in the Scottish newspapers and *The List* magazine for reviews.
- **To avoid queues** at the venue and telephone booking fees, visit one of the Fringe sales points at the Festival Fringe office, The Hub, Waterstones booksellers (83 George Street) or HMV (129 Princes Street).
- **Spontaneous festival-goers** should head for one of the top Fringe venues, such as the Pleasance (60 The Pleasance), Assembly Rooms (54 George Street) or Gilded Balloon (Cowgate).

The Edinburgh Mela

Information tel: 557 1400, www.edinburgh-mela.co.uk Season and duration vary from year to year. A vibrant multi-cultural festival organised by representatives of the city's ethnic minority communities.

Sport

Participant Sports

SPORTS CENTRES

Craiglockhart Tennis and Sports Centre, 177 Colinton Road, tel: 443 0101. Open Monday–Thursday 10am–11pm, Saturday and Sunday 9am–10.30pm. Noted especially for its tennis courts (indoor and outdoor) but also has squash and badminton courts, a fitness room, a boating pond and a crèche.

Marco's Leisure Centre, 55 Grove Street, tel: 228 2141. A private club, but facilities are open to non-members (you must pay in advance if you pre-book). Squash courts, gym, snooker and pool tables, and numerous fitness classes, as well as a bar, bistro and children's soft play area.

Meadowbank Sports Centre, 139 London Road, tel: 661 5351. Open daily 9.00am–10.30pm. Scotland's premier athletic arena. Facilities for all dry sports, from archery to football. Also a climbing wall, gym and numerous dance and fitness classes.

Saughton Sports Complex, Stevenson Drive, tel: 444 0422. Open Sunday–Friday 9am–10pm, Saturday 8.30am–6.30pm. Caters mainly for outdoor sports: football, rugby, tennis and athletics. All-weather Astroturf. Small indoor fitness centre.

CLIMBING

Alien Rock, 8 Pier Place, Newhaven, tel: 552 7211. Open Monday–Friday noon–10pm, Saturday and Sunday 10am–7pm. A moulded rock face in a converted church which is just as challenging

as the real thing. Children's sessions at weekends, (10am–noon, 1pm–3pm).

FISHING

It is possible to fish in Edinburgh itself (on the Water of Leith) as well as around Scotland. However, a permit is generally required (except for sea fishing) and limits may be set on the quantity and size of fish. Guides are available from most fishing tackle shops in Edinburgh, as are permits for certain areas. The book *Trout and Salmon Rivers and Lochs Of Scotland*, by Bruce Saunderson, is one of the most comprehensive available.

For the Water of Leith contact the Parks Unit, 49 York Place, Edinburgh EH1 3JD; for the reservoirs around Edinburgh, tel: 445 6462 (east of Scotland Water); for the lochs in Holyrood Park, tel: 556 1761 (Crown Office); for the Union Canal, tel: 0141 332 6936 (British Waterways). The **Scottish Anglers National Association** tel: 558 3644 can also offer advice.

GOLF

Municipal courses are open seven days a week and are unaffected by public holidays except Christmas Day. The following are the municipal courses within the bounds of the city. A round costs from £10–£15 and clubs may be hired. In addition, Edinburgh has a number of private golf clubs (and there are plenty more within striking distance), most of which welcome visitors.

Braid Hills, No. 1 and No. 2 courses, Braid Hills, tel: 447 6666. The main course is closed on Sunday, but you can play on No. 2 course.

Carrick Knowe Golf Course, Balgreen Road, tel: 337 1096.

Craigentinny Golf Course, Craigentinny Avenue, tel: 554 7501.

Portobello Golf Course, (9 holes), Stanley Street, tel: 669 4361.

Silverknowes Golf Course,
Silverknowes Parkway, tel:
336 3843.

HILLWALKING AND MOUNTAINEERING

There are numerous opportunities
to take part in this pursuit around
Edinburgh and beyond.
Contact **The Mountaineering
Council of Scotland,** The Old
Grannery, West Mill Street, Perth
Ph1 5QP, PH1 5SE, tel: (01738)
638227, www.mountaineering-
scotland.org.uk.

HORSE RIDING

Riding is an excellent way to
see the countryside around
Edinburgh, and there are many
riding schools operating throughout
the Lothians and Border regions.
For full details of approved
operators contact the Scottish
branch of the **British Horse Society**,
tel: (01764) 656334,
www.bhs.org.uk. The following
riding schools all offer child and
group sessions:
Appin Equestrian Centre, Drem,
East Lothian, tel: 01620 880 366.
Houston Farm Riding School,
Broxburn, West Lothian, tel: 01506
811 351.
Pentland Hills Icelandics,
Windy Gowl Farm, nr. West Linton,
tel: 01968 661 095. Hill rides on
rare Icelandic horses.
Tower Farm Riding Stables, 85
Liberton Drive, tel: 664 3375.

SWIMMING

The city's big swim centres are:
Royal Commonwealth Pool, 21
Dalkeith Road, tel: 667 7211.
Open Monday–Friday 6am–9.30pm,
Saturday 6–8am and
10am–4.30pm, Sunday
10am–4.30pm. Restricted access
at certain times (check in
advance). Olympic-sized municipal
pool with separate diving and
children's pools. Other facilities

Hot Air Ballooning

Hot air balloon flights over
Edinburgh, Lothians, Borders
and Fife. For more information
contact: **Alba Ballooning,** 12
Gladstone Terrace, tel: 667
4251, www.albaballooning.co.uk.

too, including a gym, sauna, soft
play and crèche.
Leith Waterworld, 377 Easter
Road, Leith, tel: 555 6000. Open
Friday–Sunday and school holidays
10am–4.45pm. Ideal for children.
Much more than a swimming pool,
it has flumes, a wave machine and
a river run.

Other Municipal Pools

Many of Edinburgh's municipal
swimming pools are worth a visit for
their architecture alone. The city
specialises in small pools built in the
Victorian era, which, with brightly
coloured changing rooms on each
side, are reminiscent of a 1920s
cruise ship. The following are
Victorian pools with women-only and
children's sessions, and fitness
centres attached. All of them restrict
access at certain times due to these
special sessions and lessons, so
ring in advance to check when you
can swim. Last admission is usually
30 minutes before closing time.
Dalry Swim Centre, 29 Caledonian
Crescent, tel: 313 3964. Open
Monday–Friday 8am–7.40pm,
Saturday noon–3.40pm, Sunday
9am–3.40pm.
Glenogle Swim Centre, Glenogle
Road, tel: 343 6376. Open
Monday–Friday 8am–7.40pm,
(closed Wednesday and Friday pm),
Saturday 10am–3.40pm, Sunday
9am–3.40pm.
Leith Victoria Swim Centre,
Junction Place, Leith, tel: 555 4728.
Open Monday–Friday 8am–9.30pm
(Tuesday closes 7.40pm, Friday
closes 2pm), Saturday and Sunday
9am–3.40pm.
Portobello Swim Centre, 57
Promenade, Portobello, tel: 669
6888. Open Monday–Friday
7am–9pm, Saturday and Sunday
9am–4pm. Authentic Turkish baths.

Warrender Swim Centre,
Thirlestane Road, tel: 447 0052.
Open Monday and Friday
8am–7.40pm Tuesday and
Thursday 8am–6.40pm, Wednesday
8am–3pm, Saturday and Sunday
9am–3.40pm.

Spectator Sports

ATHLETICS

Meadowbank Stadium, 139 London
Road, tel: 661 5351. Scotland's
premier athletic arena which hosts
all the major tournaments.

FOOTBALL

Edinburgh has two Scottish Premier
League teams: Heart of Midlothian
(Hearts) play at **Tynecastle
Stadium,** Gorgie Road, tel: 200
7200, www.heartsfc.co.uk;
Hibernian (Hibs) play at **Easter
Road Park,** tel: 661 2159,
www.hibs.co.uk.

HORSE RACING

Musselburgh Racecourse,
Linkfield Road, tel: 665 2859,
www.musselburgh-racecourse.co.uk
Events take place throughout the
year, with flat racing March to
November and National Hunt events
from December to February. The
Scottish Sprint Cup is held in June.

RUGBY

Murrayfield Stadium, Riversdale
Crescent, tel: 346 5000.
Scottish and international games
take place here throughout the
season. International matches are
held in November, February–March.

OTHER SPORTS

Basketball
The Edinburgh Rocks (tel: 0208
554 8400) is the only Scottish
team in the Budweiser League.
Weekend matches are played

Winter Sports

Apart from curling, the following sports may, in fact, be engaged in most of the year.
Skiing: Midlothian Ski Centre, Hillend, Biggar Road, tel: 445 4433. Open daily 9.30am–9pm (closes 7pm Sunday and summer Saturdays). The longest artificial ski slope in Europe, with challenging routes for all abilities. Lessons, ski hire, snowboarding and information on trips to Scotish ski resorts available.
Ice Skating: Murrayfield Ice Rink, 13 Riversdale Crescent, tel: 337 6933. Open Monday, Tuesday, Thursday, 2.30–9pm, Wednesday 2.30–10pm, Friday 2.30–10.30pm, Saturday 10am–10.30pm, Sunday noon–4.30pm. Skating sessions are restricted so call first to check. Tuition and family sessions are available, with disco evenings on Friday and Saturday.
Curling: Murrayfield Curling, Riversdale Crescent, tel: 346 4477. Curling is a pastime popular in Scotland, North America and Northern Europe, similar to playing bowls on ice. It can be enjoyed both as a participant and spectator sport, with a season which runs from October to March. Note that the facilities close during the summer.

September to April at **Meadowbank Sports Centre** (139 London Road, tel: 661 5351).

Ice Hockey
The Edinburgh Capitals (tel: 313 2977) is the local team, with a season from September to March (games played on Sunday). They are based at **Murrayfield Ice Rink** (13 Riversdale Crescent, tel: 337 6933).

Sailing
Port Edgar Marina and Sailing School, Shore Road, South Queensferry, tel: 331 3330.

Shopping

Where to Shop

Those who enjoy wandering up back streets and stumbling across a treasure of a shop will find plenty in Edinburgh to divert them. Once you get away from Princes Street and the same array of shops which dominates every high street in Britain, there is a host of specialist shops and idiosyncratic traders to choose from.

THE OLD TOWN

The **Royal Mile** is mostly given over to souvenirs and tartan, with a vast but predictable range. However, running off the High Street (Royal Mile) is **Cockburn Street** for the trendy shopper, with such shop names as Whiplash Trash and Return to Sender. The **Grassmarket** these days has only a smattering of interesting small shops and boutiques amidst the restaurants and bars, but adjoining **Victoria Street** offers an exceptional range of curio shopping, with the indoor Byzantium Market at the top featuring a range of craft, antique and bric-a-brac stalls.

THE NEW TOWN

Princes Street is Edinburgh's main shopping street, with the predictable presence of department stores **Marks & Spencer** (No. 91 for ladieswear, No. 54 for men's and children's wear and food, **BhS** (No.64), **Debenhams** (No. 109) and **Frasers** (No. 145), as well as the chemist **Boots** (No. 101), record store **Virgin Megastore** (No. 124) and **Waterstone's** bookshop (Nos.

13 and 128). **Jenners** (No. 47) is the last of the independently owned department stores on Princes Street.
Streets parallel to Princes Street, namely pedestrianised **Rose Street** and **Thistle Street**, provide a range of smaller shops, while the larger, upmarket **George Street** has designer fashion outlets such as Cruise, Moss Bros and Karen Millen and the independent department store Aitken and Niven. A major redevelopment of **St Andrew Square** features the upmarket fashion emporium **Harvey Nichols** as its flagship store.
Stockbridge (see the chapter on *Villages, pages 208 and 210*) and **Broughton Street** (see *The Greater New Town, page 159*) are good for antique hunters.

Indoor Shopping Centres
There are two indoor shopping centres at the east end of Princes Street: the large, bland **St James Centre** (with a big **John Lewis**) and the more tourist-oriented **Princes Mall** in a light modern, underground building, on top of which is the Tourist Information Centre. Out-of-centre malls include The Gyle (west), Ocean Terminal (north), Cameron toll (south-east) and The Fort (south-east), not covered.

Specialist Stores

ANTIQUES

Auchinleck, 86 Grassmarket.
Bacchus, 95 West Bow.
Bow Well Antiques, 103 West Bow.
Carson Clark Gallery, 181–183 Canongate. Antique maps.
James Scott, 43 Dundas Street.
Laurence Black, 60 Thistle Street.
Old Toys and Antiques, 9 West Crosscauseway.
Phillips, 65 George Street.
Sotheby's, 112 George Street.
Unicorn Antiques, 65 Dundas Street.

ART

See *Culture: Art Galleries* for details.
Bourne Fine Art, 6 Dundas Street.
Calton Gallery, 10 Royal Terrace.

The Edinburgh Gallery, 18 Dundas Street.
Edinburgh Printmakers Workshop and Gallery, 23 Union Street.
Ingleby Gallery, 6 Carlton Terrace.
Open Eye Gallery, 75 Cumberland Street.
The Scottish Gallery, 16 Dundas Street.
Torrance Gallery, 36 Dundas Street.

BAGPIPES

Bagpipe Centre, 49 Blackfriars Street.
Kilberry Bagpipes, 38 Lochrin Buildings, Gilmore Place, Tolcross.

BOOKSHOPS

Armchair Books, 72 West Port. Second-hand books.
Bauermeister, 19 George IV Bridge.
Beyond Words, 42–44 Cockburn Street.
James Thin, 53 South Bridge, 29 Buccleuch Street and 59 George Street.
McNaughtan's Bookshop, 3a–4a Haddington Place. Second-hand and antiquarian books.
Waterstone's, 83 George Street, 13–14 Princes Street and 128 Princes Street.

CLOTHING

Highland Dress and Tartan
Ecossais, 3 Canonmills Bridge.
Geoffrey (Tailor) Kiltmakers, 57–59 High Street, www.geoffreykilts.co.uk.
Hector Russell Kiltmakers, 95 Princes Street, 137–141 High Street and 509 Lawnmarket.
Hugh Macpherson (Scotland), 17 West Maitland Street.
The Kiltmaker, 95 Princes Street.
Kinloch Anderson, Commercial Street/Dock Street, Leith, www.kinlochanderson.com.
Kiltmakers to the Royal Family.
Manacraft, 88 Bruntsfield Place.
McCalls of the Royal Mile, 11 High Street.
See also Outdoor Pursuits.

Traditional Outfitters
Burberry's and the Scotch House, 39/41 Princes Street.
Crombie, 63 George Street.

Designer Scottish Cashmere
Belinda Robertson Cashmere, 22 Palmerston Place.
Cashmere Store, 67 George Street.
Designs on Cashmere, 28 High Street.
Glentress Cashmere, 14 Bank Street.
Hawick Cashmere, 71–81 Grassmarket.

Scottish Woollens
Bill Baber Knitwear Design, 66 Grassmarket.
Edinburgh Woollen Mill, 139 Princes Street.
Number Two, 2 St Stephen Place.
Old Town Knitwear, 125 Canongate.
Ragamuffin, 276 Canongate.
Royal Mile Knitwear Store, 51 High Street.
Scoosh, 30 St Mary's Street.
Sheeps Clothing for Ewe, 46 High Street.
The Shetland Connection, 491 Lawnmarket.
The Woollen Mill, 179 High Street.

CRAFTS

The Adam Pottery, 76 Henderson Row.
Byzantium, 9a Victoria Street.
Celtic Craft Centre, 101 High Street.
Clarksons, 87 West Bow.
Flux Scottish Artisans Gallery, 55 Bernard Street, Leith.
Geoffrey (Tailor) Highland Crafts, 555 Castlehill.
Helios Fountain, 7 Grassmarket.
One World Shop, St John's Church Hall, Princes Street.

JEWELLERY

Scottish Jewellery
Alison & Roy Murray, 20 Thistle Street.
Alistair Tait, 116a Rose Street.
Clarksons of Edinburgh, 87 West Bow.
Hamilton & Inches, 87 George Street.
Joseph Bonnar, 72 Thistle Street.

VAT Refund

Some shops operate a VAT refund scheme for visitors, which allows you to claim back tax on goods you buy and take out of the country. Ask the shopkeeper for details.

Antique and Period Jewellery
Laing the Jeweller, 29 Frederick Street.
Mappin & Webb, 88 George Street.
Ortak Jewellery, Princes Mall, Princes Street.
Ringmaker, 19 Princes Mall.
Royal Mile Antiques, 363 High Street.
Scottish Gems, 24 High Street.

OUTDOOR PURSUITS

Blacks, 24 Frederick Street and 13–14 Elm Row.
Camping and Outdoor Centre, 77 South Bridge.
Graham Tiso, 123 Rose Street and 41 Commercial Street, Leith.
Dickson & MacNaughton, 21 Frederick Street (guns and fishing tackle).
Rohan Designs, 86 George Street.

SPECIALITY FOODS

The Fudge House, 197 Canongate.
Hanover Health Foods, 40 Hanover Street.
Herbie of Edinburgh, 66 Raeburn Place.
Ian Mellis Cheesemonger, 30a Victoria Street and 205 Bruntsfield Place.
Lupe Pintos, 24 Leven Street.
Peckhams, 155–159 Bruntsfield Place and Waverley Station.
Real Foods, 37 Broughton Street and 8 Brougham Place.
Valvona & Crolla, 19 Elm Row.

Haggis
Crombie's of Edinburgh, 97–101 Broughton Street.

SCOTCH WHISKY

Cadenheads Whisky Shop, 172 Canongate.
Royal Mile Whiskies, 379 High Street.
The Whisky Shop, Princes Mall, Princes Street.

SCOTTISH HERALDRY

Heraldic Art and Design, 204 Canongate.

Shopping Hours

High Street and Princes Street shops are open 9am–5.30pm Monday to Saturday, and until 7 or 8pm on Thursday. Smaller shops may not open until 10am, and may close at 6pm or later. Since Waterstone's introduced competition to the bookselling market, the big bookshops open until 10pm during the week, and are open on Sunday afternoons. Most large shops in Princes Street open on Sunday, generally from around noon until 4 or 5pm.

Customer Complaints

Contact Advice Shop at 85–87 South Bridge, tel: 225 1255.

Further Reading

History and Architecture

Cant, Malcolm, **Villages of Edinburgh: North Edinburgh,** Malcolm Cant Publications (1997). A concise look at some of the city's many picturesque suburbs. Also South Edinburgh volume available (1999).

Chambers, Robert, **Traditions of Edinburgh,** Chambers (1996). Originally written in 1824 about the historic traditions of Scotland's capital.

Dick, David, **Who Was Who in the Royal Mile,** Clerkington Publishing (1997). Dips into the rich history of Edinburgh's oldest thoroughfare.

Durie, Alastair J., **Vanishing Edinburgh,** Aberdeen University (1994). Fantastic photographic guide to the city's past and present.

Hardie, Alastair M.R., **Close Encounters in the Royal Mile,** John Donald Publishers (1995). Learn the fascinating history of the many closes and alleys along the Royal Mile.

Henderson, Jan-Andrew, **The Town Below The Ground – Edinburgh's Legendary Underground City,** Mainstream (1999). Discover what lies beneath your feet in the many miles of Vaults hidden below the city's streets.

Hendrie, William, **Discovering The River Forth,** John Donald Publishers (1996). The fascinating history of one of Scotland's most important waterways.

Macgregor, Forbes, **Greyfriars Bobby.** Steve Savage Publishers (2002). Learn the enchanting tale of the faithful dog who sat on his master's grave. Or did he?

Mackay, John, **Edinburgh Castle Stories of Horror and Adventure** , Lang Syne (1990). Relates some of the more macabre events at the Castle over the years.

McKean, Charles, **Edinburgh: An Illustrated Architectural Guide,** Rutland Press, (1992). The Royal Institute of Architects in Scotland's definitive guide to the city's many wonderful buildings.

Mitchell, Robin, **The Secret Life of Edinburgh Castle,** Cadies (1999). There's more to the Castle than meets the eye.

Murray, Anthony, **The Forth Railway Bridge: A Celebration,** Mainstream (2000). Affectionate look at one of Edinburgh's most famous landmarks.

Smith, Donald, **John Knox House: Gateway to Edinburgh's Old Town,** John Donald Publishing (1997). The history of one of Scotland's most important medieval buildings associated with the famous Protestant reformer.

Turnbull, Michael, **Edinburgh and Lothians Holy Corners,** Saint Andrew Press (1996). A look at some of the city's ecclesiastical buildings, past and present.

Wilson, Alan J., **Hidden Underground Edinburgh,** Mercat Tours (1999). Ghostly tales of Edinburgh's hidden Vaults, including the fascinating tale of Mary King's Close.

Sightseeing Guides

Baldwin, John, **Edinburgh, Lothians and the Borders,** The Stationery Office (1997). Features excursions, industrial monuments, palaces, Roman forts and more.

Chalmers, John, **One Hundred Hill Walks Around Edinburgh,** Mainstream (1999). Escape from the car fumes and head to the hills with this handy guide. Derek Storey's **100 Countryside Walks Around Edinburgh,** Mainstream (2000). in the same format, is easier on the calf muscles.

Gauldie, Robin, **Walking Edinburgh,** New Holland (2000). Best routes to the most interesting places.

Hallewell's **Edinburgh On Foot,** (2000). Handy guide to getting places under your own steam.

Smith, Roger, **25 Walks in Edinburgh and Lothian,** The Stationery Office (1997). Good selection of medium length, interesting walks in the city centre and beyond.

Wills, Michael and Elspeth, **Walks in Edinburgh's Old Town**, Mercat Press (1997), and **Walks in Edinburgh's New Town**, Mercat Press (1998). Find your way around and learn the odd interesting fact along the way.

Reference

Mullay, Sandy, **The Edinburgh Encyclopaedia**, Mainstream (1996). An A–Z of the city, from banks and cinemas to parks and wildlife. Current information as well as historical details.

Other Insight Guides

Apa Publications produces three series of guidebooks to suit the needs of every traveller. The **Insight Guides** series places destinations in their cultural context and features some of the world's top photo-journalism. The intensely practical **Compact Guides** series structures information for handy on-the-spot reference, with text, pictures and maps all carefully cross-indexed. These are the books to look for when you are exploring particular areas of Great Britain in detail. The **Insight Pocket Guides** series provides specific recommendations from a local host, aimed especially at visitors with limited time to spare, and most titles include a full-size fold-out map which can be used separately from the book.

The *Compact* and *Pocket* series are not cut-down versions of *Insight Guides* – they contain original material and are designed to complement the parent series.

● *Insight Guides* to the British Isles include: *Great Britain, England, Scotland, Wales, Oxford, Glasgow, Edinburgh, Channel Islands, Ireland* and *Dublin*.

● *Insight Pocket Guides* cover: *Southwark and the South Bank, London, Scotland* and *Ireland*.

● The *Compact Guides* series includes: *Scotland, Scottish Highlands, Edinburgh, Glasgow, London, Dublin, Shakespeare Country, Bath, Oxford, Cambridge & East Anglia, Cornwall, Devon, The Cotswolds, New Forest, South Downs, Lake District, York, Yorkshire Dales, Snowdonia, Peak District* and *Northumbria*.

Feedback

We do our best to ensure the information in our books is as accurate and up-to-date as possible. The books are updated on a regular basis, using local contacts, who painstakingly add, amend and correct as required. However, some mistakes and omissions are inevitable and we are ultimately reliant on our readers to put us in the picture.

We would welcome your feedback on any details related to your experiences using the book "on the road". Maybe we recommended a hotel that you liked (or another that you didn't), as well as interesting new attractions, or facts and figures you have found out about the country itself. The more details you can give us (particularly with regard to addresses, e-mails and telephone numbers), the better.

We will acknowledge all contributions, and we'll offer an Insight Guide to the best letters received.

Please write to us at:
Insight Guides
PO Box 7910
London SE1 1WE
United Kingdom
Or send e-mail to:
insight@apaguide.demon.co.uk

ART & PHOTO CREDITS

Cartographic Editor **Zoë Goodwin**
Production **Linton Donaldson**
Design Consultants
Carlotta Junger, Graham Mitchener
Picture Research **Hilary Genin**

Index

Numbers in italics refer to photographs

A
B
·
D
E
F
G
H
I
J
a
b
c
d
e
f
g
h
j
k
l

66 I was first drawn to the Insight Guides by the excellent "Nepal" volume. I can think of no book which so effectively captures the essence of a country. Out of these pages leaped the Nepal I know – the captivating charm of a people and their culture. I've since discovered and enjoyed the entire Insight Guide series. Each volume deals with a country in the same sensitive depth, which is nowhere more evident than in the superb photography. 99

Sir Edmund Hillary

INSIGHT GUIDES

The classic series that puts you in the picture

Alaska
Amazon Wildlife
American Southwest
Amsterdam
Argentina
Arizona & Grand Canyon
Asia, East
Asia, Southeast
Australia
Austria
Bahamas
Bali
Baltic States
Bangkok
Barbados
Barcelona
Beijing
Belgium
Belize
Berlin
Bermuda
Boston
Brazil
Brittany
Brussels
Buenos Aires
Burgundy
Burma (Myanmar)
Cairo
California
California, Southern
Canada
Caribbean
Channel Islands
Chicago
Chile
China
Continental Europe
Corsica
Costa Rica
Crete
Cuba
Cyprus
Czech & Slovak Republics
Delhi, Jaipur & Agra
Denmark
Dominican Rep. & Haiti

Dublin
East African Wildlife
Eastern Europe
Ecuador
Edinburgh
Egypt
England
Finland
Florence
Florida
France
France, Southwest
French Riviera
Gambia & Senegal
Germany
Glasgow
Gran Canaria
Great Britain
Great Railway Journeys
   of Europe
Greece
Greek Islands
Guatemala, Belize
   & Yucatán
Hawaii
Hong Kong
Hungary
Iceland
India
India, South
Indonesia
Ireland
Israel
Istanbul
Italy
Italy, Northern
Italy, Southern
Jamaica
Japan
Jerusalem
Jordan
Kenya
Korea
Laos & Cambodia
Lisbon
London
Los Angeles

Madeira
Madrid
Malaysia
Mallorca & Ibiza
Malta
Mauritius, Réunion
   & Seychelles
Melbourne
Mexico
Miami
Montreal
Morocco
Moscow
Namibia
Nepal
Netherlands
New England
New Orleans
New York City
New York State
New Zealand
Nile
Normandy
Norway
Oman & The UAE
Oxford
Pacific Northwest
Pakistan
Paris
Peru
Philadelphia
Philippines
Poland
Portugal
Prague
Provence
Puerto Rico
Rajasthan
Rio de Janeiro

Rome
Russia
St Petersburg
San Francisco
Sardinia
Scandinavia
Scotland
Seattle
Sicily
Singapore
South Africa
South America
Spain
Spain, Northern
Spain, Southern
Sri Lanka
Sweden
Switzerland
Sydney
Syria & Lebanon
Taiwan
Tenerife
Texas
Thailand
Tokyo
Trinidad & Tobago
Tunisia
Turkey
Tuscany
Umbria
USA: On The Road
USA: Western States
US National Parks: West
Venezuela
Venice
Vienna
Vietnam
Wales

INSIGHT GUIDES

The world's largest collection of visual travel guides & maps